Natural Language Processing with Java Cookbook

Over 70 recipes to create linguistic and language translation
applications using Java libraries

Richard M. Reese

BIRMINGHAM - MUMBAI

Natural Language Processing with Java Cookbook

Commissioning Editor: Pravin Dhandre
Acquisition Editor: Nelson Morris
Content Development Editor: Ronnel Mathew
Technical Editor: Dinesh Pawar
Copy Editor: Safis Editing
Project Coordinator: Namrata Swetta
Proofreader: Safis Editing
Indexer: Pratik Shirodkar
Graphics: Tom Scaria
Production Coordinator: Jayalaxmi Raja

First published: April 2019

Production reference: 1220419

Published by Packt Publishing Ltd.
Livery Place
35 Livery Street
Birmingham
B3 2PB, UK.

ISBN 978-1-78980-115-6

www.packtpub.com

`mapt.io`

Mapt is an online digital library that gives you full access to over 5,000 books and videos, as well as industry leading tools to help you plan your personal development and advance your career. For more information, please visit our website.

Why subscribe?

- Spend less time learning and more time coding with practical eBooks and Videos from over 4,000 industry professionals

- Improve your learning with Skill Plans built especially for you

- Get a free eBook or video every month

- Mapt is fully searchable

- Copy and paste, print, and bookmark content

Packt.com

Did you know that Packt offers eBook versions of every book published, with PDF and ePub files available? You can upgrade to the eBook version at `www.packt.com` and as a print book customer, you are entitled to a discount on the eBook copy. Get in touch with us at `customercare@packtpub.com` for more details.

At `www.packt.com`, you can also read a collection of free technical articles, sign up for a range of free newsletters, and receive exclusive discounts and offers on Packt books and eBooks.

Contributors

About the author

Richard M. Reese has worked in both industry and academia. For 17 years, he worked in the telephone and aerospace industries, serving in several capacities, including research and development, software development, supervision, and training. He currently teaches at Tarleton State University, where he has the opportunity to apply his years of industry experience to enhance his teaching. Richard has written several Java books and a C pointer book. He uses a concise and easy-to-follow approach to the topics at hand. His Java books have addressed EJB 3.1, updates to Java 7 and 8, certification, jMonkeyEngine, natural language processing, functional programming, networks, and data science.

About the reviewer

Jennifer L. Reese studied computer science at Tarleton State University. She also earned her M.Ed. from Tarleton in December 2016. She currently teaches computer science to high-school students. Her interests include the integration of computer science concepts with other academic disciplines, increasing diversity in computer science courses, and the application of data science to the field of education. She has co-authored two books: *Java for Data Science*, and *Java 7 New Features Cookbook*. She previously worked as a software engineer. In her free time, she enjoys reading, cooking, and traveling—especially to any destination with a beach. She is a musician and appreciates a variety of musical genres.

Packt is searching for authors like you

If you're interested in becoming an author for Packt, please visit authors.packtpub.com and apply today. We have worked with thousands of developers and tech professionals, just like you, to help them share their insight with the global tech community. You can make a general application, apply for a specific hot topic that we are recruiting an author for, or submit your own idea.

Table of Contents

Preface

NLP is a rapidly changing field with numerous supporting APIs. Keeping abreast of changes to these technologies and APIs can be challenging. In addition, there are numerous languages that provide access to NLP functionality.

This cookbook covers many of these techniques with a series of recipes using Java. Each recipe addresses one or more NLP technique and provides a template for using these techniques. Step-by-step instructions will guide the user through each recipe. This facilitates the reader's learning of these technologies and the development of their understanding of how to use them.

The book is organized around common NLP tasks. The chapters do not need to be followed sequentially and can be read in any order.

Who this book is for

This book is designed for Java developers who want to learn how to incorporate NLP techniques into their applications using Java. The reader is assumed to have a good working knowledge of Java 8. Ideally, they will have some experience with Eclipse and Maven as well, though this is not required.

What this book covers

Chapter 1, *Preparing Text for Analysis and Tokenization*, demonstrates numerous approaches for performing tokenization. This is the process of extracting the individual words and elements of a document, and forms the basis for most NLP tasks. This process can be difficult to perform correctly. There are many specialized tokenizers available to address a number of different specialized texts.

Chapter 2, *Isolating Sentences within a Document*, covers how the process of sentence isolation is also a key NLP task. The process involves more than finding a period, exclamation mark, or question mark and using them as sentence delimiters. The process often requires the use of trained neural network models to work correctly.

Chapter 3, *Performing Name Entity Recognition*, explains how to isolate the key elements of a text in terms of entities such as names, dates, and places. It is not feasible to create an exhaustive list of entities, so neural networks are frequently used to perform this task.

Chapter 4, *Detecting POS Using Neural Networks*, covers the topic of POS, which refers to parts of speech and corresponds to sentence elements such as nouns, verbs, and adjectives. Performing POS is critical to extract meaning from a text. This chapter will illustrate various POS techniques and show how these elements can be depicted.

Chapter 5, *Performing Text Classification*, outlines a common NLP activity: classifying text into one or more categories. This chapter will demonstrate how this is accomplished, including the process of performing sentiment analysis. This is often used to access a customer's opinion of a product or service.

Chapter 6, *Finding Relationships within Text*, explains how identifying the relationships between text elements can be used to extract meaning from a document. While this is not a simple task, it is becoming increasingly important to many applications. We will examine various approaches to accomplish this goal.

Chapter 7, *Language Identification and Translation*, covers how language translation is critical to many problem domains, and takes on increased importance as the world becomes more and more interconnected. In this chapter, we will demonstrate several cloud-based approaches to performing natural language translation.

Chapter 8, *Identifying Semantic Similarities within Text*, explains how texts can be similar to each other at various levels. Similar words may be used, or there may be similarities in text structure. This capability is useful for a variety of tasks ranging from spell checking to assisting in determining the meaning of a text. We will demonstrate various approaches in this chapter.

Chapter 9, *Common Text Processing and Generation Tasks*, outlines how the NLP techniques illustrated in this book are all based on a set of common text-processing activities. These include using data structures such as inverted dictionaries and generating random numbers for training sets. In this chapter, we will demonstrate many of these tasks.

Chapter 10, *Extracting Data for Use in NLP Analysis*, emphasizes how important it is to be able to obtain data from a variety of sources. As more and more data is created, we need mechanisms for extracting and then processing the data. We will illustrate some of these techniques, including extracting data from Word/PDF documents, websites, and spreadsheets.

Chapter 11, *Creating a Chatbot*, discusses an increasingly common and important NLP application: chatbots. In this chapter, we will demonstrate how to create a chatbot, and how a Java application interface can be used to enhance the functionality of the chatbot.

Appendix, *Installation and Configuration*, covers the different installations and configurations for **Google Cloud Platform (GCP)** and **Amazon Web Services (AWS)**.

To get the most out of this book

The reader should be proficient with Java in order to understand and use many of the APIs covered in this book. The recipes used here are presented as Eclipse projects. Familiarity with Eclipse is not an absolute requirement, but will speed up the learning process. While it is possible to use another IDE, the recipes are written using Eclipse.

Most, but not all, of the recipes use Maven to import the necessary API libraries for the recipes. A basic understanding of how to use a POM file is useful. In some recipes, we will directly import JAR files into a project when they are not available in a Maven repository. In these situations, instructions for Eclipse will be provided.

In the last chapter, Chapter 11, *Creating a Chatbot*, we will be using the AWS Toolkit for Eclipse. This can easily be installed in most IDEs. For a few chapters, we will be using GCP and various Amazon AWS libraries. The reader will need to establish accounts on these platforms, which are free as long as certain usage quotas are not exceeded.

Download the example code files

You can download the example code files for this book from your account at www.packt.com. If you purchased this book elsewhere, you can visit www.packt.com/support and register to have the files emailed directly to you.

You can download the code files by following these steps:

1. Log in or register at www.packt.com.
2. Select the **SUPPORT** tab.
3. Click on **Code Downloads & Errata**.
4. Enter the name of the book in the **Search** box and follow the onscreen instructions.

Once the file is downloaded, please make sure that you unzip or extract the folder using the latest version of:

- WinRAR/7-Zip for Windows
- Zipeg/iZip/UnRarX for Mac
- 7-Zip/PeaZip for Linux

The code bundle for the book is also hosted on GitHub at `https://github.com/PacktPublishing/Natural-Language-Processing-with-Java-Cookbook`. In case there's an update to the code, it will be updated on the existing GitHub repository.

We also have other code bundles from our rich catalog of books and videos available at `https://github.com/PacktPublishing/`. Check them out!

Conventions used

There are a number of text conventions used throughout this book.

`CodeInText`: Indicates code words in text, database table names, folder names, filenames, file extensions, pathnames, dummy URLs, user input, and Twitter handles. Here is an example: "Start by adding the following `import` statement to your project's class."

A block of code is set as follows:

```
while (scanner.hasNext()) {
    String token = scanner.next();
    list.add(token);
}
```

Bold: Indicates a new term, an important word, or words that you see onscreen. For example, words in menus or dialog boxes appear in the text like this. Here is an example: "Select the **Create Intent** button."

Warnings or important notes appear like this.

Tips and tricks appear like this.

Sections

In this book, you will find several headings that appear frequently (*Getting ready*, *How to do it...*, *How it works...*, *There's more...*, and *See also*).

To give clear instructions on how to complete a recipe, use these sections as follows:

Getting ready

This section tells you what to expect in the recipe and describes how to set up any software or any preliminary settings required for the recipe.

How to do it...

This section contains the steps required to follow the recipe.

How it works...

This section usually consists of a detailed explanation of what happened in the previous section.

There's more...

This section consists of additional information about the recipe in order to make you more knowledgeable about the recipe.

See also

This section provides helpful links to other useful information for the recipe.

Get in touch

Feedback from our readers is always welcome.

General feedback: If you have questions about any aspect of this book, mention the book title in the subject of your message and email us at customercare@packtpub.com.

Errata: Although we have taken every care to ensure the accuracy of our content, mistakes do happen. If you have found a mistake in this book, we would be grateful if you would report this to us. Please visit www.packt.com/submit-errata, selecting your book, clicking on the Errata Submission Form link, and entering the details.

Piracy: If you come across any illegal copies of our works in any form on the Internet, we would be grateful if you would provide us with the location address or website name. Please contact us at copyright@packt.com with a link to the material.

If you are interested in becoming an author: If there is a topic that you have expertise in and you are interested in either writing or contributing to a book, please visit authors.packtpub.com.

Reviews

Please leave a review. Once you have read and used this book, why not leave a review on the site that you purchased it from? Potential readers can then see and use your unbiased opinion to make purchase decisions, we at Packt can understand what you think about our products, and our authors can see your feedback on their book. Thank you!

For more information about Packt, please visit packt.com.

Preparing Text for Analysis and Tokenization

1

One of the first steps required for **Natural Language Processing** (**NLP**) is the extraction of tokens in text. The process of tokenization splits text into tokens—that is, words. Normally, tokens are split based upon delimiters, such as white space. White space includes blanks, tabs, and carriage-return line feeds. However, specialized tokenizers can split tokens according to other delimiters. In this chapter, we will illustrate several tokenizers that you will find useful in your analysis.

Another important NLP task involves determining the stem and lexical meaning of a word. This is useful for deriving more meaning about the words beings processed, as illustrated in the fifth and sixth recipe. The stem of a word refers to the root of a word. For example, the stem of the word *antiquated* is *antiqu*. While this may not seem to be the correct stem, the stem of a word is the ultimate base of the word.

The lexical meaning of a word is not concerned with the context in which it is being used. We will be examining the process of performing **lemmatization** of a word. This is also concerned with finding the root of a word, but uses a more detailed dictionary to find the root. The stem of a word may vary depending on the form the word takes. However, with lemmatization, the root will always be the same. Stemming is often used when we will be satisfied with possibly a less than precise determination of the root of a word. A more thorough discussion of stemming versus lemmatization can be found at: `https://blog.bitext.com/what-is-the-difference-between-stemming-and-lemmatization/`.

The last task in this chapter deals with the process of text normalization. Here, we are concerned with converting the token that is extracted to a form that can be more easily processed during later analysis. Typical normalization activities include converting cases, expanding abbreviations, removing stop words along with stemming, and lemmatization. *Stop words* are those words that can often be ignored with certain types of analyses. For example, in some contexts, the word *the* does not always need to be included.

In this chapter, we will cover the following recipes:

- Tokenization using the Java SDK
- Tokenization using OpenNLP
- Tokenization using maximum entropy
- Training a neural network tokenizer for specialized text
- Identifying the stem of a word
- Training an OpenNLP lemmatization model
- Determining the lexical meaning of a word using OpenNLP
- Removing stop words using LingPipe

Technical requirements

In this chapter, you will need to install the following software, if they have not already been installed:

- Eclipse Photon 4.8.0
- Java JDK 8 or later

We will be using the following APIs, which you will be instructed to add for each recipe as appropriate:

- OpenNLP 1.9.0
- LingPipe 4.1.0

The code files for this chapter can be found at `https://github.com/PacktPublishing/Natural-Language-Processing-with-Java-Cookbook/tree/master/Chapter01`.

Tokenization using the Java SDK

Tokenization can be achieved using a number of Java classes, including the `String`, `StringTokenizer`, and `StreamTokenizer` classes. In this recipe, we will demonstrate the use of the `Scanner` class. While frequently used for console input, it can also be used to tokenize a string.

Getting ready

To prepare, we need to create a new Java project.

How to do it...

Let's go through the following steps:

1. Add the following import statement to your project's class:

```
import java.util.ArrayList;
import java.util.Scanner;
```

2. Add the following statements to the main method to declare the sample string, create an instance of the `Scanner` class, and add a list to hold the tokens:

```
String sampleText =
    "In addition, the rook was moved too far to be effective.";
Scanner scanner = new Scanner(sampleText);
ArrayList<String> list = new ArrayList<>();
```

3. Insert the following loops to populate the list and display the tokens:

```
while (scanner.hasNext()) {
    String token = scanner.next();
    list.add(token);
}

for (String token : list) {
    System.out.println(token);
}
```

4. Execute the program. You should get the following output:

```
In
addition,
the
rook
was
moved
too
far
to
be
effective.
```

How it works...

The `Scanner` class's constructor took a string as an argument. This allowed us to apply the `Scanner` class's methods against the text we used in the `next` method, which returns a single token at a time, delimited by white spaces. While it was not necessary to store the tokens in a list, this permits us to use it later for different purposes.

Tokenization using OpenNLP

In this recipe, we will create an instance of the OpenNLP `SimpleTokenizer` class to illustrate tokenization. We will use its `tokenize` method against a sample text.

Getting ready

To prepare, we need to do the following:

1. Create a new Java project
2. Add the following POM dependency to your project:

```
<dependency>
    <groupId>org.apache.opennlp</groupId>
    <artifactId>opennlp-tools</artifactId>
    <version>1.9.0</version>
</dependency>
```

How to do it...

Let's go through the following steps:

1. Start by adding the following `import` statement to your project's class:

```
import opennlp.tools.tokenize.SimpleTokenizer;
```

2. Next, add the following `main` method to your project:

```
public static void main(String[] args) {
    String sampleText =
        "In addition, the rook was moved too far to be effective.";
    SimpleTokenizer simpleTokenizer = SimpleTokenizer.INSTANCE;
    String tokenList[] = simpleTokenizer.tokenize(sampleText);
    for (String token : tokenList) {
        System.out.println(token);
    }
}
```

After executing the program, you should get the following output:

```
In
addition
,
the
rook
was
moved
too
far
to
be
effective
.
```

How it works...

The `SimpleTokenizer` instance represents a tokenizer that will split text using white space delimiters, which are accessed through the class's `INSTANCE` field. With this tokenizer, we use its `tokenize` method to pass a single string returning an array of strings, as shown in the following code:

```
String sampleText =
    "In addition, the rook was moved too far to be effective.";
SimpleTokenizer simpleTokenizer = SimpleTokenizer.INSTANCE;
String tokenList[] = simpleTokenizer.tokenize(sampleText);
```

We then iterated through the list of tokens and displayed one per line. Note how the tokenizer treats the comma and the period as tokens.

See also

- The OpenNLP API documentation can be found at `https://opennlp.apache.org/docs/1.9.0/apidocs/opennlp-tools/index.html`

Tokenization using maximum entropy

Maximum entropy is a statistical classification technique. It takes various characteristics of a subject, such as the use of specialized words or the presence of whiskers in a picture, and assigns a weight to each characteristic. These weights are eventually added up and normalized to a value between 0 and 1, indicating the probability that the subject is of a particular kind. With a high enough level of confidence, we can conclude that the text is all about high-energy physics or that we have a picture of a cat.

If you're interested, you can find a more complete explanation of this technique at `https://nadesnotes.wordpress.com/2016/09/05/natural-language-processing-nlp-fundamentals-maximum-entropy-maxent/`. In this recipe, we will demonstrate the use of maximum entropy with the OpenNLP `TokenizerME` class.

Getting ready

To prepare, we need to do the following:

1. Create a new Maven project.
2. Download the `en-token.bin` file from `http://opennlp.sourceforge.net/models-1.5/`. Save it at the root directory of the project.
3. Add the following POM dependency to your project:

```
<dependency>
    <groupId>org.apache.opennlp</groupId>
    <artifactId>opennlp-tools</artifactId>
    <version>1.9.0</version>
</dependency>
```

How to do it...

Let's go through the following steps:

1. Add the following imports to the project:

```
import java.io.FileNotFoundException;
import java.io.IOException;
import java.io.File;
import java.io.FileInputStream;
import java.io.InputStream;
import opennlp.tools.tokenize.Tokenizer;
import opennlp.tools.tokenize.TokenizerME;
import opennlp.tools.tokenize.TokenizerModel;
```

2. Next, add the following code to the `main` method. This sequence initializes the text to be processed and creates an input stream to read in the tokenization model. Modify the first argument of the `File` constructor to reflect the path to the model files:

```
String sampleText =
    "In addition, the rook was moved too far to be effective.";
try (InputStream modelInputStream = new FileInputStream(
        new File("...", "en-token.bin"))) {
    ...
} catch (FileNotFoundException e) {
    // Handle exception
} catch (IOException e) {
    // Handle exception
}
```

3. Add the following code to the `try` block. It creates a tokenizer model and then the actual tokenizer:

```
TokenizerModel tokenizerModel =
    new TokenizerModel(modelInputStream);
Tokenizer tokenizer = new TokenizerME(tokenizerModel);
```

4. Insert the following code sequence that uses the `tokenize` method to create a list of tokens and then display the tokens:

```
String tokenList[] = tokenizer.tokenize(sampleText);
for (String token : tokenList) {
    System.out.println(token);
}
```

5. Next, execute the program. You should get the following output:

```
In
addition
,
the
rook
was
moved
too
far
to
be
effective
.
```

How it works...

The `sampleText` variable holds the test string. A try-with-resources block is used to automatically close the `InputStream`. The new `File` statement throws a `FileNotFoundException`, while the new `TokenizerModel(modelInputStream)` statement throws an `IOException`, both of which need to be handled.

 The code examples in this book that deal with exception handling include a comment suggesting that exceptions should be handled. The user is encouraged to add the appropriate code to deal with exceptions. This will often include print statements or possibly logging operations.

An instance of the `TokenizerModel` class is created using the `en-token.bin` model. This model has been trained to recognize English text. An instance of the `TokenizerME` class represents the tokenizer where the `tokenize` method is executed against it using the sample text. This method returns an array of strings that are then displayed. Note that the comma and period are treated as separate tokens.

See also

- The OpenNLP API documentation can be found at `https://opennlp.apache.org/docs/1.9.0/apidocs/opennlp-tools/index.html`

Training a neural network tokenizer for specialized text

Sometimes, we need to work with specialized text, such as an uncommon language or text that is unique to a problem domain. In such cases, the standard tokenizers are not always sufficient. This necessitates the creation of a unique model that will work better with the specialized text. In this recipe, we will demonstrate how to train a model using OpenNLP.

Getting ready

To prepare, we need to do the following:

1. Create a new Maven project
2. Add the following dependency to the POM file:

```
<dependency>
    <groupId>org.apache.opennlp</groupId>
    <artifactId>opennlp-tools</artifactId>
    <version>1.9.0</version>
</dependency>
```

How to do it...

Let's go through the following steps:

1. Create a file called `training-data.train`. Add the following to the file:

```
The first sentence is terminated by a period<SPLIT>. We will want
to be able to identify tokens that are separated by something other
than whitespace<SPLIT>. This can include commas<SPLIT>, numbers
such as 100.204<SPLIT>, and other punctuation characters including
colons:<SPLIT>.
```

2. Next, add the following imports to the program:

```
import java.io.BufferedOutputStream;
import java.io.File;
import java.io.FileInputStream;
import java.io.FileNotFoundException;
import java.io.FileOutputStream;
import java.io.IOException;
import java.io.InputStream;
```

```
import opennlp.tools.tokenize.TokenSample;
import opennlp.tools.tokenize.TokenSampleStream;
import opennlp.tools.tokenize.Tokenizer;
import opennlp.tools.tokenize.TokenizerFactory;
import opennlp.tools.tokenize.TokenizerME;
import opennlp.tools.tokenize.TokenizerModel;
import opennlp.tools.util.InputStreamFactory;
import opennlp.tools.util.ObjectStream;
import opennlp.tools.util.PlainTextByLineStream;
import opennlp.tools.util.TrainingParameters;
```

3. Next, add the following `try` block to the project's `main` method that contains the code needed to obtain the training data:

```
InputStreamFactory inputStreamFactory = new InputStreamFactory() {
    public InputStream createInputStream()
            throws FileNotFoundException {
        return new FileInputStream(
            "C:/NLP Cookbook/Code/chapter2a/training-data.train");
    }
};
```

4. Insert the following code segment into the `try` block that will train the model and save it:

```
try (
    ObjectStream<String> stringObjectStream =
        new PlainTextByLineStream(inputStreamFactory, "UTF-8");
    ObjectStream<TokenSample> tokenSampleStream =
        new TokenSampleStream(stringObjectStream);) {
    TokenizerModel tokenizerModel = TokenizerME.train(
        tokenSampleStream, new TokenizerFactory(
            "en", null, true, null),
            TrainingParameters.defaultParams());
    BufferedOutputStream modelOutputStream =
        new BufferedOutputStream(new FileOutputStream(
            new File(
                "C:/NLP Cookbook/Code/chapter2a/mymodel.bin")));
    tokenizerModel.serialize(modelOutputStream);
} catch (IOException ex) {
    // Handle exception
}
```

5. To test the new model, we will reuse the code found in the *Tokenization using OpenNLP* recipe. Add the following code after the preceding `try` block:

```
String sampleText = "In addition, the rook was moved too far to be
effective.";
try (InputStream modelInputStream = new FileInputStream(
        new File("C:/Downloads/OpenNLP/Models", "mymodel.bin"));) {
    TokenizerModel tokenizerModel =
        new TokenizerModel(modelInputStream);
    Tokenizer tokenizer = new TokenizerME(tokenizerModel);
    String tokenList[] = tokenizer.tokenize(sampleText);
    for (String token : tokenList) {
        System.out.println(token);
    }
} catch (FileNotFoundException e) {
    // Handle exception
} catch (IOException e) {
    // Handle exception
}
```

6. When executing the program, you will get an output similar to the following. Some of the training model output has been removed to save space:

```
Indexing events with TwoPass using cutoff of 5

Computing event counts... done. 36 events
 Indexing... done.
Sorting and merging events... done. Reduced 36 events to 12.
Done indexing in 0.21 s.
Incorporating indexed data for training...
done.
 Number of Event Tokens: 12
 Number of Outcomes: 2
 Number of Predicates: 9
...done.
Computing model parameters ...
Performing 100 iterations.
 1: ... loglikelihood=-24.95329850015802 0.8611111111111112
 2: ... loglikelihood=-14.200654164477221 0.8611111111111112
 3: ... loglikelihood=-11.526745527757855 0.8611111111111112
 4: ... loglikelihood=-9.984657035211438 0.8888888888888888
 ...
 97: ... loglikelihood=-0.7805227945549726 1.0
 98: ... loglikelihood=-0.7730211829010772 1.0
 99: ... loglikelihood=-0.765664507836384 1.0
100: ... loglikelihood=-0.7584485899716518 1.0
In
addition
```

```
,
the
rook
was
moved
too
far
to
be
effective
.
```

How it works...

To understand how this all works, we will explain the training code, the testing code, and the output. We will start with the training code.

To create a model, we need test data that was saved in the `training-data.train` file. Its contents are as follows:

```
These fields are used to provide further information about how tokens
should be identified<SPLIT>.  They can help identify breaks between
numbers<SPLIT>, such as 23.6<SPLIT>, punctuation characters such as
commas<SPLIT>.
```

The `<SPLIT>` markup has been added just before the places where the tokenizer should split code, in locations rather than white spaces. Normally, we would use a larger set of data to obtain a better model. For our purposes, this file will work.

We created an instance of the `InputStreamFactory` to represent the training data file, as shown in the following code:

```
InputStreamFactory inputStreamFactory = new InputStreamFactory() {
    public InputStream createInputStream()
            throws FileNotFoundException {
        return new FileInputStream("training-data.train");
    }
};
```

An object stream is created in the `try` block that read from the file. The
`PlainTextByLineStream` class processes plain text line by line. This stream was then used
to create another input stream of `TokenSample` objects, providing a usable form for
training the model, as shown in the following code:

```
try (
    ObjectStream<String> stringObjectStream =
        new PlainTextByLineStream(inputStreamFactory, "UTF-8");
    ObjectStream<TokenSample> tokenSampleStream =
        new TokenSampleStream(stringObjectStream);) {

    ...
} catch (IOException ex) {
    // Handle exception
}
```

The `train` method performed the training. It takes the token stream,
a `TokenizerFactory` instance, and a set of training parameters.
The `TokenizerFactory` instance provides the basic tokenizer. Its arguments include the
language used and other factors, such as an abbreviation dictionary. In this example,
English is the language, and the other arguments are not used. We used the default set of
training parameters, as shown in the following code:

```
TokenizerModel tokenizerModel = TokenizerME.train(
    tokenSampleStream, new TokenizerFactory("en", null, true, null),
    TrainingParameters.defaultParams());
```

Once the model was trained, we saved it to the `mymodel.bin` file using the `serialize`
method:

```
BufferedOutputStream modelOutputStream = new BufferedOutputStream(
    new FileOutputStream(new File("mymodel.bin")));
tokenizerModel.serialize(modelOutputStream);
```

To test the model, we reused the tokenization code found in the *Tokenization using
the OpenNLP* recipe. You can refer to that recipe for an explanation of the code.

The output of the preceding code displays various statistics, such as the number of passes and iterations performed. One token was displayed per line, as shown in the following code. Note that the comma and period are treated as separate tokens using this model:

```
In
addition
,
the
rook
was
moved
too
far
to
be
effective
.
```

There's more...

The training process can be tailored using training parameters. Details of how to use these parameters are hard to find; however, cut-off and iteration are described at: `https://stackoverflow.com/questions/30238014/what-is-the-meaning-of-cut-off-and-iteration-for-trainings-in-opennlp`.

See also

- The OpenNLP API can be found at: `https://opennlp.apache.org/docs/1.9.0/apidocs/opennlp-tools/index.html`
- See the *Tokenization using OpenNLP* recipe for an explanation of how the model is tested

Identifying the stem of a word

Finding the stem of a word is easy to do. We will illustrate this process using OpenNLP's `PorterStemmer` class.

Getting ready

To prepare, we need to do the following:

1. Create a new Maven project
2. Add the following dependency to the POM file:

```
<dependency>
    <groupId>org.apache.opennlp</groupId>
    <artifactId>opennlp-tools</artifactId>
    <version>1.9.0</version>
</dependency>
```

How to do it...

Let's go through the following steps:

1. Add the following `import` statement to the program:

```
import opennlp.tools.stemmer.PorterStemmer;
```

2. Then, add the following code to the `main` method:

```
String wordList[] =
    { "draft", "drafted", "drafting", "drafts",
        "drafty", "draftsman" };
PorterStemmer porterStemmer = new PorterStemmer();
for (String word : wordList) {
    String stem = porterStemmer.stem(word);
    System.out.println("The stem of " + word + " is " + stem);
}
```

3. Execute the program. The output should be as follows:

```
The stem of drafted is draft
The stem of drafting is draft
The stem of drafts is draft
The stem of drafty is drafti
The stem of draftsman is draftsman
```

How it works...

We start by creating an array of strings that will hold words that we will use with the stemmer:

```
String wordList[] =
    { "draft", "drafted", "drafting", "drafts", "drafty", "draftsman" };
```

The OpenNLP `PorterStemmer` class supports finding the stem of a word. It has a single default constructor that is used to create an instance of the class, as shown in the following code. This is the only constructor available for this class:

```
PorterStemmer porterStemmer = new PorterStemmer();
```

The remainder of the code iterates over the array and invokes the `stem` method against each word in the array, as shown in the following code:

```
for (String word : wordList) {
    String stem = porterStemmer.stem(word);
    System.out.println("The stem of " + word + " is " + stem);
}
```

See also

- The OpenNLP API can be found at `https://opennlp.apache.org/docs/1.9.0/apidocs/opennlp-tools/index.html`
- The process of lemmatization is discussed in the *Determining the lexical meaning of a word* recipe
- An comparison of stemming versus lemmatization can be found at `https://blog.bitext.com/what-is-the-difference-between-stemming-and-lemmatization/`

Training an OpenNLP lemmatization model

We will train a model using OpenNLP, which can be used to perform lemmatization. The actual process of performing lemmatization is illustrated in the following recipe, *Determining the lexical meaning of a word using OpenNLP*.

Getting ready

The most straightforward technique to train a model is to use the OpenNLP command-line tools. Download these tools from the OpenNLP page at `https://opennlp.apache.org/download.html`. We will not need the source code for these tools, so download the file named `apache-opennlp-1.9.0-bin.tar.gz`. Selecting that file will take you to a page that lists mirror sites for the file. Choose one that will work best for your location.

Once the file has been saved, expand the file. This will extract a `.tar` file. Next, expand this file, which will create a directory called `apache-opennlp-1.9.0`. In its `bin` subdirectory, you will find the tools that we need.

We will need training data for the training process. We will use the `en-lemmatizer.dict` file found at `https://raw.githubusercontent.com/richardwilly98/elasticsearch-opennlp-auto-taqqing/master/src/main/resources/models/en-lemmatizer.dict`. Use a browser to open this page and then save this page using the file name `en-lemmatizer.dict`.

How to do it...

Let's go through the following steps:

1. Open a command-line window. We used the Window's cmd program in this example
2. Set up a path for the OpenNLP tool's `bin` directory and then navigate to the directory containing the `en-lemmatizer.dict` file.
3. Execute the following command:

```
opennlp LemmatizerTrainerME -model en-lemmatizer.bin -lang en -data
en-lemmatizer.dict -encoding UTF-8
```

You will get the following output. It has been shortened here to save space:

```
Indexing events with TwoPass using cutoff of 5
        Computing event counts...  done. 301403 events
Indexing...  done.

Sorting and merging events... done. Reduced 301403 events to
297777.
Done indexing in 9.09 s.

Incorporating indexed data for training...
done.
```

```
       Number of Event Tokens: 297777
       Number of Outcomes: 432
       Number of Predicates: 69122
...done.

Computing model parameters ...
Performing 100 iterations.
  1:  ... loglikelihood=-1829041.6775780176
3.317817009120679E-6
  2:  ... loglikelihood=-452333.43760414346    0.876829361353404
  3:  ... loglikelihood=-211099.05280473927    0.9506806501594212
  4:  ... loglikelihood=-132195.3981804198     0.9667554735686108
 ...
 98:  ... loglikelihood=-6702.5821153954375    0.9988420818638168
 99:  ... loglikelihood=-6652.6134177562335    0.998845399680826
100:  ... loglikelihood=-6603.518040975329     0.9988553531318534

Writing lemmatizer model
... done (1.274s)
Wrote lemmatizer model to
path: C:\Downloads\OpenNLP\en-lemmatizer.bin

Execution time: 275.369 seconds
```

How it works...

To understand the output, we need to explain the following command:

```
opennlp LemmatizerTrainerME -model en-lemmatizer.bin -lang en -data en-
lemmatizer.dict -encoding UTF-8
```

The opennlp command is used with a number of OpenNLP tools. The tool to be used is specified by the command's first argument. In this example, we used the LemmatizerTrainerME tool. The arguments that follow control how the training process works. The LemmatizerTrainerME arguments are documented at https://opennlp. apache.org/docs/1.9.0/manual/opennlp.html#tools.cli.lemmatizer. LemmatizerTrainerME.

We use the -model, -lang, –data, and –encoding arguments, as detailed in the following list:

- The -model argument specifies the name of the model output file. This is the file that holds the trained model that we will use in the next recipe.
- The –lang argument specifies the natural language used. In this case, we use en, which indicates the training data is English.
- The –data argument specifies the file containing the training data. We used the en-lemmatizer.dict file.
- The –encoding parameter specifies the character set used by the training data. We used UTF-8, which indicates the data is Unicode data.

The output shows the training process. It displays various statistics, such as the number of passes and iterations performed. During each iteration, the probability increases, as shown in the following code. With the 100th iteration, the probability approaches 100.

```
Performing 100 iterations:

  1:   ... loglikelihood=-1829041.6775780176     3.317817009120679E-6
  2:   ... loglikelihood=-452333.43760414346     0.876829361353404
  3:   ... loglikelihood=-211099.05280473927     0.9506806501594212
  4:   ... loglikelihood=-132195.3981804198      0.9667554735686108
...
 98:   ... loglikelihood=-6702.5821153954375     0.9988420818638168
 99:   ... loglikelihood=-6652.6134177562335     0.998845399680826
100:   ... loglikelihood=-6603.518040975329      0.9988553531318534
Writing lemmatizer model ... done (1.274s)
```

The final part of the output shows where the file is written. We wrote the lemmatizer model to the path :\Downloads\OpenNLP\en-lemmatizer.bin.

There's more...

If you have specialized lemmatization needs, then you will need to create a training file. The training data file consists of a series of lines. Each line consists of three entries separated by spaces. The first entry contains a word. The second entry is the POS tag for the word. The third entry is the lemma for the word.

For example, in `en-lemmatizer.dict`, there are several lines for variations of the word *bump*, as shown in the following code:

```
bump      NN            bump
bump      VB             bump
bump      VBP          bump
   bumped               VBD       bump
   bumped               VBN       bump
   bumper  JJ              bumper
   bumper  NN           bumper
```

As you can see, a word may be used in different contexts and with different suffixes. Other datasets can be used for training. These include the Penn Treebank (`https://web.archive.org/web/19970614160127/http://www.cis.upenn.edu/~treebank/`) and the CoNLL 2009 datasets (`https://www.ldc.upenn.edu/`).

Training parameters other than the default parameters can be specified depending on the needs of the problem.

In the next recipe, *Determining the lexical meaning of a word using OpenNLP,* we will use the model to develop and determine the lexical meaning of a word.

See also

- The OpenNLP API can be found at `https://opennlp.apache.org/docs/1.9.0/apidocs/opennlp-tools/index.html`

Determining the lexical meaning of a word using OpenNLP

In this recipe, we will use the model we created in the previous recipe to perform lemmatization. We will perform lemmatization on the following sentence:

```
The girls were leaving the clubhouse for another adventurous afternoon.
```

In the example, the lemmas for each word in the sentence will be displayed.

Getting ready

To prepare, we need to do the following:

1. Create a new Maven project
2. Add the following dependency to the POM file:

```
<dependency>
    <groupId>org.apache.opennlp</groupId>
    <artifactId>opennlp-tools</artifactId>
    <version>1.9.0</version>
</dependency>
```

How to do it...

Let's go through the following steps:

1. Add the following imports to the project:

```
import java.io.FileInputStream;
import java.io.FileNotFoundException;
import java.io.IOException;
import java.io.InputStream;
import opcnnlp.tools.lemmatizer.LemmatizerME;
import opennlp.tools.lemmatizer.LemmatizerModel;
```

2. Add the following try block to the main method. An input stream and model are created, followed by the instantiation of the lemmatization model:

```
LemmatizerModel lemmatizerModel = null;
try (InputStream modelInputStream = new FileInputStream(
        "C:\\Downloads\\OpenNLP\\en-lemmatizer.bin")) {
    lemmatizerModel = new LemmatizerModel(modelInputStream);
    LemmatizerME lemmatizer = new LemmatizerME(lemmatizerModel);
    ...
} catch (FileNotFoundException e) {
    // Handle exception
} catch (IOException e) {
    // Handle exception
}
```

3. Add the following code to the end of the `try` block. It sets up arrays holding the words of the sample text and their POS tags. It then performs the lemmatization and displays the results:

```
String[] tokens = new String[] {
    "The", "girls", "were", "leaving", "the",
    "clubhouse", "for", "another", "adventurous",
    "afternoon", "." };
String[] posTags = new String[] { "DT", "NNS", "VBD",
    "VBG", "DT", "NN", "IN", "DT", "JJ", "NN", "." };
String[] lemmas = lemmatizer.lemmatize(tokens, posTags);
for (int i = 0; i < tokens.length; i++) {
    System.out.println(tokens[i] + " - " + lemmas[i]);
}
```

4. Upon executing the program, you will get the following output that displays each word and then its lemma:

```
The - the
girls - girl
were - be
leaving - leave
the - the
clubhouse - clubhouse
for - for
another - another
adventurous - adventurous
afternoon - afternoon
. - .
```

How it works...

We performed lemmatization on the sentence *The girls were leaving the clubhouse for another adventurous afternoon*. A LemmatizerModel was declared and instantiated from the en-lemmatizer.bin file. A try-with-resources block was used to obtained an input stream for the file, as shown in the following code:

```
LemmatizerModel lemmatizerModel = null;
try (InputStream modelInputStream = new FileInputStream(
        "C:\\Downloads\\OpenNLP\\en-lemmatizer.bin")) {
    lemmatizerModel = new LemmatizerModel(modelInputStream);
```

Next, the lemmatizer was created using the `LemmatizerME` class, as shown in the following code:

```
LemmatizerME lemmatizer = new LemmatizerME(lemmatizerModel);
```

The following sentence was processed, and is represented as an array of strings. We also need an array of POS tags for the lemmatization process to work. This array was defined in parallel with the sentence array. As we will see in `Chapter 4`, *Detecting POS Using Neural Networks*, there are often alternative tags that are possible for a sentence. For this example, we used tags generated by the Cognitive Computation Group's online tool at `http://cogcomp.org/page/demo_view/pos`:

```
String[] tokens = new String[] {
    "The", "girls", "were", "leaving", "the",
    "clubhouse", "for", "another", "adventurous",
    "afternoon", "." };
String[] posTags = new String[] { "DT", "NNS", "VBD",
    "VBG", "DT", "NN", "IN", "DT", "JJ", "NN", "." };
```

The lemmatization then occurred, where the `lemmatize` method uses the two arrays to build an array of lemmas for each word in the sentence, as shown in the following code:

```
String[] lemmas = lemmatizer.lemmatize(tokens, posTags);
```

The lemmas are then displayed, as shown in the following code:

```
for (int i = 0; i < tokens.length; i++) {
    System.out.println(tokens[i] + " - " + lemmas[i]);
}
```

See also

- The OpenNLP API can be found at `https://opennlp.apache.org/docs/1.9.0/apidocs/opennlp-tools/index.html`
- The *Training an OpenNLP lemmatization model* recipe shows how the model was trained

Removing stop words using LingPipe

Normalization is the process of preparing text for subsequent analysis. This is frequently performed once the text has been tokenized. Normalization activities include such tasks as converting the text to lowercase, validating data, inserting missing elements, stemming, lemmatization, and removing stop words.

We have already examined the stemming and lemmatization process in earlier recipes. In this recipe, we will show how stop words can be removed. Stop words are those words that are not always useful. For example, some downstream NLP tasks do not need to have words such as *a*, *the*, or *and*. These types of words are the common words found in a language. Analysis can often be enhanced by removing them from a text.

Getting ready

To prepare, we need to do the following:

1. Create a new Maven project
2. Add the following dependency to the POM file:

```
<dependency>
    <groupId>de.julielab</groupId>
    <artifactId>aliasi-lingpipe</artifactId>
    <version>4.1.0</version>
</dependency>
```

How to do it...

Let's go through the following steps:

1. Add the following import statements to your program:

```
import com.aliasi.tokenizer.IndoEuropeanTokenizerFactory;
import com.aliasi.tokenizer.Tokenizer;
import com.aliasi.tokenizer.TokenizerFactory;
import com.aliasi.tokenizer.EnglishStopTokenizerFactory;
```

2. Add the following code to the `main` method:

```
String sentence =
    "The blue goose and a quiet lamb stopped to smell the roses.";
TokenizerFactory tokenizerFactory =
    IndoEuropeanTokenizerFactory.INSTANCE;
tokenizerFactory =
    new EnglishStopTokenizerFactory(tokenizerFactory);
Tokenizer tokenizer =tokenizerFactory.tokenizer(
    sentence.toCharArray(), 0, sentence.length());
for (String token : tokenizer) {
    System.out.println(token);
}
```

3. Execute the program. You will get the following output:

```
The
blue
goose
quiet
lamb
stopped
smell
roses

.
```

How it works...

The example started with the declaration of a sample sentence. The program will return a list of words found in the sentence with the stop words removed, as shown in the following code:

```
String sentence =
    "The blue goose and a quiet lamb stopped to smell the roses.";
```

An instance of LingPipe's `IndoEuropeanTokenizerFactory` is used to provide a means of tokenizing the sentence. It is used as the argument to the `EnglishStopTokenizerFactory` constructor, which provides a stop word tokenizer, as shown in the following code:

```
TokenizerFactory tokenizerFactory =
    IndoEuropeanTokenizerFactory.INSTANCE;
tokenizerFactory = new EnglishStopTokenizerFactory(tokenizerFactory);
```

The `tokenizer` method is invoked against the sentence, where its second and third parameters specify which part of the sentence to tokenize. The `Tokenizer` class represents the tokens extracted from the sentence:

```
Tokenizer tokenizer = tokenizerFactory.tokenizer(
    sentence.toCharArray(), 0, sentence.length());
```

The `Tokenizer` class implements the `Iterable<String>` interface that we utilized in the following `for-each` statement to display the tokens:

```
for (String token : tokenizer) {
    System.out.println(token);
}
```

Note that in the following duplicated output, the first word of the sentence, `The`, was not removed, nor was there a terminating period. Otherwise, common stop words were removed, as shown in the following code:

```
The
blue
goose
quiet
lamb
stopped
smell
roses
.
```

See also

- The LingPipe API can be found at `http://alias-i.com/lingpipe/docs/api/index.html`

2
Isolating Sentences within a Document

The process of extracting sentences from text is known as **Sentence Boundary Disambiguation (SBD)**. While this process may initially appear to be simple, there are many complicating factors that ultimately demand more sophisticated approaches, such as using neural networks.

The end of a sentence is typically marked with a period. However, there are other terminators used, such as question marks and exclamation marks. If these were the only considerations, then the process would be easy. However, even limiting the problem to periods, we find that periods are used in many places including abbreviations, numbers, and ellipses. A sentence might use periods such as *Mr. Smith, 2.005*, or *3.12.18*. Ellipses may be simply three periods back, to back or a Unicode character might be used.

Specialized text such as scientific text may contain unusual uses of periods. Sometimes, one sentence may be embedded inside of another sentence such as *Here is a simple example.*, which complicates the SBD process. We will examine how SBD is accomplished using the `BreakIterator` Java class in the first recipe. This technique is easy to use and may well suffice for many applications. When it does split sentences correctly, then the use of neural network models becomes important. Several of these models are illustrated in later recipes. We may find that there are situations where even the readily available models do not work for the specialized data we may be using. When this is the case, then training our own model may be the ideal thing to do (this approach is demonstrated in the last recipe).

In this chapter, we will cover the following recipes:

- Finding sentences using the Java core API
- Performing SBD using the `BreakIterator` class
- Using OpenNLP to perform SBD
- Using the Stanford NLP API to perform SBD
- Using the LingPipe and chunking to perform SBD
- Performing SBD on specialized text
- Training a neural network to perform SBD with specialized text

Technical requirements

In this chapter, you will need to install the following software if it has not already been installed:

- Eclipse Photon 4.8.0
- Java JDK 8 or later

We will be using the following APIs, which you will be instructed to add for each recipe as appropriate:

- OpenNLP 1.9.0
- Stanford NLP 3.8.0
- LingPipe 4.1.0

The code files for this chapter can be found at `https://github.com/PacktPublishing/Natural-Language-Processing-with-Java-Cookbook/tree/master/Chapter02`.

Finding sentences using the Java core API

There are several approaches to performing SBD using the Java core JDK. While they will not always yield good results as do other more advanced SBD techniques, they may prove quite useful in some situations while not incurring the expense of specialized NLP models.

In this recipe, we will examine two approaches:

- The first approach will use the `split` method of the `String` class
- The second approach uses a simple regular expression

Getting ready

Create a new Java project. Since we will not be using any specialized libraries, the project does not need to be a Maven project.

How to do it...

The necessary steps include the following:

1. Add the following imports to the project:

```
import java.util.regex.Matcher;
import java.util.regex.Pattern;
```

2. Add the following sample text to the main method:

```
String text =
    "We will start with a simple sentence. However, is it "
    + "possible for a sentence to end with a question "
    + "mark? Obviously that is possible! Another "
    + "complication is the use of a number such as 56.32 "
    + "or ellipses such as ... Ellipses may be found ... "
    + "with a sentence! Of course, we may also find the "
    + "use of abbreviations such as Mr. Smith or "
    + "Dr. Jones.";
```

3. Add the following code to split sentences using the String class:

```
String sentenceDelimiters = "[.?!]";
String[] sentences = (text.split(sentenceDelimiters));
for (String sentence : sentences) {
    System.out.println(sentence);
}
```

4. Next, add the following sequence, which illustrates using a regular expression:

```
Pattern sentencePattern = Pattern.compile("\\s+[^.!?]*[.!?]");
Matcher matcher = sentencePattern.matcher(text);
while (matcher.find()) {
    System.out.println(matcher.group());
}
```

5. Executing the code, you will get the following output:

```
We will start with a simple sentence
However, is it possible for a sentence to end with a question mark
Obviously that is possible
Another complication is the use of a number such as 56
32 or ellipses such as

Ellipses may be found

 with a sentence
 Of course, we may also find the use of abbreviations such as Mr
 Smith or Dr
 Jones
 will start with a simple sentence.
 However, is it possible for a sentence to end with a question
mark?
 Obviously that is possible!
 Another complication is the use of a number such as 56.
 or ellipses such as .
 Ellipses may be found .
 with a sentence!
 Of course, we may also find the use of abbreviations such as Mr.
 Smith or Dr.
 Jones.
```

How it works...

The first code sequence splits the sentences using a simple set of delimiters. These delimiters consisted of a period, question mark, and exclamation mark, which represent the more common sentence delimiters. The split method was applied against the sample sentences using the delimiters as its argument. The method returned an array of strings, which represent the sentences identified:

```
String sentenceDelimiters = "[.?!]";
String[] sentences = (text.split(sentenceDelimiters));
for (String sentence : sentences) {
    System.out.println(sentence);
}
```

The output of this sequence did not handle numbers very well. The number 56.32 was split into two integer values between lines 4 and 5 of the output of step 5 in the previous section. In addition, each dot of an ellipsis was treated as a separate sentence. Using a period as a delimiter easily explains why we get this output. However, understanding the limitations of this technique allows us to choose those situations where it is applicable.

The next sequence used a simple regular expression to isolate sentences. This regular expression was used as the argument of the `compile` method, which returned an instance of the `Pattern` class. The `matcher` method of this class created a `Matcher` object. Its `find` method is used to iterate through the sample text. The `Matcher` object's group method returns the current sentence, which was displayed:

```
Pattern sentencePattern = Pattern.compile("\\s+[^.!?]*[.!?]");
Matcher matcher = sentencePattern.matcher(text);
while (matcher.find()) {
    System.out.println(matcher.group());
}
```

The output from this code sequence also has problems. These are ultimately traceable to the overly simplistic regular expression used in the code. There are other regular expression variations that will perform better. A better performing regular expression for sentences is found at `https://stackoverflow.com/questions/5553410/regular-expression-match-a-sentence`.

See also

- Regular expressions, by their very nature, are often hard to read and follow. The *Performing SBD using the BreakIterator class* recipe that follows does a better job.

Performing SBD using the BreakIterator class

There are several Java core techniques that can be used to perform sentence boundary detection. In this recipe, we will use the `BreakIterator` class. This class supports the identification of more than just sentences. It can also be used to isolate lines and words.

Getting ready

Create a new Java project. This does not need to be a Maven project since we will not be using a specialized NLP library.

How to do it...

The necessary steps include the following:

1. Add the following import statement to the project:

    ```
    import java.text.BreakIterator;
    ```

2. Next, add the declaration for text as an instance variable:

    ```
    private static String text =
        "We will start with a simple sentence. However, is it "
        + "possible for a sentence to end with a question "
        + "mark? Obviously that is possible! Another "
        + "complication is the use of a number such as 56.32 "
        + "or ellipses such as ... Ellipses may be found ... "
        + "with a sentence! Of course, we may also find the "
        + "use of abbreviations such as Mr. Smith or "
        + "Dr. Jones.";
    ```

3. Add the following code to the `main` method to set up the `BreakIterator` instance:

    ```
    BreakIterator breakIterator = BreakIterator.getSentenceInstance();
    breakIterator.setText(text);
    ```

4. Next, add the code sequence that follows to use the `BreakIterator` instance to find and display sentences:

    ```
    int startPosition = breakIterator.first();
    int endingPosition = breakIterator.first();
    while (true) {
        endingPosition = breakIterator.next();
        if (endingPosition == BreakIterator.DONE) {
            break;
        } else {
            System.out.println(startPosition + "-" +
                endingPosition + " [" +
                text.substring(startPosition, endingPosition) + "]");
            startPosition = endingPosition;
        }
    }
    ```

5. Execute the program. You will get the following output:

```
0-38 [We will start with a simple sentence. ]
38-106 [However, is it possible for a sentence to end with a
question mark? ]
106-135 [Obviously that is possible! ]
135-217 [Another complication is the use of a number such as 56.32
or ellipses such as ... ]
217-260 [Ellipses may be found ... with a sentence! ]
260-325 [Of course, we may also find the use of abbreviations such
as Mr. ]
325-338 [Smith or Dr. ]
338-344 [Jones.]
```

How it works...

As the name of the BreakIterator class implies, it breaks up text and provides techniques for iterating between the result. The class can be used for different types of breaks. For our purposes, we used it to break up sentences. The getSentenceInstance static method returns a BreakIterator instance for sentences. The setText method associates the iterator with the sample text:

```
BreakIterator breakIterator = BreakIterator.getSentenceInstance();
breakIterator.setText(text);
```

The startPosition and endingPosition variables are used to hold the indexes of the beginning and ending positions within a sentence. These variables were initialized to the first break, which is the beginning of the text:

```
int startPosition = breakIterator.first();
int endingPosition = breakIterator.first();
```

The while loop iterated though the text processing one sentence at a time and terminates when the end of the text is reached, as shown next. In each iteration, the ending position was set using the next method. This method moved through the text until it found the next sentence break. If this ending position was equal to BreakIterator.DONE, the loop terminated and we have processed the text.

Otherwise, the starting and ending positions were used to display the sentence using the `substring` method. The `startPosition` was set to the current ending position. At the beginning of the loop, the next sentence break is assigned to the `endingPosition` variable. Keep in mind that there is only one break between each sentence. Hence, the ending position of one sentence becomes the beginning position of the next:

```
while (true) {
    endingPosition = breakIterator.next();
    if (endingPosition == BreakIterator.DONE) {
        break;
    } else {
        System.out.println(startPosition + "-" + endingPosition " [" +
            text.substring(startPosition, endingPosition) + "]");
        startPosition = endingPosition;
    }
}
```

We used brackets around the sentences to clearly show where the break iterator delineates sentences.

There's more...

The `BreakIterator` class possesses other methods that may be of interest. If we need to, we can find and display only the first sentence of the text. This process is illustrated in the following: we use the `setText` method to reset the iterator. We then obtain the first break using the `first` method. The `next` method is then applied to find the break between the first and subsequent sentences. These break indexes are then used to find the substring that makes up the first sentence:

```
breakIterator.setText(text);
startPosition = breakIterator.first();
endingPosition = breakIterator.next();
System.out.println("First sentence: [" +
    text.substring(startPosition, endingPosition) + "]");
```

When this code is executed, you will get the following output:

```
First sentence: [We will start with a simple sentence. ]
```

It is also possible to isolate just the last sentence. In the next sequence, we reset the iterator and then find the last sentence break using the `last` method. This value is then assigned to the `endingPosition` variable. The `previous` method is then applied to the iterator, which returns the starting position of the last sentence. The sentence is then displayed:

```
breakIterator.setText(text);
endingPosition = breakIterator.last();
startPosition = breakIterator.previous();
System.out.println("Last sentence: [" +
    text.substring(startPosition, endingPosition) + "]");
```

Executing this code sequence will generate the following output:

```
Last sentence: [Jones.]
```

There are also different types of `BreakIterator` instances. The `getCharacterInstance`, `getWordInstance`, and `getLineInstance` methods return iterators that will find breaks between characters, words, and lines respectively.

See also

- Documentation of the `BreakIterator` class is found at `https://docs.oracle.com/javase/10/docs/api/java/text/BreakIterator.html`

Using OpenNLP to perform SBD

OpenNLP is a popular NLP library that supports the SBD process among other NLP tasks. As we will see, it is easy to use. We will use the `SentenceDetectorME` class to demonstrate this process. This is a maximum entropy model that is based on a statistical classification approach.

Getting ready

To prepare, we need to do the following:

1. Create a new Maven project.
2. Add the following POM dependency to your project:

```
<dependency>
    <groupId>org.apache.opennlp</groupId>
    <artifactId>opennlp-tools</artifactId>
    <version>1.9.0</version>
</dependency>
```

3. Download the `en-sent.bin` file from `http://opennlp.sourceforge.net/models-1.5/`. Save the file in your project's root directory.

How to do it...

The necessary steps include the following:

1. Add the following imports to your project:

```
import java.io.File;
import java.io.FileInputStream;
import java.io.FileNotFoundException;
import java.io.IOException;
import java.io.InputStream;
import opennlp.tools.sentdetect.SentenceDetectorME;
import opennlp.tools.sentdetect.SentenceModel;
import opennlp.tools.util.Span;
```

2. Next, add the declaration for the sample text as an instance variable:

```
private static String text =
    "We will start with a simple sentence. However, is it "
    + "possible for a sentence to end with a question "
    + "mark? Obviously that is possible! Another "
    + "complication is the use of a number such as 56.32 "
    + "or ellipses such as ... Ellipses may be found ... "
    + "with a sentence! Of course, we may also find the "
    + "use of abbreviations such as Mr. Smith or "
    + "Dr. Jones.";
```

3. Add the following `try` block to your `main` method:

```
try (InputStream inputStream = new FileInputStream(
        new File("en-sent.bin"))) {
    ...
} catch (FileNotFoundException ex) {
    // Handle exceptions
} catch (IOException ex) {
    // Handle exceptions
}
```

4. Insert this next sequence into the `try` block. This will instantiate the model, perform sentence detection, and then display the results:

```
SentenceModel sentenceModel = new SentenceModel(inputStream);
SentenceDetectorME sentenceDetector =
    new SentenceDetectorME(sentenceModel);
String sentences[] = sentenceDetector.sentDetect(text);
for (String sentence : sentences) {
    System.out.println("[" + sentence + "]");
}
```

5. Execute your program. You will get the following output:

```
[We will start with a simple sentence.]
[However, is it possible for a sentence to end with a question
mark?]
[Obviously that is possible!.]
[Another complication is the use of a number such as 56.32 or
ellipses such as ... Ellipses may be found ... within a sentence!]
[Of course, we may also find the use of abbreviations such as Mr.
Smith or Dr. Jones.]
```

How it works...

The `en-sent.bin` file holds the model used for identifying sentences in text. We created an input stream using this file and then used the input stream as the argument of the `SentenceModel` constructor. An instance of `SentenceDetectorME` was created based on the sentence model:

```
try (InputStream inputStream = new FileInputStream(
        new File("en-sent.bin"))) {
    SentenceModel sentenceModel = new SentenceModel(inputStream);
    SentenceDetectorME sentenceDetector =
        new SentenceDetectorME(sentenceModel);
    ...
```

```
    } catch (FileNotFoundException ex) {
        // Handle exceptions
    } catch (IOException ex) {
        // Handle exceptions
    }
```

The `sentDetect` method was passed along with the text to be processed. The method returns an array of strings where each element represents one sentence. The sentences were then displayed:

```
String sentences[] = sentenceDetector.sentDetect(text);
for (String sentence : sentences) {
    System.out.println("[" + sentence + "]");
}
```

We used brackets around the sentences to clearly show where the model delineates sentences. This model was not successful in detecting the sentence that ended with ellipses, as found in the fourth line of the output produced in step 5 of the previous section. It is duplicated here:

```
[Another complication is the use of a number such as 56.32 or ellipses such
as ... Ellipses may be found ... with a sentence!]
```

There's more...

The `SentenceDetectorME` class possesses a `sentPosDetect` method that passes a string and returns an array of `Span` objects. A `Span` object holds the beginning and ending positions within a string. In this case, it holds the beginning and ending indexes of a sentence. The following code illustrates how to use it to obtain the indexes of each sentence in the text:

```
Span spans[] = sentenceDetector.sentPosDetect(text);
for (Span span : spans) {
    System.out.println(span);
}
```

Add this code to your project and you will get the following output:

```
[0..37)
[38..105)
[106..134)
[135..259)
[260..344)
```

We can also determine the probability that the sentences found are valid by using the `getSentenceProbabilities` method, which generates an array of probabilities, as shown next:

```
double probablities[] = sentenceDetector.getSentenceProbabilities();
for(int i=0; i<sentences.length; i++) {
    System.out.printf("Sentence %d: %6.4f\n",i, probablities[i]);
}
```

When this code is executed, you will get the following output:

```
Sentence 0: 0.9999
Sentence 1: 0.8117
Sentence 2: 0.9157
Sentence 3: 0.9953
Sentence 4: 0.9706
```

See also

- The OpenNLP documentation is found at `https://opennlp.apache.org/docs/1.9.0/apidocs/opennlp-tools/index.html`

Using the Stanford NLP API to perform SBD

The Stanford NLP API possesses several techniques for detecting SBD. We will use the `WordToSentenceProcessor` class to illustrate how this can be performed. This provides an alternate approach to using OpenNLP.

Getting ready

To prepare, we need to do the following:

1. Create a new Maven project
2. Add the following dependency to the project's POM file:

```
<dependency>
    <groupId>edu.stanford.nlp</groupId>
    <artifactId>stanford-corenlp</artifactId>
    <version>3.8.0</version>
</dependency>
```

How to do it...

The necessary steps include the following:

1. Insert the following imports to the project:

```
import java.io.StringReader;
import java.util.List;
import edu.stanford.nlp.ling.CoreLabel;
import edu.stanford.nlp.process.CoreLabelTokenFactory;
import edu.stanford.nlp.process.PTBTokenizer;
import edu.stanford.nlp.process.WordToSentenceProcessor;
```

2. Add the following instance variable, which will hold the series of sentences to be processed:

```
private static String text =
    "We will start with a simple sentence. However, is it "
    + "possible for a sentence to end with a question "
    + "mark? Obviously that is possible! Another "
    + "complication is the use of a number such as 56.32 "
    + "or ellipses such as ... Ellipses may be found ... "
    + "with a sentence! Of course, we may also find the "
    + "use of abbreviations such as Mr. Smith or "
    + "Dr. Jones.";
```

3. Add the following code to the `main` method:

```
PTBTokenizer<CoreLabel> ptbTokenizer = new PTBTokenizer<CoreLabel>(
    new StringReader(text),
    new CoreLabelTokenFactory(), null);
WordToSentenceProcessor<CoreLabel> wordToSentenceProcessor =
    new WordToSentenceProcessor<CoreLabel>();
List<List<CoreLabel>> sentenceList =
    wordToSentenceProcessor.process(ptbTokenizer.tokenize());

for (List<CoreLabel> sentence : sentenceList) {
    System.out.println(sentence);
}
```

4. Execute the code. You will get the following output:

```
[We, will, start, with, a, simple, sentence, .]
[However, ,, is, it, possible, for, a, sentence, to, end, with, a,
question, mark, ?]
[Obviously, that, is, possible, !]
[Another, complication, is, the, use, of, a, number, such, as,
56.32, or, ellipses, such, as, ..., Ellipses, may, be, found, ...,
```

```
with, a, sentence, !]
[Of, course, ,, we, may, also, find, the, use, of, abbreviations,
such, as, Mr., Smith, or, Dr., Jones, .]
```

How it works...

The `PTBTokenizer` class is a tokenizer for the English language. Most NLP APIs have tokenizers that are trained to work with various languages. The `CoreLabel` class is used as a generic for the class and represents information regarding words. The Java `StringReader` class was used to obtain data from the text string:

```
PBTokenizer<CoreLabel> ptbTokenizer = new PTBTokenizer<CoreLabel>(
    new StringReader(text), new CoreLabelTokenFactory(), null);
```

The `WordToSentenceProcessor` class was used to group words into sentences. Its process method returns a list of lists—effectively a list of sentences:

```
WordToSentenceProcessor<CoreLabel> wordToSentenceProcessor =
    new WordToSentenceProcessor<CoreLabel>();
List<List<CoreLabel>> sentenceList =
    wordToSentenceProcessor.process(ptbTokenizer.tokenize());
```

The list of sentences was then displayed:

```
for (List<CoreLabel> sentence : sentenceList) {
    System.out.println(sentence);
}
```

The first sentence in the text was as follows:

```
We will start with a simple sentence.
```

Let's examine the output for the first sentence as shown next. Notice that it is a list of words separated by commas. The sentence is enclosed in a set of brackets. Also, notice that the terminating period was included:

```
[We, will, start, with, a, simple, sentence, .]
```

In the second line of output, we find three commas back-to-back. The middle comma was in the original sentence and is treated as a word:

```
[However, ,, is, it, possible, for, a, sentence, to, end, with, a,
question, mark, ?]
```

There's more...

We can get a cleaner set of sentences by using the `CoreLabel` objects that are part of the list of sentences. In the next sequence, we iterate over the list and use the default `toString` method of the `CoreLabel` class to display the sentences:

```
for (List<CoreLabel> sentence : sentenceList) {
    for (CoreLabel coreLabel : sentence) {
        System.out.print(coreLabel + " ");
    }
    System.out.println();
}
```

When this code is executed you will get the following results:

```
We will start with a simple sentence .
However , is it possible for a sentence to end with a question mark ?
Obviously that is possible !
Another complication is the use of a number such as 56.32 or ellipses such
as ... Ellipses may be found ... with a sentence !
Of course , we may also find the use of abbreviations such as Mr. Smith or
Dr. Jones .
```

If we are interested in the position of each word in the sentence, the `beginPosition` and `endPosition` methods will return the beginning and ending index for each word. The `word` method returns the actual word. This technique is demonstrated here:

```
for (List<CoreLabel> sentence : sentenceList) {
    for (CoreLabel coreLabel : sentence) {
        System.out.print(coreLabel.word() + " - " +
            coreLabel.beginPosition() + ":" +
            coreLabel.endPosition() + " ");
    }
}
System.out.println();
```

The output is shown here:

```
We - 0:2 will - 3:7 start - 8:13 with - 14:18 a - 19:20 simple - 21:27
sentence - 28:36 . - 36:37
However - 38:45 , - 45:46 is - 47:49 it - 50:52 possible - 53:61 for -
62:65 a - 66:67 sentence - 68:76 to - 77:79 end - 80:83 with - 84:88 a -
89:90 question - 91:99 mark - 100:104 ? - 104:105
Obviously - 106:115 that - 116:120 is - 121:123 possible - 124:132 ! -
132:133
. - 133:134
Another - 135:142 complication - 143:155 is - 156:158 the - 159:162 use -
```

```
163:166 of - 167:169 a - 170:171 number - 172:178 such - 179:183 as -
184:186 56.32 - 187:192 or - 193:195 ellipses - 196:204 such - 205:209 as -
210:212 ... - 213:216 Ellipses - 217:225 may - 226:229 be - 230:232 found -
233:238 ... - 239:242 with - 243:247 a - 248:249 sentence - 250:258 ! -
258:259
Of - 260:262 course - 263:269 , - 269:270 we - 271:273 may - 274:277 also -
278:282 find - 283:287 the - 288:291 use - 292:295 of - 296:298
abbreviations - 299:312 such - 313:317 as - 318:320 Mr. - 321:324 Smith -
325:330 or - 331:333 Dr. - 334:337 Jones - 338:343 . - 343:344
```

See also

- The Stanford NLP documentation is found at `https://nlp.stanford.edu/nlp/javadoc/javanlp/`

Using the LingPipe and chunking to perform SBD

Chunking is a technique that breaks up text into units referred to as chunks. The LingPipe libraries contain classes that support SBD. In this recipe, we will demonstrate how to perform SBD using chunking.

Getting ready

To prepare, we need to do the following:

1. Create a new Maven project
2. Add the following dependency to the project's POM file:

```xml
<dependency>
    <groupId>de.julielab</groupId>
    <artifactId>aliasi-lingpipe</artifactId>
    <version>4.1.0</version>
</dependency>
```

How to do it...

The necessary steps include the following:

1. Insert the following import statements:

    ```
    import java.util.ArrayList;
    import java.util.List;
    import com.aliasi.sentences.IndoEuropeanSentenceModel;
    import com.aliasi.sentences.SentenceModel;
    import com.aliasi.tokenizer.IndoEuropeanTokenizerFactory;
    import com.aliasi.tokenizer.Tokenizer;
    import com.aliasi.tokenizer.TokenizerFactory;
    ```

2. Next, add the following code segment to the `main` method, which creates a tokenizer and sentence model:

    ```
    String text =
        "We will start with a simple sentence. However, is it "
        + "possible for a sentence to end with a question "
        + "mark? Obviously that is possible! Another "
        + "complication is the use of a number such as 56.32 "
        + "or ellipses such as ... Ellipses may be found ... "
        + "with a sentence! Of course, we may also find the "
        + "use of abbreviations such as Mr. Smith or "
        + "Dr. Jones.";
    TokenizerFactory tokenizerFactory =
        IndoEuropeanTokenizerFactory.INSTANCE;
    SentenceModel sentenceModel = new IndoEuropeanSentenceModel();
    ```

3. Add the following lists, which will hold the tokens and white space:

    ```
    List<String> tokenList = new ArrayList<>();
    List<String> whiteList = new ArrayList<>();
    ```

4. Insert the next code sequence to populate these lists and find the sentence boundaries:

    ```
    Tokenizer tokenizer = tokenizerFactory.tokenizer(
        text.toCharArray(), 0, text.length());
    tokenizer.tokenize(tokenList, whiteList);

    int[] sentenceBoundaries = sentenceModel.boundaryIndices(
        tokenList.toArray(new String[tokenList.size()]),
        whiteList.toArray(new String[whiteList.size()]));
    ```

5. Add the following code to display the sentences detected:

```
int start = 0;
for (int boundary : sentenceBoundaries) {
    System.out.print("[");
    while (start <= boundary) {
        System.out.print(tokenList.get(start) +
            whiteList.get(start + 1));
        start++;
    }
    System.out.println("]");
}
```

6. Execute the program. You will see the following output displayed:

```
[We will start with a simple sentence. ]
[However, is it possible for a sentence to end with a question
mark? ]
[Obviously that is possible!. ]
[Another complication is the use of a number such as 56.32 or
ellipses such as ... Ellipses may be found ... with a sentence! ]
[Of course, we may also find the use of abbreviations such as Mr.
Smith or Dr. Jones.]
```

How it works...

We needed a tokenizer to use in conjunction with our model. We used the
`IndoEuropeanTokenizerFactory` class to obtain an instance of a tokenizer. Once the
factory has been obtained, we used it to obtain a tokenizer using the `tokenizer` method.

The first argument of this method is the text to be tokenized. The second argument specifies
the starting index in the string, and the third argument specifies the ending position. The
incorporation of these last two arguments provides more flexibility in what text is
processed:

```
TokenizerFactory tokenizerFactory  =
    IndoEuropeanTokenizerFactory.INSTANCE;
Tokenizer tokenizer = tokenizerFactory.tokenizer(
    text.toCharArray(), 0, text.length());
```

Before the text was tokenized, it was necessary to create two lists. One is used to hold the tokens and the other is used to hold white spaces. The `tokenize` method was then executed as shown here:

```
List<String> tokenList = new ArrayList<>();
List<String> whiteList = new ArrayList<>();
tokenizer.tokenize(tokenList, whiteList);
```

An instance of the `IndoEuropeanSentenceModel` class was created next. Its `boundaryIndices` method created an array of integer sentence boundaries. The arguments of this method needed to be two arrays holding the tokens and the white spaces of the text. These were created using the `toArray` method, which is applied against the two lists, as shown here:

```
SentenceModel sentenceModel = new IndoEuropeanSentenceModel();
int[] sentenceBoundaries = sentenceModel.boundaryIndices(
    tokenList.toArray(new String[tokenList.size()]),
    whiteList.toArray(new String[whiteList.size()]));
```

The boundaries are word indexes. In order to display the sentences, we iterated through the `sentenceBoundaries` array. Each element of the array is an index into the lists corresponding to the sentence boundary position. For the first sentence, its boundary index was 7. The inner `while` loop, shown next, uses a starting index for a sentence and advances through the lists until the next sentence boundary index is encountered. The sentence is displayed with open and close brackets to clarify what tokens and white spaces make up the sentence:

```
int start = 0;
for (int boundary : sentenceBoundaries) {
    System.out.print("[");
    while (start <= boundary) {
        System.out.print(tokenList.get(start) +
            whiteList.get(start + 1));
        start++;
    }
    System.out.println("]");
}
```

Notice how the sentence that ends in an ellipsis was not detected with this model. Every model has its own limitations, which may need to be worked around if possible. At other times, it is necessary to train a model to address specific types of text.

There's more...

We can more clearly illustrate the sentence boundaries using the following code sequence. This will display the sentence boundaries, where the beginning and ending indexes are shown, separated by a colon:

```
int begin = 0;
for (int boundary : sentenceBoundaries) {
    System.out.println(begin + ":" + boundary);
    begin — boundary;
}
```

When this sequence is executed, you will see the following output displayed, showing the indexes for each of the five sentences:

```
0:7
7:22
22:27
27:52
52:73
```

See also

- The documentation for the LingPipe classes and methods are found at `http://alias-i.com/lingpipe/docs/api/index.html`

Performing SBD on specialized text

Unique types of text, such as medical or unusual languages, pose challenges when performing SBD. The frequent heavy use of specialized words and numeric values will not always yield good result with a model trained on a normal text. As a result, there are numerous models that have been trained on specialized datasets. In this recipe, we will demonstrate the use of a LingPipe model that has been trained to handle medical text.

The model will be demonstrated against an actual paragraph from a medical research article found in the *Journal of Biomedical Science* in 2018, *Association between heavy metal levels and acute ischemic stroke*, by Ching-Huang Lin, Yi-Ting Hsu, Cheng-Chung Yen, Hsin-Hung Chen, Ching-Jiunn Tseng, Yuk-Keung Lo, and Julie Y. H. Chan at `https://jbiomedsci.biomedcentral.com/articles/10.1186/s12929-018-0446-0`.

Specifically, we will use the paragraph found in the *Results* section of the article. It is shown here:

"In total, 33 patients with AIS and 39 healthy controls were enrolled in this study. The major findings were as follows: (1) The stroke group had a significantly lower level of serum Hg (6.4?±?4.3 µg/L vs. 9.8?±?7.0 µg/L, P =?0.032, OR?=?0.90, 95% CI?=?0.81–0.99) and a lower level of urine Hg (0.7?±?0.7 µg/L vs. 1.2?±?0.6 µg/L, P =?0.006, OR?=?0.27, 95% CI?=?0.11–0.68) than the control group. (2) No significant difference in serum Pb (S-Pb), As (S-As), and Cd (S-Cd) levels and urine Pb (U-Pb), As (U-As) and Cd (U-Cd) levels was observed in either group."

Getting ready

To prepare, we need to do the following:

1. Create a new Maven project
2. Add the following dependency to the POM file:

```
<dependency>
    <groupId>de.julielab</groupId>
    <artifactId>aliasi-lingpipe</artifactId>
    <version>4.1.0</version>
</dependency>
```

How to do it...

The necessary steps include the following:

1. Add the following imports to the project:

```
import com.aliasi.chunk.Chunk;
import com.aliasi.chunk.Chunking;
import com.aliasi.sentences.MedlineSentenceModel;
import com.aliasi.sentences.SentenceChunker;
import com.aliasi.tokenizer.IndoEuropeanTokenizerFactory;
import com.aliasi.tokenizer.TokenizerFactory;
```

2. Next, add the following string declaration for a sample series of sentences to the `main` method:

```
String text = "In total, 33 patients with AIS and 39 healthy "
    + "controls were enrolled in this study. The major "
    + "findings were as follows: (1) The stroke group had "
    + "a significantly lower level of serum Hg (6.4?±?4.3 "
    + "μg/L vs. 9.8?±?7.0 μg/L, P =?0.032, OR?=?0.90, 95% "
    + "CI?=?0.81-0.99) and a lower level of urine Hg "
    + "(0.7?±?0.7 μg/L vs. 1.2?±?0.6 μg/L, P =?0.006, "
    + "OR?=?0.27, 95% CI?=?0.11-0.68) than the control "
    + "group. (2) No significant difference in serum "
    + "Pb (S-Pb), As (S-As), and Cd (S-Cd) levels and "
    + "urine Pb (U-Pb), As (U-As) and Cd (U-Cd) levels "
    + "was observed in either group.";
```

3. Add the following code to create a tokenizer and specialized model:

```
TokenizerFactory tokenizerfactory =
IndoEuropeanTokenizerFactory.INSTANCE;
MedlineSentenceModel medlineSentenceModel =
    new MedlineSentenceModel();
```

4. Next, add the following sequence to perform the SBD:

```
SentenceChunker sentenceChunker =
    new SentenceChunker(tokenizerfactory,  medlineSentenceModel);
Chunking chunking =
    sentenceChunker.chunk(text.toCharArray(),0, text.length());
String slice = chunking.charSequence().toString();
```

5. Complete the code sequence with the following code to display the sentences:

```
for (Chunk chunk : chunking.chunkSet()) {
    System.out.println("[" +  slice.substring(chunk.start(),
        chunk.end()) + "]");
}
```

6. Execute the code. You will get the following output:

```
[In total, 33 patients with AIS and 39 healthy controls were
enrolled in this study.]
[The major findings were as follows: (1) The stroke group had a
significantly lower level of serum Hg (6.4?±?4.3 µg/L vs. 9.8?±?7.0
µg/L, P =?0.032, OR?=?0.90, 95% CI?=?0.81-0.99) and a lower level
of urine Hg (0.7?±?0.7 µg/L vs. 1.2?±?0.6 µg/L, P =?0.006,
OR?=?0.27, 95% CI?=?0.11-0.68) than the control group.]
[(2) No significant difference in serum Pb (S-Pb), As (S-As), and
Cd (S-Cd) levels and urine Pb (U-Pb), As (U-As) and Cd (U-Cd)
levels was observed in either group.]
```

How it works...

The string, `text`, was initialized with the paragraph's text. Next, we used an instance of the `IndoEuropeanTokenizerFactory` class and created an instance of the `MedlineSentenceModel` class, which has been trained on medical data:

```
TokenizerFactory tokenizerfactory =
    IndoEuropeanTokenizerFactory.INSTANCE;
MedlineSentenceModel medlineSentenceModel = new MedlineSentenceModel();
```

`SentenceChunker` used the tokenizer and model to create an instance of the class. Its `chunk` method returned a `Chunking` instance. The chunks represent sequences of text based on the chunker used. In this case, it generated sentence chunks. The first argument of the method requires an array character, hence, the use of the `toCharArray` method. The second and third arguments specify which part of the text will be processed:

```
SentenceChunker sentenceChunker = new
    SentenceChunker(tokenizerfactory, medlineSentenceModel);
Chunking chunking = sentenceChunker.chunk(text.toCharArray(),0,
    text.length());
```

The final step used a for-each statement to display each sentence enclosed in brackets. The `start` and `end` methods of the `Chunk` class return the index for the beginning and ending of each sentence:

```
for (Chunk chunk : chunking.chunkSet()) {
    System.out.println("[" +
        slice.substring(chunk.start(), chunk.end()) + "]");
}
```

See also

- The documentation for the LingPipe classes and methods are found at `http://alias-i.com/lingpipe/docs/api/index.html`
- The next recipe, *Training a neural network to perform SBD with specialized text*, illustrates how a model can be trained for other specialized text

Training a neural network to perform SBD with specialized text

When there are no specialized models for SBD, it becomes necessary to train a new model. In this recipe, we will illustrate how this can be performed using the OpenNLP API. We will create a set of training data and use it to train a neural network model. The model will then be tested using the OpenNLP technique illustrated in the *Using OpenNLP to perform SBD* recipe.

Getting ready

To prepare, we need to do the following:

1. Create new Maven project
2. Add the following dependency to the POM file:

```
<dependency>
    <groupId>org.apache.opennlp</groupId>
    <artifactId>opennlp-tools</artifactId>
    <version>1.9.0</version>
</dependency>
```

How to do it...

The necessary steps include the following:

1. Add the following imports to the project:

```
import java.io.BufferedOutputStream;
import java.io.ByteArrayInputStream;
import java.io.FileInputStream;
import java.io.FileNotFoundException;
```

```
import java.io.FileOutputStream;
import java.io.IOException;
import java.io.InputStream;
import java.io.OutputStream;
import java.nio.charset.Charset;
import opennlp.tools.sentdetect.SentenceDetectorFactory;
import opennlp.tools.sentdetect.SentenceDetectorME;
import opennlp.tools.sentdetect.SentenceModel;
import opennlp.tools.sentdetect.SentenceSample;
import opennlp.tools.sentdetect.SentenceSampleStream;
import opennlp.tools.util.ObjectStream;
import opennlp.tools.util.PlainTextByLineStream;
import opennlp.tools.util.TrainingParameters;
```

2. Add the following code to the `main` method of the project. This will create a set of data used to train the model:

```
String terminators[] = { ".", "!", "?", "..." };
String sampleSentences[] = {
    "A simple sentence",
    "Another sentence a bit longer",
    "Last sentence"};

StringBuilder stringBuilder = new StringBuilder();
for (String sentenceTerminator : terminators) {
    for (String sentence : sampleSentences) {
        stringBuilder.append(sentence).append(sentenceTerminator);
        stringBuilder.append(System.lineSeparator());
    }
}

String trainingSentences = stringBuilder.toString();
```

3. Next, add a try-with-resources block to set up a stream that will be used by the trainer:

```
try (ObjectStream<String> lineStream = new PlainTextByLineStream(
        () -> new ByteArrayInputStream(trainingSentences.getBytes()),
            Charset.forName("UTF-8"));
    ObjectStream<SentenceSample> sampleStream =
            new SentenceSampleStream(lineStream)) {
        ...
} catch (FileNotFoundException ex) {
    // Handle exceptions
} catch (IOException ex) {
    // Handle exceptions
}
```

4. Within the `try` block, add the following code sequence to train the model:

```
SentenceDetectorFactory sentenceDetectorFactory =
new SentenceDetectorFactory("en", true, null, null);
SentenceModel sentenceModel = SentenceDetectorME.train(
    "en", sampleStream, sentenceDetectorFactory,
TrainingParameters.defaultParams());
```

5. Add the following code to serialize the model for later use:

```
OutputStream modelOutputStream =
    new BufferedOutputStream(new FileOutputStream("modelFile"));
sentenceModel.serialize(modelOutputStream);
```

6. Add the next code sequence, which is duplicated from the *Using OpenNLP to perform SBD* recipe. It is used to show how well the trained model works with the sample text. A detailed explanation of the code segment is found in that recipe:

```
String text =
    "We will start with a simple sentence. However, is it "
    + "possible for a sentence to end with a question "
    + "mark? Obviously that is possible! Another "
    + "complication is the use of a number such as 56.32 "
    + "or ellipses such as ... Ellipses may be found ... "
    + "with a sentence! Of course, we may also find the "
    + "use of abbreviations such as Mr. Smith or "
    + "Dr. Jones.";

SentenceDetectorME sentenceDetector = null;
InputStream inputStrean = new FileInputStream("modelFile");
sentenceModel = new SentenceModel(inputStrean);
sentenceDetector = new SentenceDetectorME(sentenceModel);
String sentences[] = sentenceDetector.sentDetect(text);
for (String sentence : sentences) {
    System.out.println("[" + sentence + "]");
}
```

7. Execute the program. You will get the following output, which has been shortened to save space:

```
Indexing events with TwoPass using cutoff of 5

    Computing event counts...  done. 81 events
    Indexing...  done.
Sorting and merging events... done. Reduced 81 events to 50.
Done indexing in 0.16 s.
Incorporating indexed data for training...
done.
```

```
        Number of Event Tokens: 50
          Number of Outcomes: 2
        Number of Predicates: 18
...done.
Computing model parameters ...
Performing 100 iterations.
  1:   ... loglikelihood=-56.14492162535558     0.9135802469135802
  2:   ... loglikelihood=-23.154515271743776    0.9135802469135802
  3:   ... loglikelihood=-18.877544062201142    0.9135802469135802
  4:   ... loglikelihood=-17.0872904013079     0.9135802469135802
  5:   ... loglikelihood=-15.783419186253273    0.9135802469135802
  6:   ... loglikelihood=-14.703634221493198    0.9259259259259259
  7:   ... loglikelihood=-13.78695051256956     0.9382716049382716
  ...
 97:   ... loglikelihood=-3.7004380366106537    1.0
 98:   ... loglikelihood=-3.6800302107269958    1.0
 99:   ... loglikelihood=-3.659894772462019     1.0
100:   ... loglikelihood=-3.640024973157977     1.0
[We will start with a simple sentence.]
[However, is it possible for a sentence to end with a question
mark?]
[Obviously that is possible!]
[Another complication is the use of a number such as 56.32 or
ellipses such as ...]
[Ellipses may be found ...]
[with a sentence!]
[Of course, we may also find the use of abbreviations such as Mr.]
[Smith or Dr.]
[Jones.]
```

How it works...

To train a model, we need training data. We used the `StringBuilder` class to build up a string using three simple sentences and sentence terminators. This provided us with a variety of sentences for our training data. A real training set would use a much larger set of sentences with greater variety in the sentence structure.

We used a try-with-resources block to create an `ObjectStream` instance. This used an instance of the `PlainTextByLineStream` class, which was created using a lambda expression. This `ObjectStream` instance was then used as the argument of the `SentenceSampleStream` class constructor to create an `ObjectStream` instance of `SentenceSample` instances, which represents sentences of the training set.

This is the instruction pattern used by the OpenNLP:

```
try (ObjectStream<String> lineStream = new PlainTextByLineStream(
        () -> new ByteArrayInputStream(trainingSentences.getBytes()),
            Charset.forName("UTF-8"));
    ObjectStream<SentenceSample> sampleStream =
            new SentenceSampleStream(lineStream)) {
```

A `SentenceDetectorFactory` instance was created, which was used in conjunction with the sample stream to create a `SentenceModel` instance. A default set of training parameters was also used. The `train` method performs the training and creates the sentence model:

```
SentenceDetectorFactory sentenceDetectorFactory =
    new SentenceDetectorFactory("en", true, null, null);
SentenceModel sentenceModel = SentenceDetectorME.train(
    "en", sampleStream, sentenceDetectorFactory,
TrainingParameters.defaultParams());
```

The model was then serialized and demonstrated with sample text. The output of the training process is shown in the following. The first part shows the training process and illustrates various aspects of the training data used such as the number of event tokens and iterations performed. Since we used the default training parameters, 100 iterations were performed on the data, with each iteration showing a higher level of confidence in the model:

```
Indexing events with TwoPass using cutoff of 5

    Computing event counts...  done. 81 events
    Indexing...  done.
Sorting and merging events... done. Reduced 81 events to 50.
Done indexing in 0.16 s.
Incorporating indexed data for training...
done.
    Number of Event Tokens: 50
        Number of Outcomes: 2
      Number of Predicates: 18
...done.
Computing model parameters ...
Performing 100 iterations.
  1:  ... loglikelihood=-56.14492162535558    0.9135802469135802
  2:  ... loglikelihood=-23.154515271743776   0.9135802469135802
  3:  ... loglikelihood=-18.877544062201142   0.9135802469135802
  4:  ... loglikelihood=-17.0872904013079    0.9135802469135802
  5:  ... loglikelihood=-15.783419186253273   0.9135802469135802
  6:  ... loglikelihood=-14.703634221493198   0.9259259259259259
  7:  ... loglikelihood=-13.78695051256956    0.9382716049382716
```

```
...
  97:   ... loglikelihood=-3.7004380366106537    1.0
  98:   ... loglikelihood=-3.6800302107269958    1.0
  99:   ... loglikelihood=-3.659894772462019     1.0
 100:   ... loglikelihood=-3.640024973157977     1.0
```

The next part of the output shows how well the model worked with the sample text. Each sentence extracted from the sample data is shown enclosed with brackets. In this case, the results were not that good as it splits sentences on ellipses and abbreviations when it shouldn't. This reflects the importance of using a complete and comprehensive set of training data. A better training set would include significantly more and varied text that used here:

```
[We will start with a simple sentence.]
[However, is it possible for a sentence to end with a question mark?]
[Obviously that is possible!]
[Another complication is the use of a number such as 56.32 or ellipses such
as ...]
[Ellipses may be found ...]
[with a sentence!]
[Of course, we may also find the use of abbreviations such as Mr.]
[Smith or Dr.]
[Jones.]
```

See also

- The OpenNLP documentation is found at `https://opennlp.apache.org/docs/1.9.0/apidocs/opennlp-tools/index.html`

3
Performing Name Entity Recognition

When documents are analyzed, we often need to extract information about its contents and relationships between elements of the document. If we encounter a person's name, we may also be expecting that person's email address or phone number. These elements are referred to as entities. **Named-entity recognition** (**NER**) is the process of locating different types of entities within a document.

There are different types of entities, including names, addresses, dates, and locations. Likewise, there are different ways of isolating entities in text. We will be illustrating many of these approaches in this chapter.

There are several techniques we will demonstrate in this chapter. The variety of techniques will provide developers with options of how to find entities depending on the problem and environment in question. We will start with illustrations of how regular expressions can be used. The first uses standard Java classes, and the second will use a technique involving chunks. These are units of text that provide a convenient way of assessing entities.

Several of the recipes use neural networks. These are models that have been trained for both general and specialized types of documents. In the last recipe, we will illustrate how to train a model to find entities.

In this chapter, we will cover the following recipes:

- Using regular expressions to find entities
- Using chunks with regular expressions to identify entities
- Using OpenNLP to find entities in text
- Isolating multiple entities types
- Using a CRF model to find entities in a document
- Using a chunker to find entities
- Training a specialized NER model

Technical requirements

In this chapter, you will need to install the following software, if they have not already been installed:

- Eclipse Photon 4.8.0
- Java JDK 8 or later

We will be using the following APIs, which you will be instructed to add for each recipe as appropriate:

- OpenNLP 1.9.0
- OpenNP models 1.5
- Stanford NLP 3.9.2
- LingPipe 4.1.0

The code files for this chapter can be found at `https://github.com/PacktPublishing/Natural-Language-Processing-with-Java-Cookbook/tree/master/Chapter03`.

Using regular expressions to find entities

Entities can be extracted using regular expressions. In this recipe, we will illustrate this process for email addresses. The code can be easily modified to address other entity types.

Regular expressions are sequences of special characters that describe a particular type of text. There will often be specialized units of text, such as email addresses or phone numbers, that possess a unique pattern. Regular expressions are used to describe these patterns and are used to find the elements in text.

Regular expressions can be difficult to read and understand. This can make the code more difficult to maintain. However, they are not as computationally intensive as neural networks can be. In addition, for many entities there are multiple, readily available regular expression variations easily found on the internet (`https://www.vogella.com/tutorials/JavaRegularExpressions/article.html`, `https://docs.oracle.com/javase/tutorial/essential/regex/`).

Getting ready

Create a new Java project.

We will not be needing a Maven project for this recipe.

How to do it...

The following are the necessary steps:

1. Add the following `import` statements to the project:

```
import java.util.regex.Matcher;
import java.util.regex.Pattern;
```

2. Add the following declarations to the `main` method. The first is the text to be
   processed, and the second is a regular expression for an email address:

```
String sampleText = "I can normally be reached at nlp@nlpworks.com.
" +
    "If not you can email me at mrnlp@nlpworks.org";
String emailRegularExpression = "[a-zA-Z0-9'._%+-]+@" +
    "(?:[a-zA-Z0-9-]+\\.)" + "+[a-zA-Z]{2,4}";
```

3. Insert the next sequence, which will create a `pattern` instance and a `matcher`
   instance for the regular expression:

```
Pattern pattern = Pattern.compile(emailRegularExpression);
Matcher matcher = pattern.matcher(sampleText);
```

4. Add the following `while` loop, which finds occurrences of email addresses
   within the text and displays them:

```
while (matcher.find()) {
    System.out.println(matcher.group());
}
```

5. Execute the program. You will get the following output:

```
nlp@nlpworks.com
mrnlp@nlpworks.org
```

How it works...

The regular expression string was defined to match a simple pattern: multiple characters followed by an ampersand, and then by more characters terminated by a period. This is followed by two to four characters typically representing an internet domain, such as .net or .com:

```
String emailRegularExpression = "[a-zA-Z0-9'._%+-]+@" +
    "(?:[a-zA-Z0-9-]+\\.)" + "+[a-zA-Z]{2,4}";
```

The Pattern class is an internal representation of a regular expression created using the static compile method executed against the regular expression string. The matcher instance finds the instance of the regular expression:

```
Pattern pattern = Pattern.compile(emailRegularExpression);
Matcher matcher = pattern.matcher(sampleText);
```

The find method was then used to identify the next embedded entity. Each invocation of the method will result in the Matcher instance pointing to the next entity. It will return true if it finds one. The group method returns the following entity:

```
while (matcher.find()) {
    System.out.println(matcher.group());
}
```

There's more...

We can also determine the position of an entity in the sample text using the start and end methods, as shown next. These represent the beginning and ending indexes in the target string. The matcher is reinitialized using the sample text. This is necessary because the Matcher instance has exhausted the string, and there are no more entities to be found. The while loop iterates through the text displaying each entity along with its beginning and ending positions within the text:

```
matcher = pattern.matcher(sampleText);
while (matcher.find()) {
    System.out.println(matcher.group() + " [" + matcher.start() + ":" +
        matcher.end() + "]");
}
```

Execute the previous example. You will get the following output:

```
nlp@nlpworks.com [29:45]
mrnlp@nlpworks.org [74:92]
```

The regular expression capabilities of Java are able to find different types of entities within the same text. We will demonstrate this in the next recipe. Regular expressions are defined for phone numbers and ZIP codes in these strings:

```
String phoneNumberRegularExpression = "\\d{3}-\\d{3}-\\d{4}";
String zipCodeRegularExpression = "[0-9]{5}(\\-?[0-9]{4})?";
```

The pattern is compiled using a string consisting of the previous patterns separated by a vertical line as shown next. A new sample text is also defined as shown:

```
pattern = Pattern.compile(phoneNumberRegularExpression + "|" +
  zipCodeRegularExpression + "|" + emailRegularExpression);
  sampleText = "Her phone number is 888-555-1111. You may also need her ZIP
code: 55555-4444";
```

A new `Matcher` instance is created next, followed by a `while` loop that displays each entity found:

```
matcher = pattern.matcher(sampleText);
while (matcher.find()) {
    System.out.println(matcher.group() + " [" + matcher.start() + ":" +
        matcher.end() + "]");
}
```

When the previous example is executed, you will get the following output:

```
888-555-1111 [20:32]
55555-4444 [66:76]
```

The accuracy of matches will depend on the quality of the regular expressions. As with most applications, effort must be expended to ensure that the results are valid and meet the requirements of the project.

See also

- A thorough explanation of regular expressions is found at `https://ryanstutorials.net/regular-expressions-tutorial/regular-expressions-basics.php`

Using chunks with regular expressions to identify entities

In this recipe, we will use LingPipe's `RegExChunker` class to illustrate another approach for finding entities. This approach is based on the concept of chucks, which are textual units representing a set of data. Specifically, we will show how to identify email addresses within text.

Getting ready

To prepare, we need to follow these steps:

1. Create a new Maven project
2. Add the following dependency to the project's POM file:

```
<dependency>
    <groupId>de.julielab</groupId>
    <artifactId>aliasi-lingpipe</artifactId>
    <version>4.1.0</version>
</dependency>
```

How to do it...

The following are the necessary steps:

1. Add the following imports to the project:

```
import java.util.Set;
import com.aliasi.chunk.Chunk;
import com.aliasi.chunk.Chunker;
import com.aliasi.chunk.Chunking;
import com.aliasi.chunk.RegExChunker;
```

2. Add the following string declarations to the `main` method. The first is a sample string containing an email address. The second string is a regular expression that matches a typical email address:

```
String sampleText = "His email address is
hisemail@somecompany.com.";
String emailRegularExpression = "[A-Za-z0-9](([_\\.\\-]?[a-zA-
Z0-9]+)*)@(" +
    "[A-Za-z0-9]+)(([\\.\\-]?[a-zA-Z0-9]+)*)\\.([A-Za-z]{2,})";
```

3. Add the following code, which creates an instance of the RegExChunker class using the regular expression:

```
Chunker chunker = new
RegExChunker(emailRegularExpression,"EMAIL",1.0);
```

4. Add the next statements, which will create a series of chunks identifying the email text:

```
Chunking chunking = chunker.chunk(sampleText);
Set<Chunk> chunkSet = chunking.chunkSet();
```

5. Next, display the chunks found using this code sequence:

```
for (Chunk chunk : chunkSet) {
    System.out.println("Entity: " +
        sampleText.substring(chunk.start(), chunk.end()) +
        "\tType: " + chunk.type());
}
```

6. Execute the code. You will get the following output:

```
Entity: hisemail@somecompany.com Type: EMAIL
```

How it works...

The first string consists of a simple text containing a single email address. The regular expression, while fairly complex, represents a typical email address.

The RegExChunker class' constructor uses three arguments:

- The first one is the regular expression.
- The second is a name used to identify the type of the entity found. We used the EMAIL string as the entity type.
- The third argument is a chunk score used by all of the chunks. This argument is not relevant to our example. This value is assigned to successful matches to indicate its importance, which we do not use in our examples.

An instance of the class is created as shown next:

```
Chunker chunker = new RegExChunker(emailRegularExpression,"EMAIL",1.0);
```

The `chunk` method returns an instance of an object that implements the `Chunking` interface. This interface's `chunkSet` method was executed against this object, and returns a set of `Chunk` instances. Each `Chunk` instance represents an entity found in the sample text:

```
Chunking chunking = chunker.chunk(sampleText);
Set<Chunk> chunkSet = chunking.chunkSet();
```

The for-each statement iterates over all of the elements of the set and displays each entity found. The `start` and `end` methods return the index in the sample text where the entity is found. The `type` method returns the entity's type:

```
for (Chunk chunk : chunkSet) {
    System.out.println("Entity: " +
        sampleText.substring(chunk.start(), chunk.end()) +
        "\tType: " + chunk.type());
}
```

There's more...

There is another approach to using regular expressions with LingPipe. This involves creating a new class specifically designed to handle entity-specific regular expressions. We will create a class to handle email addresses.

Add a new class to your project called `EmailRegExChunker`. Derive the class from `RegExChunker`, as shown next:

```
import com.aliasi.chunk.RegExChunker;

public class EmailRegExChunker extends RegExChunker {
    ...
}
```

We need to include a regular expression for email addresses, so we will use the same one shown earlier in this recipe. Add the following statement to declare the regular expression:

```
private final static String EMAIL_REGULAR_EXPRESSION =
    "[A-Za-z0-9](([_\\.\\-]?[a-zA-Z0-9]+)*)@([A-Za-z0-9]+)(([\\.\\-]?[a-zA-Z0-9]+)*)\\.([A-Za-z]{2,})";
```

We also need to define a chunk type and score for the class. Add the following declarations to the class:

```
private final static String CHUNK_TYPE = "EMAIL";
private final static double CHUNK_SCORE = 1.0;
```

Next, add the default constructor that follows:

```
public EmailRegExChunker() {
    super(EMAIL_REGULAR_EXPRESSION,CHUNK_TYPE,CHUNK_SCORE);
}
```

The constructor calls the basic class constructor with the `super` keyword, passing it the regular expression, a chunk type, and a score. The basic class, `RegExChunker`, will then initialize the object to handle email regular expressions.

Replace the following statement that we used previously in the `main` method:

```
Chunker chunker = new RegExChunker(emailRegularExpression,"EMAIL",1.0);
```

Replace it with the following statement:

```
Chunker chunker = new EmailRegExChunker();
```

Execute the program again. You will get the same output as before.

See also

- An additional discussion of regular expressions is found at `https://ryanstutorials.net/regular-expressions-tutorial/`
- The LingPipe API documentation is found at `http://alias-i.com/lingpipe/docs/api/index.html`

Using OpenNLP to find entities in text

In this recipe, we will show one way of using OpenNLP to identify entities in a document. This technique does not use regular expressions, but rather a neural network model trained on date type entities.

Specifically, we will use the `NameFinderME` class, which uses the maximum entropy approach. We will download and use a model trained to detect dates in text. We will use another model to tokenize the text.

Getting ready

To prepare, we need to do the following:

1. Create a new Maven project.

2. Add the following dependency to the POM file:

```
<dependency>
    <groupId>org.apache.opennlp</groupId>
    <artifactId>opennlp-tools</artifactId>
    <version>1.9.0</version>
</dependency>
```

3. Download the `en-token.bin` and `en-ner-time.bin` files from `http://opennlp.sourceforge.net/models-1.5/`. Add the files to the root level of your project.

How to do it...

The following are the necessary steps:

1. Insert the following `import` statements to the project:

```
import java.io.File;
import java.io.FileInputStream;
import java.io.InputStream;
import opennlp.tools.namefind.NameFinderME;
import opennlp.tools.namefind.TokenNameFinderModel;
import opennlp.tools.tokenize.Tokenizer;
import opennlp.tools.tokenize.TokenizerME;
import opennlp.tools.tokenize.TokenizerModel;
import opennlp.tools.util.Span;
```

2. Add the following try-with-resources block to the `main` method:

```
try (InputStream tokenStream = new FileInputStream(new File("en-
token.bin"));
 InputStream entityModelInputStream =
 new FileInputStream(new File("en-ner-date.bin"));) {
 ...
} catch (Exception ex) {
 // Handle exception
}
```

3. Insert the next set of code into the `try` block to create models for the `Tokenizer` instance and token name `finder` models:

```
TokenizerModel tokenizerModel = new TokenizerModel(tokenStream);
Tokenizer tokenizer = new TokenizerME(tokenizerModel);
TokenNameFinderModel tokenNameFinderModel =
    new TokenNameFinderModel(entityModelInputStream);
```

4. Next, add this sequence to create the instance that will find dates:

```
NameFinderME nameFinderME = new NameFinderME(tokenNameFinderModel);
```

5. Use the following declaration to test the model:

```
String text = "The city was founded in the 1850s and its first
mayor was born March 3, 1832.";
```

6. Insert the next sequence to create an array of tokens and spans representing the position of tokens in the text:

```
String tokens[] = tokenizer.tokenize(text);
Span dateSpans[] = nameFinderME.find(tokens);
```

7. Finally, display the entities using the following `for` loop:

```
for (int i = 0; i < dateSpans.length; i++) {
    System.out.print("Entity: [" +
tokens[dateSpans[i].getStart()]);
    System.out.print("] was a " + dateSpans[i].getType() +
        " entity found starting at " + dateSpans[i].getStart());
    System.out.println(" and ending at " + dateSpans[i].getEnd());
}
```

8. Execute the code. The following output will be displayed:

```
Entity: [1850s] was a date entity found starting at 6 and ending at
7
Entity: [March] was a date entity found starting at 13 and ending
at 15
```

How it works...

The try-with-resources block created input streams for both the tokenizer and entity date models. If we needed to find a different type of entity, we could have used a different model other than en-ner-date.bin:

```
try (InputStream tokenInputStream = new FileInputStream(
        new File("en-token.bin"));
    InputStream entityModelInputStream = new FileInputStream(
        new File("en-ner-date.bin"));) {
```

These input streams were used to as the constructor arguments for the tokenizer and token name finder models. The tokenizer used was one based on maximum entropy:

```
TokenizerModel tokenizerModel = new TokenizerModel(tokenInputStream);
Tokenizer tokenizer = new TokenizerME(tokenizerModel);
```

Likewise, an instance of the TokenNameFinderModel class was instantiated using the entityModelInputStream instance. The NameFinderME instance also uses the maximum entropy approach:

```
TokenNameFinderModel tokenNameFinderModel =
    new TokenNameFinderModel(entityModelInputStream);
NameFinderME nameFinderME = new NameFinderME(tokenNameFinderModel);
```

The tokenize and find methods were used to extract the tokens from the text and the spans of the entities respectively. A span represents the indexes into the text and the type of the entity found:

```
String tokens[] = tokenizer.tokenize(text);
Span dateSpans[] = nameFinderME.find(tokens);
```

The for loop displays the entity enclosed in brackets. The Span class' getStart method returns an index of the token that the model identified as an entity. Its getType returned the type of entity found. Since we were using a date model, then only that type will be found in this example. The Span class' getEnd method returns the index of the token that follows the entity:

```
for (int i = 0; i < dateSpans.length; i++) {
    System.out.print("Entity: [" + tokens[dateSpans[i].getStart()]);
    System.out.print("] was a " + dateSpans[i].getType() +
        " entity found starting at " + dateSpans[i].getStart());
    System.out.println(" and ending at " + dateSpans[i].getEnd());
}
```

Notice that the `March` date starts at index 13 and ends at index 15. However, only the month was displayed. We will address this issue next:

```
Entity: [March] was a date entity found starting at 13 and ending at 15
```

There's more...

If we desire to get the actual span displayed, we need to add the following code to the `for` loop:

```
String date = "";
for(int j=dateSpans[i].getStart(); j< dateSpans[i].getEnd(); j++) {
    date += tokens[j] + " ";
}
System.out.println("Date: " + date);
```

This will produce the following output:

```
Entity: [1850s] was a date entity found starting at 6 and ending at 7
Date: 1850s
Entity: [March] was a date entity found starting at 13 and ending at 15
Date: March 3
```

This still does not give us an entire date that includes the year. Unfortunately, this is a limitation of the model. It treats the comma as the end of the date and ignores the year. If you remove the comma from the text, then the entire date will be retrieved.

We can also determine the probability that an entity was identified correctly. This is done using the `NameFinderME` class, `probs` method, which, when applied to the array of `Span` objects, will return an array of doubles representing the probability for each entity.

Replace the following statement that we used previously:

```
System.out.println("Date: " + date);
```

Add the following code sequence and re-execute the following code:

```
double[] spanProbs = nameFinderME.probs(dateSpans);
System.out.println("Date: " + date + " Probability: " + spanProbs[i]);
```

You will get the following output:

```
Entity: [1850s] was a date entity found starting at 6 and ending at 7
Date: 1850s Probability: 0.878211895731101
Entity: [March] was a date entity found starting at 13 and ending at 16
Date: March 3 Probability: 0.9937399307548391
```

The output reflects a high level of confidence that the date entities were identified correctly. The values returned will range from `0.0` to `1.0`. The closer the value is to `1.0`, the higher the level of confidence in the results

See also

- The OpenNLP API documentation is found at `https://opennlp.apache.org/docs/1.9.0/apidocs/opennlp-tools/index.html`

Isolating multiple entities types

When an application is identifying entities in text, it is often interested in more than one type of entity. For example, we may be interested in identifying both the names of individual and dates associated with them, such as a birth date or hire date. In this recipe, we will use OpenNLP to illustrate the process of identifying multiple types of entities in text.

We will download several OpenNLP models that will allow us to find people, locations, organizations, money, and time. We will also use the `NameFinderME` class to identify the entities.

Getting ready

To prepare, we need to do the following:

1. Create a new Maven project.
2. Add the following dependency to the POM file:

```
<dependency>
    <groupId>org.apache.opennlp</groupId>
    <artifactId>opennlp-tools</artifactId>
    <version>1.9.0</version>
</dependency>
```

3. Download the `en-token.bin`, `en-ner-person.bin`, `en-ner-location.bin`, `en-ner-organization.bin`, `en-ner-money.bin`, and `en-ner-time.bin` files from `http://opennlp.sourceforge.net/models-1.5/`. Add the files to the root level of your project.

How to do it...

The following are the necessary steps:

1. Add the following `import` statements to the project:

```
import java.io.File;
import java.io.FileInputStream;
import java.io.InputStream;
import java.util.ArrayList;
import opennlp.tools.namefind.NameFinderME;
import opennlp.tools.namefind.TokenNameFinderModel;
import opennlp.tools.tokenize.Tokenizer;
import opennlp.tools.tokenize.TokenizerME;
import opennlp.tools.tokenize.TokenizerModel;
import opennlp.tools.util.Span;
```

2. Add the following declaration for an array of sentences:

```
String sentences[] = {
    "Sam and Mary left on Friday, November 12. ",
    "They stopped in Boston at an ATM to get $300 for expenses. ",
    "While they were there Sam bumped into an old friend who was on
his way to work at ATT. ",
    "They decided to leave together and departed for Maine" };
```

3. Add the following try-with-resources block to load the tokenizer model:

```
try (InputStream tokenStream = new FileInputStream(new File("en-
token.bin"))) {
TokenizerModel tokenModel = new TokenizerModel(tokenStream);
...
} catch (Exception ex) {
// Handle exceptions
}
```

4. Next, insert the following code to create the `Tokenizer` instance:

```
Tokenizer tokenizer = new TokenizerME(tokenModel);
```

5. We will be using several entity models. Use the following declaration that holds their names:

```
String modelNames[] = {
    "en-ner-person.bin", "en-ner-location.bin",
    "en-ner-organization.bin", "en-ner-money.bin",
    "en-ner-time.bin"
};
```

6. Process one sentence at a time by adding the next `for` loop:

```
for (int i = 0; i < sentences.length; i++) {
 System.out.println("Sentence " + (i + 1));
  ...
}
```

7. Insert the next `for` loop, nested inside the previous `for` loop, to load and create the `NameFinderME` instances:

```
for (String name : modelNames) {
    TokenNameFinderModel entityModel = new TokenNameFinderModel(
        new FileInputStream(new File(name)));
    NameFinderME nameFinderME = new NameFinderME(entityModel);
    ...
}
```

8. We will now process one sentence using the loaded model:

```
String tokens[] = tokenizer.tokenize(sentences[i]);
...
```

9. Add the next code sequence to find the location of the entities and display them:

```
Span spans[] = nameFinderME.find(tokens);
for (Span span : spans) {
    System.out.print("\tEntity: ");
    for (int j = span.getStart(); j < span.getEnd(); j++) {
        System.out.print(tokens[j]);
    }
    System.out.println(" - Entity Type: " + span.getType());
}
```

10. Execute the program. You will get the following output:

```
Sentence 1
    Entity: Sam - Entity Type: person
    Entity: Mary - Entity Type: person
Sentence 2
    Entity: Boston - Entity Type: location
    Entity: $300 - Entity Type: money
Sentence 3
    Entity: Mr.Smith - Entity Type: person
Sentence 4
    Entity: Maine - Entity Type: location
```

How it works...

The following try-with-resources block loaded the tokenizer model and handles any exceptions thrown. The tokenizer was then created. The `modelNames` array holds the names of the entity models we used.

We decided to display all of the entities found in a sentence, one sentence at a time. The following `for` loop allows us to do this:

```
for (int i = 0; i < sentences.length; i++) {
    System.out.println("Sentence " + (i + 1));
    ...
}
```

The `TokenNameFinderModel` class represents an entity model. It was created using the model names defined in the `modelNames` array. The next `for` loop will load one model at a time, and then use it on a sentence. Once the entities, if any, are found, then it loads another model and repeats the process:

```
for (String name : modelNames) {
    TokenNameFinderModel entityModel = new TokenNameFinderModel(
        new FileInputStream(new File(name)));
    NameFinderME nameFinderME = new NameFinderME(entityModel);
    ...
}
```

The `tokenize` method returns a list of tokens for that sentence. The `find` method then isolates entities within those tokens:

```
String tokens[] = tokenizer.tokenize(sentences[i]);
Span spans[] = nameFinderME.find(tokens);
```

The last `for` loop displays the entities for the current sentence. The `span` object holds information about the entity. Its `getStart` and `getEnd` methods return the beginning and ending indexes of the entity in the `tokens` array. Its `getType` method returns the type of entity found:

```
for (Span span : spans) {
    System.out.print("\tEntity: ");
    for (int j = span.getStart(); j < span.getEnd(); j++) {
        System.out.print(tokens[j]);
    }
    System.out.println(" - Entity Type: " + span.getType());
}
```

See also

- The OpenNLP API documentation is found at `https://opennlp.apache.org/docs/1.9.0/apidocs/opennlp-tools/index.html`

Using a CRF model to find entities in a document

CRF stands for **conditional random field**. This is the name a statistical model that is used for many purposes, including the of text. In this recipe, we will illustrate how to use this CRF model to identify entities within a document. Specifically, we will use the Stanford NLP `CRFClassifier` class and a trained model.

Getting ready

To prepare, we need to do the following:

1. Create a new Maven project.
2. Add the following dependency to the POM file:

```
<dependency>
    <groupId>edu.stanford.nlp</groupId>
    <artifactId>stanford-corenlp</artifactId>
    <version>3.9.2</version>
</dependency>
```

3. Download the `english.conll.4class.distsim.crf.ser.gz` file from `https://github.com/sosolimited/recon_backend/blob/master/named-entity/classifiers/english.conll.4class.distsim.crf.ser.gz`. Add it to the project's root directory.

How to do it...

The following are the necessary steps:

1. Add the following `import` statements to the project:

```
import java.util.List;
import edu.stanford.nlp.ie.crf.CRFClassifier;
import edu.stanford.nlp.ling.CoreAnnotations;
import edu.stanford.nlp.ling.CoreLabel;
```

2. Add the following statement to the `main` method. It will create an instance of the `CRFClassifier` class:

```
CRFClassifier<CoreLabel> classifier = CRFClassifier
.getClassifierNoExceptions("english.conll.4class.distsim.crf.ser.gz
");
```

3. Insert the following statement, which will create a list of lists of entities based on the string argument of the `classify` method:

```
List<List<CoreLabel>> entityList = classifier.classify("Sam and
Mary left on Friday, November 12. ");
```

4. Add the following code, which iterates overs the entities found, displaying the entity and its type:

```
for (CoreLabel coreLabel : entityList.get(0)) {
    String category =
coreLabel.get(CoreAnnotations.AnswerAnnotation.class);
    System.out.println(coreLabel.word() + ":" + category);
}
```

5. Execute the code. It will generate the following output:

```
Sam:PERSON
and:O
Mary:PERSON
left:O
on:O
Friday:O
,:O
November:O
12:O
.:O
```

How it works...

The `CRFClassifier` class represents a CRF classifier and the `CoreLabel` class will hold information about an entity. `getClassifierNoExceptions` will use the model specified by its argument—`english.conll.4class.distsim.crf.ser.gz`:

```
CRFClassifier<CoreLabel> classifier =
    CRFClassifier.getClassifierNoExceptions(
        "english.conll.4class.distsim.crf.ser.gz");
```

When the `classify` method was executed, it processed its string argument, which is a simple statement. The method returned a list of `CoreLabel` objects. Returning this list of lists allows it to process multiple sentences at a time if needed:

```
List<List<CoreLabel>> entityList = classifier.classify(
    "Sam and Mary left on Friday, November 12. ");
```

The `for` loop iterated over the first and only list used in this example, contained in `entityList`. This list represents a sentence. The list's `get` method returned a `CoreLabel` instance that corresponded to the sentence being processed. The `CoreLabel` class' `get` method obtained access to the type of entity found. For entities other than standard categories, such as PERSON, ORGANIZATION, or LOCATION, it returns an O, effectively representing other category. The `word` method returns the string for the entity:

```
for (CoreLabel coreLabel : entityList.get(0)) {
    String category =
coreLabel.get(CoreAnnotations.AnswerAnnotation.class);
    System.out.println(coreLabel.word() + ":" + category);
}
```

There's more...

If we want to avoid other category entities, we can use the following sequence instead:

```
for (CoreLabel coreLabel : entityList.get(0)) {
    String category =
coreLabel.get(CoreAnnotations.AnswerAnnotation.class);
    if (!"O".equals(category)) {
        System.out.println(coreLabel.word() + ":" + category);
    }
}
```

When this code is executed, you will get this simplified output:

```
Sam:PERSON
Mary:PERSON
```

See also

- The Stanford API documentation is found at `https://nlp.stanford.edu/nlp/javadoc/javanlp/`

Using a chunker to find entities

In this recipe, we will illustrate another chunker to find entities. A chunk is an object that represents information about data. In this case, it will represent information about entities. We will use the LingPipe NLP API to illustrate this approach.

This use of a chunker differs in that it does not use regular expressions. Instead, we will use a model trained to find entities and use the model in conjunction with a chunker.

Getting ready

To prepare, we need to do the following:

1. Create a new Maven project.
2. Add the following dependency to the POM file:

```
<dependency>
    <groupId>de.julielab</groupId>
    <artifactId>aliasi-lingpipe</artifactId>
    <version>4.1.0</version>
</dependency
```

3. Download the `ne-en-news-muc6.AbstractCharLmRescoringChunker` file from `https://github.com/gregmoreno/lingpipe/tree/master/demos/models`. Save the file to the root directory of the project.

How to do it...

The following are the necessary steps:

1. Add the following `import` statements to the project:

    ```
    import java.io.File;
    import java.io.IOException;
    import java.util.Set;
    import com.aliasi.chunk.Chunk;
    import com.aliasi.chunk.Chunker;
    import com.aliasi.chunk.Chunking;
    import com.aliasi.util.AbstractExternalizable;
    ```

2. Add the following string to the `main` method:

    ```
    String sentences[] = { "Sam and Mary left on Friday, November 12.
    ",
        "They stopped in Boston at an ATM to get $300 for expenses. ",
        "While they were there Sam bumped into an old friend, Mr.
    Smith, " +
        "who was on his way to work at ATT. ",
        "They decided to leave together and departed for Maine" };
    ```

3. Next, add the following `try` block to deal with exceptions:

    ```
    try {
        ...
    } catch (IOException | ClassNotFoundException ex) {
        // Handle exception
    }
    ```

4. Insert the next statements into the `try` block to load a model and create a `Chunker` instance:

    ```
    File modelFile = new File("ne-en-news-
    muc6.AbstractCharLmRescoringChunker");
    Chunker chunker = (Chunker)
    AbstractExternalizable.readObject(modelFile);
    ```

5. Add the following `for` loop, which will process one sentence at a time:

    ```
    for (int index = 0; index < sentences.length; index++) {
        System.out.println("Sentence " + (index + 1));
        ...
    }
    ```

6. Next, add these statements to the previous `for` loop, which will create a set of chunks:

```
Chunking chunking = chunker.chunk(sentences[index]);
Set<Chunk> set = chunking.chunkSet();
```

7. Insert the next `for` loop to display each chunk:

```
for (Chunk chunk : set) {
    System.out.println("\tEntity: " +
        sentences[index].substring(chunk.start(), chunk.end()) +
        "\tType: "+ chunk.type());
}
```

8. Execute the code. You will get the following output:

```
Sentence 1
 Entity: Sam Type: PERSON
Sentence 2
 Entity: Boston Type: LOCATION
 Entity: ATM Type: ORGANIZATION
Sentence 3
 Entity: Sam Type: PERSON
 Entity: Smith Type: PERSON
 Entity: ATT Type: ORGANIZATION
Sentence 4
 Entity: Maine Type: LOCATION
```

How it works...

A series of sentences were used for the sample text:

```
String sentences[] = { "Sam and Mary left on Friday, November 12. ",
 "They stopped in Boston at an ATM to get $300 for expenses. ",
"While they were there Sam bumped into an old friend, Mr. Smith, " +
"who was on his way to work at ATT. ",
"They decided to leave together and departed for Maine" };
```

The `ne-en-news-muc6.AbstractCharLmRescoringChunker` file is a pretrained model for finding entities. The `AbstractExternalizable` class' `readObject` method read the file and created an instance of a `Chunker` class:

```
File modelFile = new File("ne-en-news-
muc6.AbstractCharLmRescoringChunker");
Chunker chunker = (Chunker) AbstractExternalizable.readObject(modelFile);
```

The outer `for` loop will process one sentence at a time. This will allow us to display the entities found for a sentence together. The `chunk` method takes a single sentence and returns a `Chunking` instance. Its `chunkSet` method returns a set of `Chunk` objects that represent the entities found:

```
Chunking chunking = chunker.chunk(sentences[index]);
Set<Chunk> set = chunking.chunkSet();
```

The inner `for` loop will display each chunk. The `start` and `end` methods returned the indexes into the sentence corresponding to the beginning and ending tokens of the entity. The `type` method returns the entity's type:

```
for (Chunk chunk : set) {
    System.out.println("\tEntity: " +
        sentences[index].substring(chunk.start(), chunk.end()) +
        "\tType: "+ chunk.type());
}
```

See also

- The LingPipe API documentation is found at `http://alias-i.com/lingpipe/docs/api/index.html`

Training a specialized NER model

When the data being processed is specialized, then we often need to train a model to address that specific problem domain. In this recipe, we will use OpenNLP to illustrate how this is done.

We will need to create a file that has been marked up to identify location entities. The `TokenNameFinderModel` class will use these markups to train a model. We will then test the model to see how well it worked.

Getting ready

To prepare, we need to do the following:

1. Create a new Maven project.
2. Add the following dependency to the POM file:

```
<dependency>
    <groupId>org.apache.opennlp</groupId>
    <artifactId>opennlp-tools</artifactId>
    <version>1.9.0</version>
</dependency>
```

3. Download the `en-token.bin` file from `http://opennlp.sourceforge.net/models-1.5/`. Add the file to the root level of your project.

4. Create a file called `training-data.train` at the root level of your project. Add the following to the file:

```
There are several interesting cities found around the world.
These include <START:location> London <END> which is located in
<START:location> Europe <END> and <START:location> Syndey <END>
which is located in <START:location> Australia <END> .
You will find <START:location> Cairo <END> in <START:location>
Africa <END>.
<START:location> Berlin <END> and <START:location> Hamburg <END>
are both located in <START:location> Europe <END>.
```

How to do it...

The following are the necessary steps:

1. Add the following `import` statements to the project:

```
import java.io.BufferedOutputStream;
import java.io.File;
import java.io.FileInputStream;
import java.io.FileOutputStream;
import java.io.IOException;
import java.io.InputStream;
import java.io.OutputStream;
import opennlp.tools.namefind.NameFinderME;
import opennlp.tools.namefind.NameSample;
import opennlp.tools.namefind.NameSampleDataStream;
import opennlp.tools.namefind.TokenNameFinderFactory;
import opennlp.tools.namefind.TokenNameFinderModel;
```

```
import opennlp.tools.tokenize.Tokenizer;
import opennlp.tools.tokenize.TokenizerME;
import opennlp.tools.tokenize.TokenizerModel;
import opennlp.tools.util.InputStreamFactory;
import opennlp.tools.util.ObjectStream;
import opennlp.tools.util.PlainTextByLineStream;
import opennlp.tools.util.Span;
import opennlp.tools.util.TrainingParameters;
```

2. Create an instance of the `InputStreamFactory` class using the next statement:

```
InputStreamFactory inputStreamFactory = new InputStreamFactory() {
    public InputStream createInputStream() throws IOException {
        return new FileInputStream("training-data.train");
    }
};
```

3. Add a try-with-resources block to the `main` method, as follows:

```
try (OutputStream modelOutputStream = new BufferedOutputStream(
            new FileOutputStream(new File("location-model.bin")));
        ObjectStream<String> stringStream = new
PlainTextByLineStream(
            inputStreamFactory, "UTF-8");
        ObjectStream<NameSample> nameSampleStream = new
            NameSampleDataStream(stringStream);) {
    ...
} catch (IOException ex) {
 // Handle exceptions
}
```

4. Insert the following statement to train the model into the `try` block:

```
TokenNameFinderModel locationModel = NameFinderME.train(
        "en", "LOCATION", nameSampleStream,
        TrainingParameters.defaultParams(), new
TokenNameFinderFactory());
```

5. Now that the model has been trained, serialize it to the model file, as shown here:

```
locationModel.serialize(modelOutputStream);
```

6. To test the model, add the following code after the try-with-resources block. It has been adapted from OpenNLP to find entities in text recipes:

```
try (InputStream tokenInputStream = new FileInputStream(
            new File("en-token.bin"));
        InputStream entityModelInputStream = new FileInputStream(
```

```
                          new File("location-model.bin"));) {
        TokenizerModel tokenizerModel = new
TokenizerModel(tokenInputStream);
        Tokenizer tokenizer = new TokenizerME(tokenizerModel);
        TokenNameFinderModel tokenNameFinderModel = new
            TokenNameFinderModel(entityModelInputStream);
        NameFinderME nameFinderME = new
NameFinderME(tokenNameFinderModel);
        String text =
            "The city of Cairo is quite large. However, Quebec is not
quite as big.";

        String tokens[] = tokenizer.tokenize(text);
        Span locationSpans[] = nameFinderME.find(tokens);
        for (int i = 0; i < locationSpans.length; i++) {
            System.out.println("Entity: [" +
                tokens[locationSpans[i].getStart()] + "]");
        }
} catch (Exception ex) {
 // Handle exceptions
}
```

7. Execute the code. You will get the following output. Some of the output has been condensed to conserve space:

```
Indexing events with Two Pass using cutoff of 5

Computing event counts... done. 40 events
 Indexing... done.
Sorting and merging events... done. Reduced 40 events to 31.
Done indexing in 0.15 s.
Incorporating indexed data for training...
done.
 Number of Event Tokens: 31
 Number of Outcomes: 2
 Number of Predicates: 26
...done.
Computing model parameters ...
Performing 100 iterations.
 1: ... loglikelihood=-27.725887222397798 0.825
 2: ... loglikelihood=-18.41476371013137 0.825
 3: ... loglikelihood=-15.45872609563646 0.825
...
 98: ... loglikelihood=-4.657280820162023 0.95
 99: ... loglikelihood=-4.644589880832584 0.95
100: ... loglikelihood=-4.632091065886678 0.95
Entity: [Cairo]
```

How it works...

An instance of the InputStreamFactory class is needed to train the model. The anonymous inner class is a convenient way of doing that.

The training-data.train file contained the training data. Each entity of type location is surrounded by a <START:location> and <END> tag. The file does not contain a very large training sample. It would be better if the file was much larger, but it will suffice for this example. A larger and more varied the file would result in a more accurate model, as there would be more data to calibrate the model.

The first try block is duplicated in the following code snippet for your convenience. It was used to create three streams:

- The first statement created an OutputStream instance for the model, which eventually serialized the model to the location-model.bin file. This file is placed in the root directory of the project.
- The second statement created an ObjectStream instance consisting of individual lines of the training file.
- The last statement created an ObjectStream instance of a NameSample type. This puts the training data into the correct format to train the model:

```
try (   OutputStream modelOutputStream = new BufferedOutputStream(
            new FileOutputStream(new File("location-model.bin")));
        ObjectStream<String> stringStream = new
PlainTextByLineStream(
            inputStreamFactory, "UTF-8");
        ObjectStream<NameSample> nameSampleStream = new
            NameSampleDataStream(stringStream);) {
```

The train method performed the actual training. It used five parameters:

- The first parameter specified the language being used. In this example, we used English.
- The second parameter is the name of the type of parameter.
- The third parameter is the ObjectStream instance holding the training data.
- The fourth parameter specifies the training parameters used during the training process. We used a default set of training parameters.
- The last parameter is an instance of the TokenNameFinderFactory class

We used the `train` method as shown next:

```
TokenNameFinderModel locationModel =
    NameFinderME.train("en", "LOCATION", nameSampleStream,
TrainingParameters.defaultParams(), new TokenNameFinderFactory());
```

The `serialize` method was then executed to save the model to the model file:

```
locationModel.serialize(modelOutputStream);
```

The second `try` block tested the serialized model. A detailed explanation of this technique is found in OpenNLP to find entities in text recipes.

Notice that the output did not detect both cities in the sample string. It missed the city of Quebec. Using a more comprehensive set of training data can overcome this problem.

See also

- The OpenNLP API documentation is found at `https://opennlp.apache.org/docs/1.9.0/apidocs/opennlp-tools/index.html`

4
Detecting POS Using Neural Networks

The Java core SDK does not provide ready techniques for detecting **Part-Of-Speech** (**POS**). This necessitates using specialized NLP APIs. Tags are an important part of identifying POS. A tag is typically an abbreviation such as NN, which specifies that the corresponding word is a noun. There are different sets of tags, which vary somewhat by API. We will reference these lists as they are encountered.

In this chapter, we will cover the following recipes:

- Finding POS using tagging
- Using a chunker to find POS
- Using a tag dictionary
- Finding POS using the Penn Treebank
- Finding POS from textese
- Using a pipeline to perform tagging
- Using a hidden Markov model to perform POS
- Training a specialized POS model

Technical requirements

In this chapter, you will need to install the following software if it has not already been installed:

- Eclipse Photon 4.8.0
- Java JDK 8 or later

We will be using the following APIs, which you will be instructed to add for each recipe as appropriate:

- OpenNLP 1.9.0
- OpenNLP models 1.5
- Stanford NLP models
- LingPipe 4.1.0

The code files for this chapter can be found at https://github.com/PacktPublishing/ Natural-Language-Processing-with-Java-Cookbook/tree/master/Chapter04.

Finding POS using tagging

In this recipe, we will use the OpenNLP API to identify POS. Specifically, we will use the POSTaggerME class to tag the words of a sentence. The process of tagging is the association of a POS tag to a word of a sentence. The POSTaggerME class uses a maximum entropy model. This type of model was discussed in the *Tokenization using maximum entropy* recipe of Chapter 1, *Preparing Text for Analysis and Tokenization*.

Getting ready

To prepare, we need to do the following:

1. Create a new Maven project.
2. Add the following dependency to the project's POM file:

```
<dependency>
    <groupId>org.apache.opennlp</groupId>
    <artifactId>opennlp-tools</artifactId>
    <version>1.9.0</version>
</dependency>
```

3. Download the file, en-pos-maxent.bin, from http://opennlp.sourceforge. net/models-1.5/. Add the files to the root level of your project.

How to do it...

The necessary steps include the following:

1. Add the following imports to your project:

    ```java
    import java.io.File;
    import java.io.FileInputStream;
    import java.io.IOException;
    import java.io.InputStream;
    import java.util.List;
    import opennlp.tools.postag.POSModel;
    import opennlp.tools.postag.POSTaggerME;
    import opennlp.tools.util.Sequence;
    ```

2. Add the following declarations for the sample text to the project's `main` method:

    ```java
    String sampleSentence = "When the mouse saw the cat it ran away.";
    String words[] = sampleSentence.split(" ");
    ```

3. Next, add the following try-with-resource block to load the model:

    ```java
    try (InputStream modelInputStream = new FileInputStream(
        new File("en-pos-maxent.bin"));) {
        ...
    } catch (IOException e) {
        // Handle exceptions
    }
    ```

4. Insert the next two statements to create the tagger:

    ```java
    POSModel posModel = new POSModel(modelInputStream);
    POSTaggerME posTaggerME = new POSTaggerME(posModel);
    ```

5. Next, add the following code sequence to tag the words and display the results:

    ```java
    String tags[] = posTaggerME.tag(words);
    for (int i = 0; i < words.length; i++) {
        System.out.print(words[i] + "/" + tags[i] + " ");
    }
    System.out.println();
    ```

6. Execute the code. You will get the following output:

    ```
    When/WRB the/DT mouse/NN saw/VBD the/DT cat/NN it/PRP ran/VBD
    away./.
    ```

How it works...

The file, en-pos-maxent.bin, contained the maximum entropy model that will identify POS in text. As shown in the following code snippet, an instance of the POSModel class was loaded with the model. The model was used to create an instance of the POSTaggerME class, which performed the tagging:

```
POSModel posModel = new POSModel(modelInputStream);
POSTaggerME posTaggerME = new POSTaggerME(posModel);
```

The tag method of the POSTaggerME class returns an array of strings that will hold the names of the tags. These names are abbreviations for the POS such as NN for noun. A list of these tags is found at https://www.ling.upenn.edu/courses/Fall_2003/ling001/penn_treebank_pos.html. As shown next, both the tokenized words and their tags are displayed:

```
String tags[] = posTaggerME.tag(words);
for (int i = 0; i < words.length; i++) {
    System.out.print(words[i] + "/" + tags[i] + " ");
}
System.out.println();
```

There's more...

For any given sentence, there are often more than one possible sequence of POS tags. The topKSequences method returns a list of possible sequences:

```
Sequence topSequences[] = posTaggerME.topKSequences(words);
```

For each sequence, we can list the each outcome along with its corresponding word. In the next set of statements, we iterate over each sequence and then, for each sequence, we use the getOutcomes method to return a list of tags. The inner for loop will display each sentence with their tags:

```
for (Sequence sequence : topSequences) {
    List<String> outcomes = sequence.getOutcomes();
    System.out.print("[");
    for(int i=0; i<outcomes.size(); i++) {
        System.out.print(words[i] + "/" + outcomes.get(i) + " ");
    }
    System.out.println("]");
}
```

When this code is executed, you will get the following output:

```
[When/WRB the/DT mouse/NN saw/VBD the/DT cat/NN it/PRP ran/VBD away./. ]
[When/WRB the/DT mouse/NN saw/VBD the/DT cat/NN it/PRP ran/VBD away./RB ]
[When/WRB the/DT mouse/NN saw/VBD the/DT cat/NN it/PRP ran/VBD away./VBG ]
```

Associated with each possible set of tags is a set of probabilities indicating the likelihood of the results being correct. The next code sequence is similar to the previous except we have used the `getProbs` method of the `Sequence` class to obtain the probabilities that are listed, along with the corresponding word and tag:

```
for (Sequence sequence : topSequences) {
    List<String> outcomes = sequence.getOutcomes();
    double probabilities[] = sequence.getProbs();
    for (int i = 0; i < outcomes.size(); i++) {
        System.out.printf("%s/%s/%5.3f ",words[i],
            outcomes.get(i), probabilities[i]);
    }
    System.out.println();
}
```

When this code is executed, you will get the following output:

```
When/WRB/0.985 the/DT/0.976 mouse/NN/0.994 saw/VBD/0.993 the/DT/0.976
cat/NN/0.985 it/PRP/0.925 ran/VBD/0.992 away./../0.358
When/WRB/0.985 the/DT/0.976 mouse/NN/0.994 saw/VBD/0.993 the/DT/0.976
cat/NN/0.985 it/PRP/0.925 ran/VBD/0.992 away./RB/0.347
When/WRB/0.985 the/DT/0.976 mouse/NN/0.994 saw/VBD/0.993 the/DT/0.976
cat/NN/0.985 it/PRP/0.925 ran/VBD/0.992 away./VBG/0.094
```

See also

- The OpenNLP API documentation is found at https://opennlp.apache.org/docs/1.8.0/apidocs/opennlp-tools/index.html?overview-summary.html

Using a chunker to find POS

The idea behind chunking is to group POS-related words together. In this recipe, we will use the OpenNLP `ChunkerME` class to perform chunking. This class uses maximum entropy to perform this task.

Getting ready

To prepare, we need to do the following:

1. Create a new Maven project.
2. Add the following dependency to the project's POM file:

```
<dependency>
    <groupId>org.apache.opennlp</groupId>
    <artifactId>opennlp-tools</artifactId>
    <version>1.9.0</version>
</dependency>
```

Download the files, `en-pos-maxent.bin` and `en-chunker.bin`, from `http://opennlp.sourceforge.net/models-1.5/`. Add the files to the root level of your project.

How to do it...

The necessary steps include the following:

1. Add the following imports to the project:

```
import java.io.FileInputStream;
import java.io.IOException;
import java.io.InputStream;
import opennlp.tools.chunker.ChunkerME;
import opennlp.tools.chunker.ChunkerModel;
import opennlp.tools.postag.POSModel;
import opennlp.tools.postag.POSTaggerME;
import opennlp.tools.util.Span;
```

2. Add the following try-with-resources block to your `main` method:

```
try (InputStream posModelInputStream =
        new FileInputStream("en-pos-maxent.bin");
    InputStream chunkerInputStream =
        new FileInputStream("en-chunker.bin");) {
    ...
} catch (IOException ex) {
    // Handle exceptions
}
```

3. Next, insert the following statements to create the `POSTaggerME` instance:

```
POSModel posModel = new POSModel(posModelInputStream);
POSTaggerME posTaggerME = new POSTaggerME(posModel);
```

4. Add the next statements to create a sample sentence and create an array of tags:

```
String sampleSentence = "When the mouse saw the cat it ran away.";
String words[] = sampleSentence.split(" ");
String tags[] = posTaggerME.tag(words);
```

5. Next, create the `ChunkerME` instance and use its `chunk` method to create the chunks:

```
ChunkerModel chunkerModel = new ChunkerModel(chunkerInputStream);
ChunkerME chunkerME = new ChunkerME(chunkerModel);
String results[] = chunkerME.chunk(words, tags);
```

6. Insert the next `for` loop to display the results:

```
for (int i = 0; i < results.length; i++) {
    System.out.println("[" + words[i] + "] " + results[i]);
}
```

7. Execute the program. You will get the following output, which displays the words, the beginning and end of a chunk, and then the chunk type. The meaning of B, I, and O will be explained in the next section:

```
[When] B-ADVP
[the] B-NP
[mouse] I-NP
[saw] B-VP
[the] B-NP
[cat] I-NP
[it] B-NP
[ran] B-VP
[away.] O
```

How it works...

The files, `en-pos-maxent.bin` and `en-chunker.bin`, contain the models for the tagger and chunker respectively. The tagger identifies the text's tags and the chunker groups them together. A `POSTaggerME` instance was created to support tagging:

```
POSModel posModel = new POSModel(posModelInputStream);
POSTaggerME posTaggerME = new POSTaggerME(posModel);
```

The `tag` method requires an array of words. The sample sentence was declared and split into words using the `split` method of the `String` class:

```
String sampleSentence = "When the mouse saw the cat it ran away.";
String words[] = sampleSentence.split(" ");
String tags[] = posTaggerME.tag(words);
```

The `ChunkerME` instance was then instantiated and its `chunk` method returned an array of chunks. The method required both the array of words and their corresponding tags:

```
ChunkerModel chunkerModel = new ChunkerModel(chunkerInputStream);
ChunkerME chunkerME = new ChunkerME(chunkerModel);
String results[] = chunkerME.chunk(words, tags);
```

The results were then displayed as shown next. Each word of the sentence was displayed in brackets, followed by a letter representing the chunk tag. Two chunk tags were used; the B tag specifies the beginning of a chunk and the I tag specifies the continuation of a tag. For some output, you may see an E tag, which marks the end of a tag. This is not shown for words consisting of a single tag. The last entry on each line is the type of chunk:

```
ADVP — Adverb chunk
NP — Noun chunk
VB — Verb chunk

[When] B-ADVP
[the] B-NP
[mouse] I-NP
[saw] B-VP
[the] B-NP
[cat] I-NP
[it] B-NP
[ran] B-VP
[away.] O
```

There's more...

We can group the words of a chunk together using the next code sequence. The `chunkAsSpans` method returns an array of `Span` objects representing the position of a chunk within the array of words. The `getStart` and `getEnd` methods return the beginning and ending indexes within the word array. The `getType` method returns the chunk's type while the `length` method returns the length of the chunk:

```
Span[] spans = chunkerME.chunkAsSpans(words, tags);
for (Span span : spans) {
    String chunk = "";
```

```
for (int j = span.getStart(); j < span.getEnd(); j++) {
    chunk += words[j] + " ";
}
System.out.printf("[%-10s]", chunk);
System.out.printf(" Type: %-4s – Begin: %d End: %d Length: %d\n",
    span.getType(), span.getStart(), span.getEnd(), span.length());
}
```

When this code is executed, you will get the following output:

```
[When ] Type: ADVP – Begin: 0 End: 1 Length: 1
[the mouse ] Type: NP – Begin: 1 End: 3 Length: 2
[saw ] Type: VP – Begin: 3 End: 4 Length: 1
[the cat ] Type: NP – Begin: 4 End: 6 Length: 2
[it ] Type: NP – Begin: 6 End: 7 Length: 1
[ran ] Type: VP – Begin: 7 End: 8 Length: 1
```

See also

- The OpenNLP API documentation is found at https://opennlp.apache.org/docs/1.8.0/apidocs/opennlp-tools/index.html?overview-summary.html

Using a tag dictionary

A tag dictionary allows a developer to control which tags are valid for a specific word. By controlling these tags, it can prevent the tagger from using an inappropriate tag for a word. In this recipe, we will use the OpenNLP's MutableTagDictionary class to illustrate this process.

Getting ready

To prepare, we need to do the following:

1. Create a new Maven project.
2. Add the following dependency to the project's POM file:

```
<dependency>
    <groupId>org.apache.opennlp</groupId>
    <artifactId>opennlp-tools</artifactId>
    <version>1.9.0</version>
</dependency>
```

Download the file, `en-pos-maxent.bin,` from `http://opennlp.sourceforge.net/models-1.5/.` Add the file to the root level of your project.

How to do it...

The necessary steps include the following:

1. Add the following imports to the project:

```
import java.io.FileInputStream;
import java.io.IOException;
import java.io.InputStream;
import java.util.ArrayList;
import opennlp.tools.postag.MutableTagDictionary;
import opennlp.tools.postag.POSModel;
import opennlp.tools.postag.POSTaggerFactory;
import opennlp.tools.postag.TagDictionary;
```

2. Add the following try-with-resources block to the `main` method:

```
try (InputStream modelInputStream = new FileInputStream(
        "en-pos-maxent.bin");) {
    ...
} catch (IOException e) {
    // Handle exceptions
}
```

3. Insert these statements into the `try` block to create a tag dictionary:

```
POSModel posModel = new POSModel(modelInputStream);
POSTaggerFactory posTaggerFactory = posModel.getFactory();
MutableTagDictionary mutableTagDictionary = (MutableTagDictionary)
posTaggerFactory.getTagDictionary();
```

4. Add the next sequence to display the existing tags for the word `process`:

```
String currentTags[] = mutableTagDictionary.getTags("process");
for (String tag : currentTags) {
    System.out.print("/" + tag);
}
System.out.println();
```

5. Execute the code. You will get the following output:

```
/VBP/NN/VB
```

How it works...

The `en-pos-maxent.bin` file contains the model for POS tags. This was used to create an instance of the `POSTaggerFactory` class. This instance was used to obtain an instance of `MutableTagDictionary`. Since the dictionary is mutable, we will be able to add new tags as needed:

```
POSModel posModel = new POSModel(modelInputStream);
POSTaggerFactory posTaggerFactory = posModel.getFactory();
MutableTagDictionary mutableTagDictionary = (MutableTagDictionary)
posTaggerFactory.getTagDictionary();
```

The `getTags` method returned an array of strings holding the tags for its string argument. For the word, `process`, we obtained the following output indicating that the word can be used as a verb or as a noun:

```
/VBP/NN/VB
```

A list of tags can be found at `https://www.ling.upenn.edu/courses/Fall_2003/ling001/penn_treebank_pos.html`.

There's more...

We can add new tags or delete old tags from a dictionary to reflect a more accurate word usage for certain problem spaces. To do this, we need to get a list of the current tags and then add or delete tags as needed. In the following sequence, we use the `currentTags` array to build a list of tags for the word, `process`, and then add a new tag, `MYTAG`:

```
ArrayList<String> newTags = new ArrayList<String>();
for (int i = 0; i < currentTags.length; i++) {
 newTags.add(currentTags[i]);
}
newTags.add("MYTAG");
```

The list is then added to the tag dictionary:

```
mutableTagDictionary.put("process", newTags.toArray(
    new String[newTags.size()]));
```

To verify that the tags were added correctly, use the following statements to display the tag list:

```
currentTags = mutableTagDictionary.getTags("process");
for (String tag : currentTags) {
    System.out.print("/" + tag);
```

```
}
System.out.println();
```

When this code is executed, you will get the following output:

```
/VBP/NN/VB/MYTAG
```

See also

- The OpenNLP API documentation is found at `https://opennlp.apache.org/docs/1.8.0/apidocs/opennlp-tools/index.html?overview-summary.html`

Finding POS using the Penn Treebank

The Penn Treebank published a set of English POS tags used by many taggers. We will be using the Stanford NLP API to demonstrate how this set of tags can be used to find POS elements in text. We will be using a Penn Treebank tag set file, `wsj-0-18-bidirectional-distsim.tagger`, for this recipe. It has been trained on a series of Wall Street Journal articles.

Getting ready

To prepare, we need to do the following:

1. Create a new Maven project.
2. Download the following JAR files:
   - `stanford-corenlp-full-2018-10-05.zip`: It can be found at `https://stanfordnlp.github.io/CoreNLP/download.html`. Extract the file, `stanford-corenlp-3.9.2.jar`.
   - `stanford-postagger-2018-10-16.zip`: It can be found at `https://nlp.stanford.edu/software/tagger.shtml`. Extract the file, `stanford-postagger-3.9.2.jar`.
   - `stanford-corenlp-models-current.jar`: Use the `corenlp-models` link found in step 6 of the *Build with Ant* section found at `https://github.com/stanfordnlp/CoreNLP`.

3. Add these three JAR files to your project. These types of files are frequently added by using a project property dialog box and modifying the Java build path to include them in the classpath.

4. Download the file, `wsj-0-18-bidirectional-distsim.tagger`, from `stanford-corenlp-2018-10-05-models\edu\stanford\nlp\models\pos-tagger` and save it in the root directory of the project.

How to do it...

The necessary steps include the following:

1. Add the following imports to your project:

```
import java.io.StringReader;
import java.util.List;
import edu.stanford.nlp.ling.HasWord;
import edu.stanford.nlp.ling.TaggedWord;
import edu.stanford.nlp.tagger.maxent.MaxentTagger;
```

2. Add the following declarations to the `main` method. These will set up the tagger:

```
String sampleSentence = "When the mouse saw the cat it ran away.";
MaxentTagger maxentTagger = new MaxentTagger(
    "wsj-0-18-bidirectional-distsim.tagger");
List<List<HasWord>> sentences = MaxentTagger.tokenizeText(
    new StringReader(sampleSentence));
```

3. Next, add the following code sequence to tag and display the sentences:

```
for (List<HasWord> sentence : sentences) {
    List<TaggedWord> taggedSentence =
        maxentTagger.tagSentence(sentence);
    for (TaggedWord taggedWord : taggedSentence) {
        System.out.print(taggedWord.word() + "/" +
            taggedWord.tag() + " ");
    }
    System.out.println();
}
```

4. Execute the program. You will get the following output:

```
When/WRB the/DT mouse/NN saw/VBD the/DT cat/NN it/PRP ran/VBD
away/RB ./.
```

How it works...

An instance of the maximum entropy tagger was created using the `wsj-0-18-bidirectional-distsim.tagger` file. This was pulled from the `stanford-corenlp-models-current.jar` file. Next, a list of `HasWord` objects was created. A `HasWord` object holds information about words. The `tokenizeText` method of the `MaxentTagger` class used the `sampleSentence` string to create the list:

```
String sampleSentence = "When the mouse saw the cat it ran away.";
MaxentTagger maxentTagger =
    new MaxentTagger( "wsj-0-18-bidirectional-distsim.tagger");
List<List<HasWord>> sentences = MaxentTagger.tokenizeText(
    new StringReader(sampleSentence));
```

The `tagSentence` method performed the actual tagging, as shown next, where it created a list of the `TaggedWord` instance. As the name implies, it represents the word and its tags. While we used a single sentence, the `for` loop will iterate over a collection of sentences if needed. For each sentence, the `word` and `tag` methods returned each word in the sentence and its tag, which were displayed:

```
for (List<HasWord> sentence : sentences) {
    List<TaggedWord> taggedSentence =
        maxentTagger.tagSentence(sentence);
    for (TaggedWord taggedWord : taggedSentence) {
        System.out.print(taggedWord.word() + "/" +
            taggedWord.tag() + " ");
    }
    System.out.println();
}
```

There's more...

We may not always want to identify each and every tag in the text. We can narrow the tags reported using a simple `if` statement as shown next. In this code sequence, we list only the nouns that make up the sentence:

```
for (TaggedWord taggedWord : taggedSentence) {
    if (taggedWord.tag().startsWith("NN")) {
        System.out.println(taggedWord.word() + " ");
    }
}
System.out.println();
```

When this code is executed, you will get the following output:

```
mouse
cat
```

See also

- The Stanford NLP API documentation is found at `https://nlp.stanford.edu/nlp/javadoc/javanlp/`

Finding POS from textese

Textese is a form of text commonly used with typed messaging applications. It consists of a series of terse abbreviations that are used as a substitute for more verbose words or phrases, for example, **BTW** (short for **by the way**). Twitter feeds is another common place where textese is used. Due to its prevalence, it can be important to determine the POS for such message types.

In this recipe, we will be using the Stanford NLP API to demonstrate how to find the POS of textese. We will use the `gate-EN-twitter.model` model in conjunction with the `MaxentTagger` class to perform this task.

Getting ready

To prepare, we need to do the following:

1. Create a new Maven project.
2. Download the following JAR files:
    - `stanford-corenlp-full-2018-10-05.zip`: This can be found at `https://stanfordnlp.github.io/CoreNLP/download.html`. Extract the file, `stanford-corenlp-3.9.2.jar`.
    - `stanford-postagger-2018-10-16.zip`: This can be found at `https://nlp.stanford.edu/software/tagger.shtml`. Extract the file, `stanford-postagger-3.9.2.jar`.
    - `stanford-corenlp-models-current.jar`: Use the `corenlp-models` link found in step 6 of the *Build with Ant* section found at `https://github.com/stanfordnlp/CoreNLP`.

3. Add these three JAR files to your project. These types of files are frequently added by using a project property dialog box and modifying the Java build path to include them in the classpath.

4. Download the file, `gate-EN-twitter.model`, from `https://gate.ac.uk/wiki/twitter-postagger.html` and save it to the root directory of the project.

How to do it...

The necessary steps include the following:

1. Add the following imports to the project:

```
import java.io.StringReader;
import java.util.List;
import edu.stanford.nlp.ling.HasWord;
import edu.stanford.nlp.ling.TaggedWord;
import edu.stanford.nlp.tagger.maxent.MaxentTagger;
```

2. Add the following string to the `main` method:

```
String sampleSentence = "JK IMA eat by EOD!";
```

It is based on the following textese phrases:

- JK: Just kidding
- IMA: I'm going to
- EOD: End of day

3. Create a `MaxentTagger` instance and invoke the tagger as shown next:

```
MaxentTagger maxentTagger = new MaxentTagger(
    "gate-EN-twitter.model");
System.out.println(maxentTagger.tagString(sampleSentence));
```

4. Execute the program. You will get the following output:

```
warning: no language set, no open-class tags specified, and no
closed-class tags specified; assuming ALL tags are open class tags
Loading POS tagger from C:\NLP Cookbook\Code\chapter5\gate-EN-
twitter.model ... done [2.1 sec].
JK_UH IMA_NNP eat_VB by_IN EOD!_NNP
```

How it works...

The MaxentTagger class was instantiated using the file, gate-EN-twitter.model. The tagString method was then used to tag the sentence:

```
MaxentTagger maxentTagger = new MaxentTagger("gate-EN-twitter.model");
System.out.println(maxentTagger.tagString(sampleSentence));
```

There's more...

We can provide a bit more control over how the words and tags are displayed using the following code sequence. This code was originally discussed in the *Finding POS using the Penn Treebank* recipe:

```
List<List<HasWord>> sentences =
    MaxentTagger.tokenizeText(new StringReader(sampleSentence));
for (List<HasWord> sentence : sentences) {
    List<TaggedWord> taggedSentence =
        maxentTagger.tagSentence(sentence);
    for (TaggedWord taggedWord : taggedSentence) {
        System.out.print(taggedWord.word() + "/" +
            taggedWord.tag() + " ");
    }
    System.out.println();
}
```

When this code is executed, you will get the following output:

```
JK/UH IMA/NNP eat/VB by/IN EOD/NNP !/.
```

We can add even more detail by replacing the following statement:

```
System.out.print(taggedWord.word() + "/" + taggedWord.tag() + " ");
```

We replace it with the following statement:

```
System.out.println(taggedWord.word() + "/" + taggedWord.tag() +
    " (" + taggedWord.beginPosition() + ", " +
    taggedWord.endPosition() + ")" );
```

This will display the word followed by its tag and then its starting and ending positions in the sentence, as shown next:

```
JK/UH (0, 2)
IMA/NNP (3, 6)
eat/VB (7, 10)
by/IN (11, 13)
EOD/NNP (14, 17)
!/. (17, 18)
```

See also

- The Stanford NLP API documentation is found at `https://nlp.stanford.edu/nlp/javadoc/javanlp/`

Using a pipeline to perform tagging

Pipelining is a technique that strings together various operations in a convenient and easily modifiable form to achieve some result. There are several APIs that support this approach. In this recipe, we will demonstrate how the Stanford NLP API supports this concept for POS tagging. This will provide the reader with an additional development technique.

Getting ready

To prepare, we need to do the following:

1. Create a new Maven project.
2. Download the following JAR files:
    - `stanford-corenlp-full-2018-10-05.zip`: This can be found at `https://stanfordnlp.github.io/CoreNLP/download.html`. Extract the file, `stanford-corenlp-3.9.2.jar`.
    - `stanford-postagger-2018-10-16.zip`: This can be found at `https://nlp.stanford.edu/software/tagger.shtml`. Extract the file, `stanford-postagger-3.9.2.jar`.
    - `stanford-corenlp-models-current.jar`: Use the `corenlp-models` link found in step 6 of the *Build with Ant* section found at `https://github.com/stanfordnlp/CoreNLP`.

3. Add these three JAR files to your project. These types of files are frequently added using a property dialog box and modifying the Java build path to include them in the classpath.

How to do it...

The necessary steps include the following:

1. Add the following imports to the project:

```
import java.util.List;
import java.util.Properties;
import
edu.stanford.nlp.ling.CoreAnnotations.PartOfSpeechAnnotation;
import edu.stanford.nlp.ling.CoreAnnotations.SentencesAnnotation;
import edu.stanford.nlp.ling.CoreAnnotations.TextAnnotation;
import edu.stanford.nlp.ling.CoreAnnotations.TokensAnnotation;
import edu.stanford.nlp.ling.CoreLabel;
import edu.stanford.nlp.pipeline.Annotation;
import edu.stanford.nlp.pipeline.StanfordCoreNLP;
import edu.stanford.nlp.util.CoreMap;
```

2. Add the following declarations to the `main` method. They set up the sample sentence and the pipeline:

```
String sampleSentence = "When the mouse saw the cat it ran away.";
Properties properties = new Properties();
properties.put("annotators", "tokenize, ssplit, pos");
properties.put("pos.model",
    "wsj-0-18-bidirectional-distsim.tagger");
properties.put("pos.maxlen", 10);
StanfordCoreNLP pipeline = new StanfordCoreNLP(properties);
Annotation annotation = new Annotation(sampleSentence);
pipeline.annotate(annotation);
```

3. Next, insert the following code sequence to obtain a list of `CoreMap` objects, which are used to identify and display the POS:

```
List<CoreMap> sentenceList =
annotation.get(SentencesAnnotation.class);
for (CoreMap sentence : sentenceList) {
    for (CoreLabel coreLabel :
            sentence.get(TokensAnnotation.class)) {
        String word = coreLabel.get(TextAnnotation.class);
        String partOfSpeech =
            coreLabel.get(PartOfSpeechAnnotation.class);
```

```
                System.out.print(word + "/" + partOfSpeech + " ");
            }
            System.out.println();
        }
```

4. Execute the code. You will get the following output:

```
Adding annotator tokenize
Adding annotator ssplit
Adding annotator pos
Loading POS tagger from wsj-0-18-bidirectional-distsim.tagger ...
done [1.4 sec].
When/WRB the/DT mouse/NN saw/VBD the/DT cat/NN it/PRP ran/VBD
away/RB ./.
```

How it works...

The `Properties` class holds a list of operations that constitutes the pipeline. In this case, we used the `annotators`, `tokenize`, `ssplit`, and `pos` operations. These operations were performed when the pipeline was executed. The model, `wsj-0-18-bidirectional-distsim.tagger`, was used for the tagging operation:

```
Properties properties = new Properties();
properties.put("annotators", "tokenize, ssplit, pos");
properties.put("pos.model", "wsj-0-18-bidirectional-distsim.tagger");
```

The `StanfordCoreNLP` instance represents the pipeline and was constructed from the operations defined in the `Properties` instance. The `Annotation` instance represents a span of text in the document being processed. The `annotate` method runs the pipeline:

```
StanfordCoreNLP pipeline = new StanfordCoreNLP(properties);
Annotation annotation = new Annotation(sampleSentence);
pipeline.annotate(annotation);
```

The `get` method, when used with the `SentencesAnnotation.class` argument, returns a list of `CoreMap` objects representing sentences. The `get` method of the `CoreMap` class returned a `CoreLabel` label containing information about a single word. Its `get` method was used twice: once with an argument of `TextAnnotation.class`, which resulted in the method returning a string representing the word, then with an argument of `PartOfSpeechAnnotation.class`, which resulted in the method returning a string representing the POS. The word/POS pairs were then displayed:

```
List<CoreMap> sentenceList = annotation.get(SentencesAnnotation.class);
for (CoreMap sentence : sentenceList) {
```

```
    for (CoreLabel coreLabel : sentence.get(TokensAnnotation.class)) {
        String word = coreLabel.get(TextAnnotation.class);
        String partOfSpeech =
            coreLabel.get(PartOfSpeechAnnotation.class);
        System.out.print(word + "/" + partOfSpeech + " ");
    }
    System.out.println();
}
```

From the following output, we can see the annotators being added to the pipeline and the model being loaded. The sentence, with its POS tags, is then displayed:

```
Adding annotator tokenize
Adding annotator ssplit
Adding annotator pos
Loading POS tagger from wsj-0-18-bidirectional-distsim.tagger ... done [1.4
sec].
When/WRB the/DT mouse/NN saw/VBD the/DT cat/NN it/PRP ran/VBD away/RB ./.
```

See also

- The Stanford NLP API documentation is found at `https://nlp.stanford.edu/nlp/javadoc/javanlp/`

Using a hidden Markov model to perform POS

A hidden Markov model is a statistical technique that has proved to be useful in many areas, including reinforcement learning, speech recognition, and detecting POS. We will use the LingPipe's `HiddenMarkovModel` class to demonstrate this model. This model will be used with a POS-trained file that we will download.

Getting ready

To prepare, we need to do the following:

1. Create a new Maven project

2. Add the following dependency to the POM file:

```
<!-- https://mvnrepository.com/artifact/de.julielab/aliasi-lingpipe
-->
<dependency>
    <groupId>de.julielab</groupId>
    <artifactId>aliasi-lingpipe</artifactId>
    <version>4.1.0</version>
</dependency>
```

3. Download the file, `pos-en-general-brown.HiddenMarkovModel`, from `http://alias-i.com/lingpipe/web/models.html` and save it to the project's root directory

How to do it...

The necessary steps include the following:

1. Add the following imports to the project:

```
import java.io.FileInputStream;
import java.io.IOException;
import java.io.ObjectInputStream;
import java.util.Arrays;
import java.util.Iterator;
import java.util.List;
import com.aliasi.hmm.HiddenMarkovModel;
import com.aliasi.hmm.HmmDecoder;
import com.aliasi.tag.ScoredTagging;
import com.aliasi.tag.Tagging;
```

2. In the `main` method, add the following statements to define a sample text and a try-with-resources block to create input streams to load a model:

```
String sampleSentence = "When the mouse saw the cat it ran away.";
try (FileInputStream fileInputStream =
    new FileInputStream("pos-en-general-brown.HiddenMarkovModel");
    ObjectInputStream objectInputStream =
            new ObjectInputStream(fileInputStream);) {
    ...
} catch (IOException ex) {
    // Handle exceptions
} catch (ClassNotFoundException ex) {
    // Handle exceptions
}
```

3. Create the model and a POS tagger with the following declarations:

```
HiddenMarkovModel hiddenMarkovModel =
    (HiddenMarkovModel) objectInputStream.readObject();
HmmDecoder hmmDecoder = new HmmDecoder(hiddenMarkovModel);
```

4. Add the following statements to find the POS elements and display them:

```
List<String> tokenList = Arrays.asList(sampleSentence.split(" "));
Tagging<String> taggingString = hmmDecoder.tag(tokenList);
for (int i = 0; i < taggingString.size(); ++i) {
    System.out.print(taggingString.token(i) + "/" +
        taggingString.tag(i) + " ");
}
System.out.println();
```

5. Execute the program. You will get the following output:

```
When/wrb the/at mouse/nn saw/vbd the/at cat/nn it/pps ran/vbd
away./nn
```

How it works...

The try-with-resources block created input streams used to load the pos-en-general-brown.HiddenMarkovModel file. HiddenMarkovModel was instantiated using the readObject method of the ObjectInputStream class. As shown next, the model was used to create an instance of the HmmDecoder class that was used to find POS elements in the text:

```
HiddenMarkovModel hiddenMarkovModel =
    (HiddenMarkovModel) objectInputStream.readObject();
HmmDecoder hmmDecoder = new HmmDecoder(hiddenMarkovModel);
```

The tag method extracted the POS elements. However, it required a list of strings containing the words of the text. The split method of the String class extracted the words while asList of the Arrays class created the list:

```
List<String> tokenList = Arrays.asList(sampleSentence.split(" "));
Tagging<String> taggingString = hmmDecoder.tag(tokenList);
```

The output of the `tag` method was a `Tagging` class instance. It possesses two methods of interest. The `token` method returns a word and the `tag` method returns a tag. Both methods used an index to identify word and tag combination. The following `for` loop displayed each of these combinations:

```
for (int i = 0; i < taggingString.size(); ++i) {
    System.out.print(taggingString.token(i) + "/" +
        taggingString.tag(i) + " ");
}
System.out.println();
```

There's more...

Since there is more than one possible set of tags for most sentences, it is often useful to examine other possible tag variations. The `tagNBest` method of the `HmmDecoder` class returns an iterator of the `ScoredTagging` instance, each of which represents alternate tagging possibilities.

In the following statement, we create such an iterator using the previously created list of words and a second argument of three meaning that only the top three variations will be returned:

```
Iterator<ScoredTagging<String>> scoredTaggingIterator =
    hmmDecoder.tagNBest(tokenList, 3);
```

The following `while` loop will iterate over the list of possibilities:

```
while (scoredTaggingIterator.hasNext()) {
    ScoredTagging<String> scoredTagging = scoredTaggingIterator.next();
    System.out.printf("Score: %7.3f Sequence: ",
        scoredTagging.score());
    for (int i = 0; i < tokenList.size(); ++i) {
        System.out.print(scoredTagging.token(i) + "/" +
            scoredTagging.tag(i) + " ");
    }
    System.out.println();
}
```

The `hasNext` method returns an instance of the `ScoredTagging` class, which provides three methods of interest:

- `score`: A score for a specific POS variation
- `token`: The word
- `tag`: The POS tag for the word

When the preceding code is executed, you will get the following output:

```
Score: -128.671 Sequence: When/wrb the/at mouse/nn saw/vbd the/at cat/nn
it/pps ran/vbd away./nn
Score: -129.263 Sequence: When/wrb the/at mouse/nn saw/vbd the/at cat/nn
it/pps ran/vbd away./np
Score: -129.551 Sequence: When/wrb the/at mouse/nn saw/vbd the/at cat/nn
it/pps ran/vbd away./vbn
```

See also

- The LingPipe API documentation is found at `http://alias-i.com/lingpipe/docs/api/index.html`

Training a specialized POS model

We will use the OpenNLP API to demonstrate how to train a specialized POS model. Training your own model is important when the pre-trained models do not work satisfactorily for the problem at hand and there are no other specialized models available for the language or problem domain.

We will use the `POSTaggerME` class to train our model. We will need to create a file that contains POS markups. Once trained, we will test the model using the technique demonstrated in the *Finding POS using tagging* recipe.

Getting ready

To prepare, we need to do the following:

1. Create a new Maven project.
2. Add the following dependency to the project's POM file:

```
<dependency>
    <groupId>org.apache.opennlp</groupId>
    <artifactId>opennlp-tools</artifactId>
    <version>1.9.0</version>
</dependency>
```

3. Create a file called `sample.train` and place it in the root level of your project. Add the following to the file:

```
We_PRP will_MD start_VB with_IN a_DT simple_JJ sentence._NN
If_IN we_PRP consider_VBP more_JJR complex_JJ sentences,_NNS we_PRP
will_MD find_VB them_PRP to_TO be_VB a_DT bit_RB more_RBR
interesting!_JJ
Or_CC we_PRP could_MD consider_VB sentence_NN with_IN different_JJ
terminators,_NNS various_JJ element_NN types,_NNS or_CC other_JJ
factors._NNS
Should_MD we_PRP do_VB that?_DT
For_IN now,_RB let's_VB just_RB keep_VBP it_PRP simple._JJ
```

How to do it...

The necessary steps include the following:

1. Add the following imports to the project:

```
import java.io.BufferedOutputStream;
import java.io.File;
import java.io.FileInputStream;
import java.io.FileOutputStream;
import java.io.IOException;
import java.io.InputStream;
import java.io.OutputStream;
import java.util.List;
import opennlp.tools.postag.POSModel;
import opennlp.tools.postag.POSSample;
import opennlp.tools.postag.POSTaggerFactory;
import opennlp.tools.postag.POSTaggerME;
import opennlp.tools.postag.WordTagSampleStream;
import opennlp.tools.util.InputStreamFactory;
import opennlp.tools.util.ObjectStream;
import opennlp.tools.util.PlainTextByLineStream;
import opennlp.tools.util.Sequence;
import opennlp.tools.util.TrainingParameters;
```

2. In the `main` method, add the following sequence to declare the `POSModel` instance variable and an anonymous inner class to create an instance of `InputStreamFactory`:

```
POSModel posTaggerMEModel = null;
InputStreamFactory inputStreamFactory = new InputStreamFactory() {
    public InputStream createInputStream() throws IOException {
        return new FileInputStream("sample.train");
```

```
    }
};
```

3. Add the following try-with-resource block to create the input streams:

```
try (
    ObjectStream<String> stringObjectStream =
        new PlainTextByLineStream(inputStreamFactory, "UTF-8");
    ObjectStream<POSSample> posSampleObjectStream =
        new WordTagSampleStream(stringObjectStream);) {
    ...
} catch (IOException e) {
    // Handle exceptions
}
```

4. Add the next statement to the `try` block, which will train the model:

```
posTaggerMEModel = POSTaggerME.train("en", posSampleObjectStream,
    TrainingParameters.defaultParams(), new POSTaggerFactory());
```

5. Save the model to a file using the next sequence:

```
try (OutputStream modelOut = new BufferedOutputStream(
        new FileOutputStream(new File("sample.bin")));) {
    posTaggerMEModel.serialize(modelOut);
    ...
} catch (IOException e) {
    // Handle exceptions
}
```

6. Next, we need to demonstrate the model in use. Add the following code, which has been adapted from the *Finding POS using tagging* recipe, to the previous `try` block:

```
String sampleSentence = "When the mouse saw the cat it ran away.";
String words[] = sampleSentence.split(" ");
try (InputStream modelInputStream =
            new FileInputStream(new File("sample.bin"));) {
    POSModel posModel = new POSModel(modelInputStream);
    POSTaggerME posTaggerME = new POSTaggerME(posModel);
    String tags[] = posTaggerME.tag(words);
    for (int i = 0; i < words.length; i++) {
        System.out.print(words[i] + "/" + tags[i] + " ");
    }
    System.out.println();
    Sequence topSequences[] = posTaggerME.topKSequences(words);
    for (Sequence sequence : topSequences) {
        List<String> outcomes = sequence.getOutcomes();
```

```
        System.out.print("[");
        for(int i=0; i<outcomes.size(); i++) {
            System.out.print(words[i] + "/" + outcomes.get(i) +
                " ");
        }
        System.out.println("]");
    }
    System.out.println();
} catch (IOException e) {
    // Handle exceptions
}
```

7. Execute the program. You will get the following abbreviated output:

```
Indexing events with TwoPass using cutoff of 5

Computing event counts... done. 48 events
 Indexing... done.
Sorting and merging events... done. Reduced 48 events to 45.
Done indexing in 0.14 s.
Incorporating indexed data for training...
done.
 Number of Event Tokens: 45
 Number of Outcomes: 14
 Number of Predicates: 19
...done.
Computing model parameters ...
Performing 100 iterations.
 1: ... loglikelihood=-126.6747518215323 0.14583333333333334
 2: ... loglikelihood=-105.18050779926939 0.4791666666666667
 3: ... loglikelihood=-93.3799222561561 0.5625
 ...
 97: ... loglikelihood=-27.01732547916605 0.7916666666666666
 98: ... loglikelihood=-26.94206884992698 0.7916666666666666
 99: ... loglikelihood=-26.868007729321025 0.7916666666666666
100: ... loglikelihood=-26.795111243187804 0.7916666666666666
When/IN the/PRP mouse/VB saw/NN the/PRP cat/JJ it/NN ran/JJ
away./NNS
[When/IN the/PRP mouse/VB saw/NN the/PRP cat/JJ it/NN ran/JJ
away./NNS ]
[When/MD the/PRP mouse/VB saw/NN the/PRP cat/JJ it/NN ran/JJ
away./NNS ]
[When/IN the/PRP mouse/VB saw/NN the/PRP cat/RB it/NN ran/JJ
away./NNS ]
```

How it works...

The file, `sample.train`, contained a series of sentences with each word annotated with a POS tag. Each word is immediately followed by the underscore character and then by the POS abbreviation for that word.

The `InputStreamFactory` anonymous inner class declaration provides a convenient technique for creating an instance of the `InputStreamFactory` class. This instance is used to obtain the training data:

```
InputStreamFactory inputStreamFactory = new InputStreamFactory() {
    public InputStream createInputStream() throws IOException {
        return new FileInputStream("sample.train");
    }
};
```

The `train` method returns an instance of `POSModel` representing the trained model. It used five parameters:

- The first parameter specified the language being used. In this example, we used English.
- The second parameter is an instance of the `ObjectStream` class holding the training data.
- The third parameter specifies the training parameters used during the training process. We used a default set of training parameters.
- The last parameter is an instance of the `POSTaggerFactory` class.

The next statement was used to train the model:

```
posTaggerMEModel = POSTaggerME.train("en", posSampleObjectStream,
    TrainingParameters.defaultParams(), new POSTaggerFactory());
```

The model was then saved to the `sample.bin` file. The model was then demonstrated using code adapted from the *Finding POS using tagging* recipe.

See also

- The OpenNLP API documentation can be found at `https://opennlp.apache.org/docs/1.8.0/apidocs/opennlp-tools/index.html?overview-summary.html`

Performing Text Classification

5

Text classification is used for many purposes such as determining the type of document, performing sentiment analysis, and spam detection. When a document is encountered, we may be interested in whether it is fiction or nonfiction. Tweets may contain positive or negative comments about a product or song. Spam detection is also another area where text classification can be useful.

In this chapter, we will examine techniques to perform classification and how to train models to address specific problem domains. We will use the OpenNLP, Stanford, and LingPipe NLP libraries to illustrate these classification techniques.

In this chapter, we will cover the following recipes:

- Training a maximum entropy model for text classification
- Classifying documents using a maximum entropy model
- Classifying documents using the Stanford API
- Training a model to classify text using LingPipe
- Using LingPipe to classify text
- Detecting spam
- Performing sentiment analysis on reviews

Technical requirements

In this chapter, you will need to install the following software if it has not already been installed:

- Eclipse Photon 4.8.0
- Java JDK 8 or later

We will be using the following APIs, which you will be instructed to add for each recipe as appropriate:

- OpenNLP 1.5.3
- OpenNLP 1.9.0
- Stanford NLP 3.9.2
- LingPipe 4.1.0

The code files for this chapter can be found at `https://github.com/PacktPublishing/Natural-Language-Processing-with-Java-Cookbook/tree/master/Chapter05`.

Training a maximum entropy model for text classification

Maximum entropy is a statistical technique that can be used to classify documents. In this recipe, we will use OpenNLP to demonstrate this approach. Specifically, we will use the OpenNLP `DocumentCategorizerME` class. In the next recipe, *Classifying documents using a maximum entropy model*, we will demonstrate the use of this model.

In order to train the model, we will need a set of training data. We will use a set of data to differentiate between text that relates to frogs and one that relates to rats.

Getting ready

To prepare, we need to do the following:

1. Create a new Maven project
2. Add the following dependency to the project's POM file:

```
<dependency>
    <groupId>org.apache.opennlp</groupId>
    <artifactId>opennlp-tools</artifactId>
    <version>1.5.3</version>
</dependency>
```

How to do it...

The necessary steps include the following:

1. Create a training file called `en-frograt.train` in the project's root directory. This text file will consist of a series of lines that are marked with either a `frog` or `rat` tag. Create the file using the first four paragraphs of the article found at `https://www.exploratorium.edu/frogs/mainstory/index.html`. Add each paragraph as a single line to the file. Prefix each line with a tag of `frog` followed by a space.

2. Add the first four paragraphs of the article found at `http://web.jhu.edu/animalcare/procedures/rat.html` to the file using a tag of `rat`. These lines are shown next, where only the first part of each line is shown:

```
frog Imagine traveling back through time millions ...
frog Surprised? Few people realize just how ancient ...
frog As amphibians, frogs have one webbed foot in ...
frog Frogs have evolved to live in an astounding ...
rat The laboratory rat, Rattus norvegicus, belongs t...
rat The rat has short hair, a long naked tail, ...
rat Rats have a pair of incisors and three pairs ...
rat Rats have a large horseshoe-shaped Harderian ...
```

3. Add the following imports to your project:

```
import java.io.BufferedOutputStream;
import java.io.File;
import java.io.FileInputStream;
import java.io.FileNotFoundException;
import java.io.FileOutputStream;
import java.io.IOException;
import java.io.InputStream;
import java.io.OutputStream;
import java.nio.charset.StandardCharsets;
import opennlp.tools.doccat.DoccatModel;
import opennlp.tools.doccat.DocumentCategorizerME;
import opennlp.tools.doccat.DocumentSample;
import opennlp.tools.doccat.DocumentSampleStream;
import opennlp.tools.util.ObjectStream;
import opennlp.tools.util.PlainTextByLineStream;
```

4. Next, add the following try-with-resources block to the `main` method:

```
try (InputStream dataInputStream = new FileInputStream(
    "en-frograt.train")) {
    ...
} catch (FileNotFoundException e) {
    // Handle exceptions
} catch (IOException e) {
    // Handle exceptions
}
```

5. Insert the following code to create an input stream for the training data:

```
ObjectStream<String> objectStream =
    new PlainTextByLineStream(dataInputStream,
StandardCharsets.UTF_8);
ObjectStream<DocumentSample> documentSampleStream =
    new DocumentSampleStream(objectStream);
```

6. Add the next statement to train the model:

```
DoccatModel documentCategorizationModel =
DocumentCategorizerME.train("en", documentSampleStream);
```

7. Next, serialize the model so that it can be used later:

```
OutputStream modelOutputStream = new BufferedOutputStream(
    new FileOutputStream(new File("en-frograt.bin")));
OutputStream modelBufferedOutputStream =
    new BufferedOutputStream(modelOutputStream);
documentCategorizationModel.serialize(modelBufferedOutputStream);
```

8. Execute the program. You will get the following output. It has been shortened to conserve space:

```
Indexing events using cutoff of 5

Computing event counts... done. 8 events
 Indexing... done.
Sorting and merging events... done. Reduced 8 events to 8.
Done indexing.
Incorporating indexed data for training...
done.
 Number of Event Tokens: 8
 Number of Outcomes: 2
 Number of Predicates: 9
...done.
Computing model parameters ...
```

```
Performing 100 iterations.
  1: ... loglikelihood=-5.545177444479562 0.5
  2: ... loglikelihood=-4.916166681408431 0.875
  3: ... loglikelihood=-4.428326368761899 0.875
...
 98: ... loglikelihood=-0.47059894102051447 1.0
 99: ... loglikelihood=-0.4658802677819042 1.0
100: ... loglikelihood=-0.46125070133272805 1.0
```

The output reflects the default training parameters used; 100 iterations were performed on the training data. The likelihood of a correct model is increased with each iteration as reflected in the latter part of the output.

How it works...

Once the input stream was created for the training file, an object stream of DocumentSample instances was created. It used an instance of the PlainTextByLineStream class, which read in the data from the file where each line was converted into a string:

```
ObjectStream<String> objectStream =
    new PlainTextByLineStream(dataInputStream, StandardCharsets.UTF_8);
ObjectStream<DocumentSample> documentSampleStream =
    new DocumentSampleStream(objectStream);
```

The train method performed the actual training. Its first argument used an abbreviation for the language used, which is English. The second argument was the DocumentSample stream:

```
DoccatModel documentCategorizationModel =
DocumentCategorizerME.train("en", documentSampleStream);
```

An instance of the BufferedOutputStream class was used to make the serialization process more efficient. The model was serialized to the en-frograt.bin file:

```
OutputStream modelOutputStream = new BufferedOutputStream(
    new FileOutputStream(new File("en-frograt.bin")));
OutputStream modelBufferedOutputStream =
    new BufferedOutputStream(modelOutputStream);
documentCategorizationModel.serialize(modelBufferedOutputStream);
```

See also

- The documentation for OpenNLP is found at https://opennlp.apache.org/docs/1.5.3/apidocs/opennlp-tools/index.html

Classifying documents using a maximum entropy model

In this recipe, we will use the model developed in the previous recipe, *Training a maximum entropy model for text classification*, to classify text. We will use the DocumentCategorizerME class to perform the classification.

The model will be read in from the en-frograt.bin file created in the previous recipe. A test sentence is used and the best category and an estimate of how good of a fit was achieved is displayed.

Getting ready

To prepare, we need to do the following:

1. Create a new Maven project
2. Add the following dependency to the project's POM file:

```
<dependency>
    <groupId>org.apache.opennlp</groupId>
    <artifactId>opennlp-tools</artifactId>
    <version>1.5.3</version>
</dependency>
```

3. Copy the en-frograt.bin file from the previous recipe's project to the root level of the new project

How to do it...

The necessary steps include the following:

1. Add the following imports to your project:

```
import java.io.File;
import java.io.FileInputStream;
import java.io.FileNotFoundException;
import java.io.IOException;
import java.io.InputStream;
import opennlp.tools.doccat.DoccatModel;
import opennlp.tools.doccat.DocumentCategorizerME;
```

2. Add the following try-with-resources block to the `main` method in order to create an input stream for the `en-frograt.bin` file:

```
try (InputStream modelInputStream = new FileInputStream(
    new File("en-frograt.bin"));) {
    ...
} catch (FileNotFoundException e) {
    // Handle exceptions
} catch (IOException e) {
    // Handle exceptions
}
```

3. Add the next statement to define a test string:

```
String testString =
    "Amphibians are animals that dwell in wet environments";
```

4. Add the following code sequence to create an instance of the `DocumentCategorizerME` class:

```
DoccatModel documentCategorizationModel =
    new DoccatModel(modelInputStream);
DocumentCategorizerME documentCategorizer =
    new DocumentCategorizerME(documentCategorizationModel);
```

5. Add these statements to perform the categorization and display the results:

```
double[] probabilities =
    documentCategorizer.categorize(testString);
String bestCategory =
    documentCategorizer.getBestCategory(probabilities);
System.out.println("The best fit is: " + bestCategory);
```

6. Execute the program. You will get the following output:

```
The best fit is: frog
```

How it works...

The `DoccatModel` model was instantiated based on the model file. It was then used as input to the `DocumentCategorizerME` constructor:

```
DoccatModel documentCategorizationModel =
    new DoccatModel(modelInputStream);
DocumentCategorizerME documentCategorizer =
    new DocumentCategorizerME(documentCategorizationModel);
```

The `categorize` method of the `DocumentCategorizerME` class then used the test string to return an array of probabilities for the possible categories. The `getBestCategory` method then took these probabilities to find the best fit:

```
double[] probabilities =
    documentCategorizer.categorize(testString);
String bestCategory =
    documentCategorizer.getBestCategory(probabilities);
System.out.println("The best fit is: " + bestCategory);
```

There's more...

We can display all of the possible categories and probabilities using the `getNumberOfCategories` method, as shown next. The `getCategory` method returns the name of the category and the `probabilities` array returns the corresponding probability:

```
for (int i = 0; i < documentCategorizer.getNumberOfCategories(); i++) {
    System.out.printf("Category: %-4s - %4.2f\n",
        documentCategorizer.getCategory(i), probabilities[i]);
}
```

When this code is executed, we get the following output:

```
Category: frog - 0.75
Category: rat - 0.25
```

There is also the `getAllResults` method, which may be of interest to the reader. It uses the `probabilities` array and returns a formatted list of the categories and probabilities, as shown next:

```
System.out.println(documentCategorizer.getAllResults(probabilities));
```

Execute this, which will result in the following output:

```
frog[0.7534] rat[0.2466]
```

See also

- The documentation for OpenNLP is found at `https://opennlp.apache.org/docs/1.5.3/apidocs/opennlp-tools/index.html`

Classifying documents using the Stanford API

The Stanford OpenNLP API provides another technique for classifying documents. In this recipe, we will demonstrate how to train a model and then use it to classify the text. We will create a training file and a test file for the purposes of classifying flowers and spices. We will also create a properties file to provide information so the classifier can work correctly. The `ColumnDataClassifier` class is used to represent the classifier.

Getting ready

To prepare, we need to do the following:

1. Create a new Maven project
2. Add the following dependency to the project's POM file:

```
<!--
https://mvnrepository.com/artifact/edu.stanford.nlp/stanford-corenl
p -->
<dependency>
    <groupId>edu.stanford.nlp</groupId>
    <artifactId>stanford-corenlp</artifactId>
    <version>3.9.2</version>
</dependency>
```

How to do it...

The necessary steps include the following:

1. Create a text file called `FlowersAndSpices.prop` and add the following to the file in the project's root directory:

```
# Features
useClassFeature=true
1.usePrefixSuffixNGrams=true
1.maxNGramLeng=4
1.minNGramLeng=1
# Training input
trainFileFlowersAndSpices.train
testFileFlowersAndSpices.test
```

2. Next, create a text file called `FlowersAndSpices.train`. This file will consist of a series of lines—one for each flower and spice annotation. An annotation consists of a number followed by a tab and then text. For flowers, we will use an integer of 1 and for spices, we will use an integer value of 2. The text will be the name of the flower or spice. The flower list was derived from the list found at `http://www.alphalists.com/list/alphabetical-list-flowers` and the spices from `https://www.spicejungle.com/list-of-spices`. The first lines of the file are shown next. The file can be downloaded from <TBD>:

```
1 Acacia
1 Achillea
1 Adam's-needle
1 African Boxwood
1 African Lily
```

3. Create a text file called `FlowersAndSpices.test`. We will use it to test the classifier. It uses the same format as the training file but is smaller. Its content is as follows:

```
1 Nigella
1 Feverfew
1 Chamelaucium
1 Big Flax
2 Chai Tea
2 Dill Pollen
2 Infusing Flavors
2 Sage
```

4. Add the following imports to your project:

```
import java.io.BufferedReader;
import java.io.BufferedWriter;
import java.io.File;
import java.io.FileNotFoundException;
import java.io.FileReader;
import java.io.FileWriter;
import java.io.IOException;
import edu.stanford.nlp.classify.Classifier;
import edu.stanford.nlp.classify.ColumnDataClassifier;
import edu.stanford.nlp.ling.Datum;
import edu.stanford.nlp.objectbank.ObjectBank;
```

5. Add the following code to the `main` method to read in the model's properties and create the classifier:

```
ColumnDataClassifier columnDataClassifier =
    new ColumnDataClassifier("FlowersAndSpices.prop");
Classifier<String, String> classifier =
    columnDataClassifier.makeClassifier(
        columnDataClassifier.readTrainingExamples(
            "FlowersAndSpices.train"));
```

6. Use the next code sequence to test the model using the test file:

```
ObjectBank<String> objectBank = ObjectBank.getLineIterator(
    "FlowersAndSpices.test", "utf-8");
for (String line : objectBank) {
    Datum<String, String> datum =
        columnDataClassifier.makeDatumFromLine(line);
    System.out.println("Datum: [" + line + "]\tPredicted Category:
" +
        classifier.classOf(datum));
}
```

7. Execute the program. It will produce the following output:

```
Datum: [1 Nigella] Predicted Category: 1
Datum: [1 Feverfew] Predicted Category: 1
Datum: [1 Chamelaucium] Predicted Category: 1
Datum: [1 Big Flax] Predicted Category: 1
Datum: [2 Chai Tea] Predicted Category: 2
Datum: [2 Dill Pollen] Predicted Category: 2
Datum: [2 Infusing Flavors] Predicted Category: 1
Datum: [2 Sage] Predicted Category: 1
```

How it works...

The `ColumnDataClassifier` instance is initialized using the properties file:

```
ColumnDataClassifier columnDataClassifier =
    new ColumnDataClassifier("FlowersAndSpices.prop");
```

This file is duplicated in the following code sequence. It consists of several feature declarations and the names of the training and test files. These features are documented at https://nlp.stanford.edu/nlp/javadoc/javanlp/edu/stanford/nlp/classify/ColumnDataClassifier.html:

```
# Features
useClassFeature=true
1.usePrefixSuffixNGrams=true
1.maxNGramLeng=4
1.minNGramLeng=1
# Training input
trainFileFlowersAndSpices.train
testFileFlowersAndSpices.test
```

The `makeClassifier` method creates the actual classifier using the training file:

```
Classifier<String, String> classifier =
    columnDataClassifier.makeClassifier(
        columnDataClassifier.readTrainingExamples(
            "FlowersAndSpices.train"));
```

To test the model using the test file, an `ObjectBank` instance implements the `Iterable` interface; each line is processed by the `makeDatumFromLine` method and returns a `Datum` instance. This object contains a test item and was used with the classifier's `classOf` method to return the best category:

```
ObjectBank<String> objectBank = ObjectBank.getLineIterator(
    "FlowersAndSpices.test", "utf-8");
for (String line : objectBank) {
    Datum<String, String> datum =
columnDataClassifier.makeDatumFromLine(line);
    System.out.println("Datum: [" + line + "]\tPredicted Category: " +
        classifier.classOf(datum));
}
```

The classifier worked well except for the following two datums:

```
Datum: [2 Infusing Flavors] Predicted Category: 1
Datum: [2 Sage] Predicted Category: 1
```

A larger, more comprehensive dataset can provide more accurate results.

There's more...

We can also test a single text sample at a time, as shown next. A string array is defined consisting of two elements. These elements correspond to a category and text. A `Datum` instance is created using the `makeDatumFromStrings` method. The `classOf` method is used again to determine the best category:

```
String testItem[] = {"2","Dill Pollen"};
Datum<String, String> datum =
    columnDataClassifier.makeDatumFromStrings(testItem);
System.out.println("[" + testItem[0] + "\t" + testItem[1] +
    "] Predicted Category: " + classifier.classOf(datum));
```

When this code is executed, you will get the following output:

```
[2 Dill Pollen] Predicted Category: 2
```

See also

- The Stanford NLP API is found at `https://nlp.stanford.edu/nlp/javadoc/javanlp/`

Training a model to classify text using LingPipe

The LingPipe NLP API provides techniques to train a model and to classify documents based upon these models. In this recipe, we will demonstrate how a model is trained. Once trained, we will then serialize the model for later use. In the next recipe, *Using LingPipe to classify text*, we will use this model to classify sample text.

LingPipe comes with a set of training data. We will use this data in this recipe. Other training datasets can be found at sites such as `http://qwone.com/~jason/20Newsgroups/`.

Getting ready

To prepare, we need to do the following:

1. Create a new Maven project.
2. Add the following dependency to the project's POM file:

```
<!-- https://mvnrepository.com/artifact/de.julielab/aliasi-lingpipe
-->
<dependency>
    <groupId>de.julielab</groupId>
    <artifactId>aliasi-lingpipe</artifactId>
    <version>4.1.0</version>
</dependency>
```

3. Download the data files that are found in the `lingpipe-4.1.2.tar.gz` file. This file can be downloaded from `http://alias-i.com/lingpipe/web/download.html`.
4. Extract the file that contains the `lingpipe-4.1.2.tar` file and save it to a convenient location. These files will be extracted to a directory called `lingpipe-4.1.2-website`. In this directory, you will find a subdirectory called `demos`, which contains the training data we will use.

How to do it...

The necessary steps include the following:

1. Add the following imports to your project:

```
import java.io.File;
import java.io.IOException;
import com.aliasi.classify.Classification;
import com.aliasi.classify.Classified;
import com.aliasi.classify.DynamicLMClassifier;
import com.aliasi.lm.NGramProcessLM;
import com.aliasi.util.AbstractExternalizable;
import com.aliasi.util.Compilable;
import com.aliasi.util.Files;
```

2. In the `main` method, add the following string declaration. This is used for the training dataset:

```
String[] categories = { "soc.religion.christian",
    "talk.religion.misc", "alt.atheism", "misc.forsale" };
```

3. Next, add the following code to set up the training directories. The location for the `rootDirectory` string will depend on where you saved the extracted files:

```
int nGramSize = 6;
DynamicLMClassifier<NGramProcessLM> dynamicLMClassifier =
    DynamicLMClassifier.createNGramProcess(categories, nGramSize);
final String rootDirectory = "../demos";
final File trainingDirectory = new File(rootDirectory +
    "/data/fourNewsGroups/4news-train");
```

4. Add the next `for` loop to access each training file:

```
for (int i = 0; i < categories.length; ++i) {
    final File trainingFilesDirectory =
        new File(trainingDirectory, categories[i]);
        ...
}
```

5. Insert the following code to obtain the training files in the directory and read the files in:

```
String[] trainingFiles = trainingFilesDirectory.list();
for (int j = 0; j < trainingFiles.length; ++j) {
    try {
        File trainingFile =
            new File(trainingFilesDirectory, trainingFiles[j]);
        String trainingText = Files.readFromFile(
            trainingFile, "ISO-8859-1");
            ...
    } catch (IOException ex) {
        // Handle exceptions
    }
}
```

6. Next, insert the next sequence to train the model:

```
Classification classification = new Classification(categories[i]);
Classified<CharSequence> classified =
    new Classified<>((CharSequence) trainingText, classification);
dynamicLMClassifier.handle(classified);
```

7. Serialize the model using the following code sequence:

```
try {
    AbstractExternalizable.compileTo((Compilable)
        dynamicLMClassifier,
        new File("classificationModel.model"));
} catch (IOException ex) {
```

```
        // Handle exceptions
    }
```

8. Execute the program. No output will be displayed if everything works correctly. The file, `classificationModel.model`, will be present in the project's root directory.

How it works...

The `categories` array holds the names of the categories found in the training file. An instance of the `DynamicLMClassifier` class was created using these categories and an `nGramSize` size of 6. This value specifies the number of contiguous elements of text in one sequence that will be used to classify the text. We specified the `4news-train` directory to be used for training:

```
int nGramSize = 6;
DynamicLMClassifier<NGramProcessLM> dynamicLMClassifier =
    DynamicLMClassifier.createNGramProcess(categories, nGramSize);
final String rootDirectory = "../demos";
final File trainingDirectory = new File(rootDirectory
    + "/data/fourNewsGroups/4news-train");
```

There are four subdirectories, `4news-train`, which match the categories names. Within the `for` loop, the `trainingFilesDirectory` variable is set to these subdirectories and were processed one subdirectory at a time:

```
for (int i = 0; i < categories.length; ++i) {
    final File trainingFilesDirectory =
        new File(trainingDirectory, categories[i]);
    ...
}
```

For each file in one of these subdirectories, its contents are read in and stored in the `trainingText` string:

```
String[] trainingFiles = trainingFilesDirectory.list();
for (int j = 0; j < trainingFiles.length; ++j) {
    try {
        File trainingFile =
            new File(trainingFilesDirectory, trainingFiles[j]);
        String trainingText =
            Files.readFromFile(trainingFile, "ISO-8859-1");
        ...
    } catch (IOException ex) {
        // Handle exceptions
```

```
        }
    }
```

An instance of the `Classification` class was created for each category. This was used to instantiate an instance of `Classified<CharSequence>` along with the training text. The `handle` method performed the actual training:

```
Classification classification = new Classification(categories[i]);
Classified<CharSequence> classified =
    new Classified<>((CharSequence) trainingText, classification);
dynamicLMClassifier.handle(classified);
```

The model was then serialized.

See also

- The documentation for LingPipe is found at `http://alias-i.com/lingpipe/docs/api/index.html`

Using LingPipe to classify text

In this recipe, we will use the model created in the previous recipe, *Training a model to classify text using LingPipe*, to classify sample text. While we could use any of the four classification categories to test the data, we will use a sample text consisting of a religion reference. Specifically, we will use the `LMClassifier` class to perform the classification.

Getting ready

To prepare, we need to do the following:

1. Create a new Maven project
2. Add the following dependency to the project's POM file:

```
<!-- https://mvnrepository.com/artifact/de.julielab/aliasi-lingpipe
-->
<dependency>
    <groupId>de.julielab</groupId>
    <artifactId>aliasi-lingpipe</artifactId>
    <version>4.1.0</version>
</dependency>
```

3. Copy the file, classificationModel.model, created in the previous recipe to the root directory of this project

How to do it...

The necessary steps include the following:

1. Add the following imports to your project:

```
import java.io.File;
import java.io.IOException;
import com.aliasi.classify.JointClassification;
import com.aliasi.classify.LMClassifier;
import com.aliasi.util.AbstractExternalizable;
```

2. In the main method, add the variables, categories and sampleText, to hold the training categories and the text to be classified. The sample text was copied from the *Taoism* section of the article at https://en.wikipedia.org/wiki/Religion. We used the defining sentence as defined next:

```
String[] categories = { "soc.religion.christian",
"talk.religion.misc",
    "alt.atheism", "misc.forsale" };

String sampleText = "An ancient tradition of philosophy and " +
    "belief rooted in Chinese worldview";
```

3. Next, add the following try block to instantiate the model:

```
try {
    LMClassifier lmClassifier = (LMClassifier)
        AbstractExternalizable.readObject(
            new File("classificationModel.model"));
    ...
} catch (IOException | ClassNotFoundException ex) {
    // Handle exceptions
}
```

4. Add the following code to classify the sample text followed by code to display the best category:

```
JointClassification jointClassification =
    lmClassifier.classify(sampleText);
String bestCategory = jointClassification.bestCategory();
System.out.println("Best Category: " + bestCategory);
```

5. Execute the program. You will get the following output:

```
Best Category: talk.religion.misc
```

How it works...

The `readObject` method instantiated the model from the `classificationModel.model` file. The `classify` method took the sample text and returned an instance of the `JointClassification` class, which represents the classification. The `bestCategory` method returned a string for the name of the category that accurately matches the sample text, which was then displayed:

```
LMClassifier lmClassifier lmClassifier = (LMClassifier)
    AbstractExternalizable.readObject(
        new File("classificationModel.model"));
JointClassification jointClassification =
lmClassifier.classify(sampleText);
String bestCategory = jointClassification.bestCategory();
System.out.println("Best Category: " + bestCategory);
```

There's more...

We can obtain additional information regarding the classification. The following methods return various information about the classification:

- `score`: A number reflecting a relative score for the classification
- `jointLog2Probability`: The probability of the classification being correct
- `category`: The name of the classification

These methods can be used in a `for` loop to display this information, as shown next:

```
for (int i = 0; i < categories.length; i++) {
    double score = jointClassification.score(i);
    double probability = jointClassification.jointLog2Probability(i);
    String category = jointClassification.category(i);
    System.out.printf("Category: %-22s Score: %4.2f jointLog2Probability:
%4.2f%n",
        category, score, probability);
}
```

When this code is executed, you will get the following output:

```
Category: talk.religion.misc Score: -2.51 jointLog2Probability: -190.76
Category: alt.atheism Score: -2.56 jointLog2Probability: -194.71
Category: soc.religion.christian Score: -2.85 jointLog2Probability: -216.53
Category: misc.forsale Score: -3.01 jointLog2Probability: -228.58
```

The closer the `score` and `jointLog2Probability` values are to zero, the more likely the classification will be correct.

See also

- The documentation for LingPipe is found at `http://alias-i.com/lingpipe/docs/api/index.html`

Detecting spam

Spam detection is an important part of most email systems and can be useful in other areas such as text messaging. In this recipe, we will demonstrate how we can use text classification to detect spam.

We will begin with the downloading and formatting of spam and ham files. Ham refers to those emails that are not spam. Next, an OpenNLP model will be trained on the email data. We will then validate the model using an additional set of email files.

Getting ready

To prepare, we need to do the following:

1. Create a new Maven project.

2. Add the following dependency to the project's POM file:

```
<dependency>
    <groupId>org.apache.opennlp</groupId>
    <artifactId>opennlp-tools</artifactId>
    <version>1.9.0</version>
</dependency>
```

3. Download the file `lingspam_public.tar.gz` and extract to a directory of your choosing using the following URL: `http://www.aueb.gr/users/ion/data/lingspam_public.tar.gz`.

4. Extract the `lingspam_public.tar` file and then extract its files to a `lingspam_public` directory. This directory consists of several subdirectories, which are explained in its `readme.txt` file.

We will be using the subdirectories in the `stop` directory. Four different versions of the spam data are found in the `lingspam_public` directory. The emails found in these directories have had different types of pre-processing performed on them. We will use the `stop` directory, which has had **stop words** removed from them. A stop word is a word that may not be needed for some NLP tasks and may include such words as *the, and,* or *an.*

The `stop` directory contains several other subdirectories. In these subdirectories are files containing either spam email or regular email, sometimes referred to as ham. Those files whose names contain the `spms` string are the spam emails. Otherwise, they are ham emails.

How to do it...

The necessary steps include the following:

1. Add the following imports to your project:

```
import java.io.BufferedReader;
import java.io.BufferedWriter;
import java.io.File;
import java.io.FileInputStream;
import java.io.FileNotFoundException;
import java.io.FileReader;
import java.io.FileWriter;
import java.io.IOException;
import java.io.InputStream;
import java.nio.charset.StandardCharsets;
import java.util.ArrayList;
import opennlp.tools.doccat.DoccatModel;
import opennlp.tools.doccat.DocumentCategorizerME;
```

```
import opennlp.tools.doccat.DocumentSample;
import opennlp.tools.doccat.DocumentSampleStream;
import opennlp.tools.util.ObjectStream;
import opennlp.tools.util.PlainTextByLineStream;
```

2. In the `main` method, add the following declaration and `try` block:

```
ArrayList<String> testList = new ArrayList();
try (BufferedWriter spamBufferedWriter = new BufferedWriter(
        new FileWriter(new File("spamtraining.train")))) {
    ...
} catch (IOException ex) {
    // Handle exceptions
}
```

3. Insert the following code to open the spam files for processing. Modify the `rootDirectoryName` string to contain the path to where you saved the spam data:

```
String rootDirectoryName = ".../lingspam_public/stop";
File rootDirectory = new File(rootDirectoryName);
for (String directoryName : rootDirectory.list()) {
    File file = new File(rootDirectoryName + "/" + directoryName);
    ...
}
```

4. Insert the next code sequence to open one file at a time. The contents of the file will be reformatted to contain either a `spam` or `ham` header followed by a tab and then the contents of the file all on a single line. This is the format required to train an OpenNLP model:

```
String fileNames[] = file.list();
if (fileNames != null) {
    for (String fileName : fileNames) {
        String filePath = rootDirectoryName + "/" + directoryName +
            "/" + fileName;
        StringBuilder lineStringBuilder = new StringBuilder();

        BufferedReader br = new BufferedReader(new FileReader(
            new File(filePath)));
        String line = null;
        if (fileName.contains("spms")) {
            lineStringBuilder.append("spam\t");
        } else {
            lineStringBuilder.append("ham\t");
        }
        while ((line = br.readLine()) != null) {
```

```
                    lineStringBuilder.append(line);
                }
                if (directoryName.equals("part10")) {
                    testList.add(lineStringBuilder.toString());
                } else {
                    spamBufferedWriter.write(lineStringBuilder.toString() +
    "\n");
                }
                lineStringBuilder.setLength(0);
            }
        }
```

5. Add the following code to test the model using the test data contained in `testList ArrayList`. This code has been adapted from the *Classifying documents using a maximum entropy model* recipe:

```
try (InputStream dataInputStream =
        new FileInputStream("spamtraining.train")) {
    ObjectStream<String> objectStream = new PlainTextByLineStream
        (dataInputStream, StandardCharsets.UTF_8);
    ObjectStream<DocumentSample> documentSampleStream =
        new DocumentSampleStream(objectStream);
    DoccatModel documentCategorizationModel =
    DocumentCategorizerME.train("en", documentSampleStream);
    DocumentCategorizerME documentCategorizer =
        new DocumentCategorizerME(documentCategorizationModel);
    for (String testItem : testList) {
        double[] probabilities =
            documentCategorizer.categorize(testItem);
        String bestCategory =
            documentCategorizer.getBestCategory(probabilities);
        System.out.println("The best fit for: [" +
            testItem.subSequence(0, 32) + "...] is: " +
            bestCategory);
    }
} catch (FileNotFoundException ex) {
    // Handle exceptions
} catch (IOException ex) {
    // Handle exceptions
}
```

6. Execute the code. You will get the following output, which has been shortened to conserve space:

```
Indexing events using cutoff of 5

Computing event counts... done. 2602 events
  Indexing... done.
```

```
Sorting and merging events... done. Reduced 2602 events to 2583.
Done indexing.
Incorporating indexed data for training...
done.
 Number of Event Tokens: 2583
 Number of Outcomes: 2
 Number of Predicates: 14818
...done.
Computing model parameters ...
Performing 100 iterations.
  1: ... loglikelihood=-1803.5689638168774 0.8339738662567256
  2: ... loglikelihood=-1692.5047127764058 0.8478093774019985
  3: ... loglikelihood=-1604.1876379047783 0.8581860107609531
...
 97: ... loglikelihood=-535.3669570755931 0.9865488086087625
 98: ... loglikelihood=-532.7649364282789 0.9865488086087625
 99: ... loglikelihood=-530.1975277899988 0.9869331283627979
100: ... loglikelihood=-527.6639609319382 0.9869331283627979
The best fit for: [ham Subject: sound patterns spon...] is: ham
The best fit for: [ham Subject: atelier des doctora...] is: ham
The best fit for: [ham Subject: journal – – informa...] is: ham
The best fit for: [ham Subject: wholes partswholes ...] is: ham
...
The best fit for: [ham Subject: books : survey amer...] is: ham
The best fit for: [ham Subject: wecol ' 98 – – west...] is: ham
The best fit for: [ham Subject: euralex ' 98 – revi...] is: ham
The best fit for: [spam Subject: secrets travel age...] is: spam
The best fit for: [spam Subject: tami , was yu ?bob...] is: ham
The best fit for: [spam Subject: internet pc user g...] is: ham
The best fit for: [spam Subject: 95 . 8 capital fmi...] is: spam
...
The best fit for: [spam Subject: stock market infor...] is: ham
The best fit for: [spam Subject: lucky !congratulat...] is: spam
The best fit for: [spam Subject: capitalfm . comis ...] is: spam
The best fit for: [spam Subject: submit 600is spam ...] is: spam
The best fit for: [spam Subject: submit 600is spam ...] is: spam
The best fit for: [spam Subject: ' t stand ! ! ! ! ...] is: ham
```

How it works...

ArrayList and testList were used to hold a set of test data. Each element of the list contains a string holding either the spam or ham tag followed by a tab and then an email message. These lines were created from the files found in the part10 folder:

```
ArrayList<String> testList = new ArrayList();
```

The file, `spamtraining.train`, holds the training data and was created in the first `try` block. The `rootDirectoryName` string held the path to the `stop` directory:

```
Strig rootDirectoryName = ".../lingspam_public/stop";
```

The `rootDirectory` variable represents the `stop` directory. The `list` method returns the names of all of the subdirectories in this directory. These will be `part1`, `part2`, `part3`, ... `part10`:

```
File rootDirectory = new File(rootDirectoryName);
for (String directoryName : rootDirectory.list()) {
    File file = new File(rootDirectoryName + "/" + directoryName);
        ...
}
```

Next, we created a list of files for each of these directories, one at a time. The contents of each file will be reformatted to include either a `spam` or `ham` header followed by a tab and then the contents of the file all on a single line. The string will be saved to either a training file or `testList`. Data from the `part10` directory was saved to `testList`.

This is the format required to train an OpenNLP model. We will use the code developed in the *Training a maximum entropy model for text classification* recipe to train a model that we will then use to classify text as either spam or ham:

```
String fileNames[] = file.list();
if (fileNames != null) {
    for (String fileName : fileNames) {
        String filePath = rootDirectoryName + "/" + directoryName +
            "/" + fileName;
        StringBuilder lineStringBuilder = new StringBuilder();
        BufferedReader br = new BufferedReader(new FileReader(
            new File(filePath)));
        String line = null;
            ...
    }
}
```

`lineStringBuilder` is an instance of the `StringBuilder` class, which provides an efficient way of concatenating string. If the file is a spam file, the `spam` tag is used, otherwise the `ham` tag is used. After that, each line of the file is added to the `lineStringBuilder` instance:

```
if (fileName.contains("spms")) {
    lineStringBuilder.append("spam\t");
} else {
    lineStringBuilder.append("ham\t");
```

```
    }
    while ((line = br.readLine()) != null) {
        lineStringBuilder.append(line);
    }
```

We will use the part10 directory for our test data. When this directory is encountered, the lineStringBuilder instance is converted into a string and then appended to testList. Otherwise, it is written to the training file. The StringBuilder class setLength method was used to effectively reset the buffer for reuse with the next file:

```
    if (directoryName.equals("part10")) {
        testList.add(lineStringBuilder.toString());
    } else {
        spamBufferedWriter.write(lineStringBuilder.toString() + "\n");
    }
    lineStringBuilder.setLength(0);
```

Now that the training data has been created, we can train the model. The training code was adapted from the *Training a maximum entropy model for text classification* recipe. However, instead of saving the model to a file for reuse, we used the model immediately.

The only other significant difference is how the best fit category was displayed. The first 32 characters of each test data line was printed to clearly show what was being processed:

```
    System.out.println("The best fit for: [" +
        testItem.subSequence(0, 32) + "...] is: " + bestCategory);
```

Notice that the model correctly identified good email every time. However, for spam, it wasn't always successful. This can be improved by using a better set of training data. However, letting spam through is not necessarily that bad. What we don't want to do is to flag good mail as spam.

There's more...

An alternate, yet simplistic, approach is to use regular expressions to detect spam. The technique demonstrated here uses a file containing strings that may be found in spam. A regular expression is created for each of these strings and then used against a sample text. As simple as this approach may be, it may be applicable in some limited situations.

Add the following imports to the project:

```
    import java.io.BufferedReader;
    import java.io.File;
    import java.io.FileNotFoundException;
    import java.io.FileReader;
```

```
import java.io.IOException;
import java.util.regex.Matcher;
import java.util.regex.Pattern;
```

Declare the sample text, as shown next:

```
String text = "Congratualtions! You have won! Click here...";
```

Create a file called `spam.txt` and save it at the root level of your project. Add the following to the file:

```
enter your password
Nigerian princess
You have won
mystery shopper
```

Use the next `try` block to create an instance of the `BufferedReader` class, which we will use to read from the file:

```
try (BufferedReader br = new BufferedReader(
    new FileReader(new File("spam.txt")))) {
    ...
} catch (FileNotFoundException e) {
    // Handle exceptions
} catch (IOException e) {
    // Handle exceptions
}
```

The `readLine` method reads in a single line, which is used to create a `Pattern` instance. A `Matcher` instance is then created using the pattern with the sample text used as an argument of the `matcher` method. If the sample text contains the pattern, then a spam detected message is displayed and we break out of the loop. Each line of the file is processed:

```
String line = null;
while ((line = br.readLine()) != null) {
    Pattern pattern = Pattern.compile(line);
    Matcher matcher = pattern.matcher(text);
    if (matcher.find() == true) {
        System.out.println("Spam detected");
        break;
    }
}
```

When this code sequence is executed, you will get the following output:

```
Spam detected
```

We could have also used the `contains` method of the `String` class to achieve the same result:

```
System.out.println(text.contains("Click here"));
```

When executed, you will get the following:

```
true
```

Spam detection is not always easy as witnessed by the continuing evolution of spam assaults and techniques used to combat them. There are other spam detection techniques that should also be considered, for example, scrutiny of email addresses can be useful.

See also

- The documentation for OpenNLP can be found at `https://opennlp.apache.org/docs/1.5.3/apidocs/opennlp-tools/index.html`
- Other spam detection techniques are discussed at `https://www.techsoupcanada.ca/en/learning_center/10_sfm_explained`

Performing sentiment analysis on reviews

Sentiment analysis is the process of obtaining some assessment of text such as a favorable or unfavorable review of a book. We will demonstrate how this type of analysis can be performed using the Stanford API. Specifically, we will use a model trained for movie reviews.

Getting ready

To prepare, we need to do the following:

1. Create a new Maven project
2. Add the following dependencies to the project's POM file:

```
<!--
https://mvnrepository.com/artifact/edu.stanford.nlp/stanford-corenlp -->
<dependency>
    <groupId>edu.stanford.nlp</groupId>
    <artifactId>stanford-corenlp</artifactId>
```

```
        <version>3.9.2</version>
    </dependency>
    <!--
    https://mvnrepository.com/artifact/edu.stanford.nlp/stanford-corenl
    p -->
    <dependency>
        <groupId>edu.stanford.nlp</groupId>
        <artifactId>stanford-corenlp</artifactId>
        <version>3.9.2</version>
        <classifier>models</classifier>
    </dependency>
```

How to do it...

The necessary steps include the following:

1. Add the following imports to the project:

```
import java.util.Properties;
import edu.stanford.nlp.ling.CoreAnnotations;
import edu.stanford.nlp.neural.rnn.RNNCoreAnnotations;
import edu.stanford.nlp.pipeline.Annotation;
import edu.stanford.nlp.pipeline.StanfordCoreNLP;
import edu.stanford.nlp.sentiment.SentimentCoreAnnotations;
import edu.stanford.nlp.trees.Tree;
import edu.stanford.nlp.util.CoreMap;
```

2. Add the following string declarations for two movie reviews:

```
String goodReview = "With its impressive action sequences, " +
    "taut economic direction, and relentlessly fast pace, " +
    "it's clear why The Terminator continues to be an " +
    "influence on sci-fi and action flicks.";
String badReview = "\r\n" +
    "There are a few jumps and bumps, but there's no real " +
    "sense of dread, unease or questioning. We simply " +
    "watch the events unfold with a full understanding " +
    "of what's going on.";
```

These reviews are found at the following:

- Good review (https://www.rottentomatoes.com/m/terminator/):
  Critics Consensus
- Bad review (https://www.rottentomatoes.com/m/the_
  possession_of_hannah_grace): Katie Walsh

3. Next, add the following code to set up the Stanford pipeline for processing:

```
Properties properties = new Properties();
properties.setProperty("annotators",
    "tokenize, ssplit, parse, sentiment");
StanfordCoreNLP pipeline = new StanfordCoreNLP(properties);
```

4. Add the next sequence to process and display the results:

```
int predicatedTotal = 0;

String[] lines = goodReview.split("\\.");
for (int i = 0; i < lines.length; i++) {
    Annotation annotation = pipeline.process(lines[i]);
    CoreMap coreMapSentence = annotation.get(
        CoreAnnotations.SentencesAnnotation.class).get(0);
    Tree tree = coreMapSentence.get(
        SentimentCoreAnnotations.SentimentAnnotatedTree.class);
    String sentiment = coreMapSentence.get(
        SentimentCoreAnnotations.SentimentClass.class);
    int predictedScore =
        RNNCoreAnnotations.getPredictedClass(tree);
    predicatedTotal = predicatedTotal + (predictedScore);
    System.out.println(lines[i].substring(0, 32) + " ... Score: "
        + predictedScore + " " + sentiment);
}
System.out.println();
System.out.printf("Average: %3.2f",
predicatedTotal/(float)lines.length);
```

5. Execute the program. You will get the following output:

```
With its impressive action seque ... Score: 3 Positive

Average: 3.00
```

The model will return integers representing different ratings as listed here:

- 0: Very negative
- 1: Negative
- 2: Neutral
- 3: Positive
- 4: Very positive

How it works...

The pipeline created used the sentiment operation to perform the analysis. The model used was made available using the second POM dependency shown earlier.

We generated a predicted score for each sentence. We also computed an average score for the entire review using the `predicatedTotal` variable. The first review possessed a single sentence so the sentence and average values were identical.

Each review was split into individual sentences using the `split` method with an argument of \\.. This meant the sentences were split on periods. As Chapter 2, *Isolating Sentences within a Document*, suggests, this simplistic approach may not always work well:

```
int predicatedTotal = 0;
String[] lines = goodReview.split("\\.");
for (int i = 0; i < lines.length; i++) {
    ...
}
System.out.println();
System.out.printf("Average: %3.2f", predicatedTotal/(float)lines.length);
```

The `Annotation` class provides information about a span of text. The `process` method returned this information about the sentence as specified by its argument. With the `Annotation` object we used, it's a `get` method to return a `CoreMap` instance that supports sentence-specific information methods. The `SentencesAnnotation.class` class was used as the argument for the `get` method. It returns a list of sentence annotations. In this case, there was only a single sentence to be retrieved. For this reason, we used the `get` method with a 0 index:

```
Annotation annotation = pipeline.process(lines[i]);
CoreMap coreMapSentence = annotation.get(
    CoreAnnotations.SentencesAnnotation.class).get(0);
```

We used the `get` method of the `CoreMap` class twice in the following sequence. The first usage returned an instance of the `Tree` class. The second returned a string containing the classification. The `Tree` class supports access to specific information about the sentiment. We used it to obtain the predicted score using the `getPredictedClass` method:

```
Tree tree = coreMapSentence.get(
    SentimentCoreAnnotations.SentimentAnnotatedTree.class);
String sentiment = coreMapSentence.get(
    SentimentCoreAnnotations.SentimentClass.class);
int predictedScore = RNNCoreAnnotations.getPredictedClass(tree);
```

This information was used to compute a total score value and display the score and its label. In the `println` statement, only the first 32 characters of a line were displayed:

```
predicatedTotal = predicatedTotal + (predictedScore);
System.out.println(lines[i].substring(0, 32) + " ... Score: " +
    predictedScore + " " + sentiment);
```

There's more...

We will change the `String[] lines = goodReview.split("\\.");` statement to the following statement:

```
String[] lines = badReview.split("\\.");
```

Execute the program again and you will get the following output:

```
There are a few jumps and bump ... Score: 1 Negative
We simply watch the events unfo ... Score: 3 Positive
Average: 2.00
```

This illustrates how multiple sentences of a review are processed. The first sentence was negative while the second sentence was considered to be positive. After averaging, we obtained a neutral score of 2.

See also

- The Stanford NLP API documentation is found at `https://nlp.stanford.edu/nlp/javadoc/javanlp/`

6
Finding Relationships within Text

In this chapter, we will demonstrate several techniques to isolate relationships between elements of text. Central to this task is the process of parsing. With this process, we will split text into units which typically corresponds to a **Part-Of-Speech** (**POS**). Once the text has been parsed, we can isolate any relationships that might exist.

We will start by demonstrating how we can graphically depict parse trees. We will use Stanford GUI tools for this purpose. By being able to graphically visualize a parse tree, we can better understand the relationships found in the tree. Next, we will examine several techniques to parse text using simple text. Parsing text in this manner is more readily used by computers for subsequent analysis as opposed to a graphical representation.

Parent-child relationships are patterned after familial relationships. However, this can also depict relationships such as the parts of a car or a toy. We will illustrate several approaches for identifying these types of relationships.

Co-references often refers to relationships between proper nouns and pronouns. In one sentence the name, *Mary*, may be used and in the next we may find the word, *she*. This is a co-reference relationship. It is a very common occurrence in text and is a useful concept to master.

In this chapter, we will cover the following recipes:

- Displaying parse trees graphically
- Using probabilistic context-free grammar to parse text
- Using OpenNLP to generate a parse tree
- Using the Google NLP API to parse text
- Identifying parent-child relationships in text
- Finding co-references in a sentence

Technical requirements

In this chapter, you will need to install the following software if it has not already been installed:

- Eclipse Photon 4.8.0
- Java JDK 8 or later

We will be using the following APIs, which you will be instructed to add for each recipe as appropriate:

- OpenNLP 1.9.0
- OpenNLP Models 1.5
- Stanford NLP 3.9.2
- GSON 2.3.1
- Google NLP 1.40.0

The code files for this chapter can be found at `https://github.com/PacktPublishing/Natural-Language-Processing-with-Java-Cookbook/tree/master/Chapter06`.

Displaying parse trees graphically

It is useful to display parse trees graphically. This representation will provide a more intuitive understanding of the tree. For example, consider the following sentence:

```
The old man sat down beside the tree.
```

One possible parse tree for this sentence displayed textually is shown next:

```
(TOP (S (NP (DT The) (JJ old) (NN man)) (VP (VBD sat) (ADVP (RB down)) (PP
(IN beside) (NP (DT the) (NN tree.))))))
```

This is confusing. We can always reformat the tree to give it a more readable structure as illustrated with the following:

```
(TOP
    (S
        (NP (DT The) (JJ old) (NN man))
        (VP (VBD sat)
            (ADVP (RB down))
            (PP (IN beside)
                (NP (DT the) (NN tree.))
            )
```

```
            )
        )
    )
```

However, it is even better if we use a graphic. In this recipe, we will demonstrate how to use the Stanford NLP API `Parser` class to generate this type of parse tree.

Getting ready

To prepare, we need to do the following:

1. Create a new Maven project
2. Add the following dependency to the POM file:

```
<dependency>
    <groupId>edu.stanford.nlp</groupId>
    <artifactId>stanford-parser</artifactId>
    <version>3.9.2</version>
</dependency>
```

In a browser, perform the following steps:

1. Navigate to `https://stanfordnlp.github.io/CoreNLP/#download`.
2. Select the download link for *English download 3.9.2*. This will download the file, `stanford-english-corenlp-2018-10-05-models.jar`.
3. Select a download directory.
4. Extract the contents of this JAR file to a convenient location.
5. In the directory, `...\stanford-english-corenlp-2018-10-05-models\edu\stanford\nlp\models\lexparser`, you will find the file, `EnglishPCFG.ser.gz`.
6. Copy it to the root directory of your project.
7. Create a file called, `StanfordDataFile.txt`, using a convenient text editor and add the following to the file:

```
The old man sat down beside the tree.
```

How to do it...

The necessary steps include the following:

1. Add this import statement to your project:

```
import edu.stanford.nlp.parser.ui.Parser;
```

2. Add the following `main` method to your project:

```
String parameters[] = new String[2];
parameters[0] = "englishPCFG.ser.gz";
parameters[1] = "StanfordDataFile.txt";
Parser.main(parameters);
```

3. Execute the program. The following window will appear:

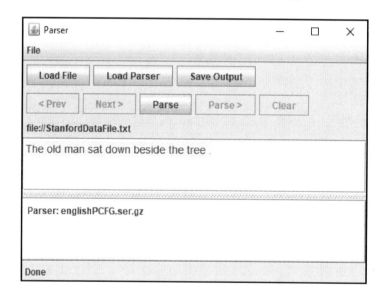

4. Select the **Parse** button. The parser will generate the tree as shown next:

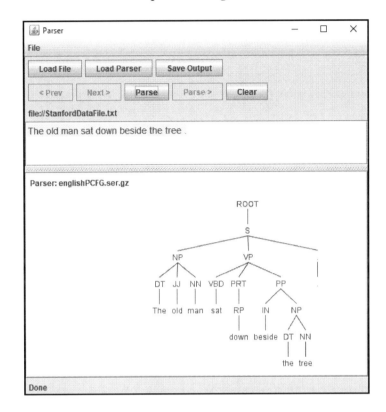

How it works...

The Parser class has a single method called main. To display a parse tree, it needs a parser model and a set of data to process. These can be provided using the main method's string array argument. The first parameter was set to the name of the parser model and the second argument was set to the name of a file containing the test data.

There's more...

There are other buttons that may be of interest:

- **Load File**: Loads a different data file.
- **Load Parser**: Loads a different model.
- **Save Output**: Save the parse tree as text. For this example, the following is saved:

```
(ROOT (S (NP (DT The) (JJ old) (NN man)) (VP (VBD sat) (PRT (RP
down)) (PP (IN beside) (NP (DT the) (NN tree)))) (. .)))
```

- **Clear**: Clears the tree.

To parse a different sentence, we can type it in the top panel replacing the original sentence.

See also

- The Stanford NLP API for the `Parser` class is found at `https://nlp.stanford.edu/nlp/javadoc/javanlp/edu/stanford/nlp/parser/ui/Parser.html`
- We will use the Stanford NLP API to also generate the textual parse tree in the next recipe, *Using probabilistic context-free grammar to parse text*

Using probabilistic context-free grammar to parse text

Probabilistic context-free grammar is grammar defined using a series of rules. Context-free refers to the idea that a rule can be applied without regard to its context. The application of a rule is assigned a probability. This type of grammar is useful for natural languages and has been used to study RNA molecular sequences.

Getting ready

To prepare, we need to do the following:

1. Create a new Maven project
2. Add the following dependency to the POM file:

```
<dependency>
    <groupId>edu.stanford.nlp</groupId>
    <artifactId>stanford-corenlp</artifactId>
    <version>3.9.2</version>
</dependency>
```

In the browser, perform the following steps:

1. Navigate to `https://stanfordnlp.github.io/CoreNLP/#download`.
2. Select the download link for *English download 3.9.2*. This will download the file, `stanford-english-corenlp-2018-10-05-models.jar`.
3. Select a download directory and extract the contents of this JAR file to a convenient location. In the directory, `...\stanford-english-corenlp-2018-10-05-models\edu\stanford\nlp\models\lexparser`, you find the file, `stanford-corenlp-models-current.jar`.
4. Copy it to the root directory of your project.

How to do it...

The necessary steps include the following:

1. Add these import statements to your project:

```
import java.util.Arrays;
import java.util.List;
import edu.stanford.nlp.parser.lexparser.LexicalizedParser;
import edu.stanford.nlp.trees.Tree;
import edu.stanford.nlp.trees.TreePrint;
```

2. Add the following to the `main` method of your project to load a model and declare a sentence:

```
LexicalizedParser lexicalizedParser =
    LexicalizedParser.loadModel("englishPCFG.ser.gz");
List<String> wordList = Arrays.asList("The", "old man", "sat",
    "down", "beside", "the", "tree", ".");
```

3. Next, add the following to parse the sentence and display the results:

```
Tree tree = lexicalizedParser.parseStrings(wordList);
tree.pennPrint();
```

4. Execute the program. You will get the following output:

```
(ROOT
  (S
  (NP (DT The) (NN old man))
  (VP (VBD sat)
  (PRT (RP down))
  (PP (IN beside)
  (NP (DT the) (NN tree))))
  (. .)))
```

How it works...

The `parseStrings` method required a list of strings. We used the `Arrays` class `asList` method to initialize the list. The `pennPrint` method displayed the parse tree, which is very similar to the one created in the previous recipe: *Displaying parse trees graphically*. It differs in how it treats the phrase `old man`. In the previous recipe, it was parsed as follows:

```
(JJ old) (NN man)
In this recipe it was parsed as:
(NN old man)
```

There's more...

The `pennPrint` method displayed a parse tree using a specific format and a limited amount of information. There are other ways of displaying the tree. As shown next, the `outputTreeFormats` method returns an array of string representing various parse tree formats that can be used. In the next code sequence, we displayed these formats:

```
for (String treeFormat : TreePrint.outputTreeFormats) {
    System.out.println(treeFormat);
}
```

When this code is executed, you will get the following output:

```
penn
oneline
rootSymbolOnly
words
```

```
wordsAndTags
dependencies
typedDependencies
typedDependenciesCollapsed
latexTree
xmlTree
collocations
semanticGraph
conllStyleDependencies
conll2007
```

We can create an instance of a `TreePrint` class using the class two argument constructor. We can use a format from the previous list as the second argument. By applying the `printTree` method against the `TreePrint` instance and using the `Tree` instance, we can display the parse based on a different format and include additional information.

In the next code sequence, we use the `typedDependenciesCollapsed` format:

```
TreePrint treePrint = new TreePrint("penn,typedDependenciesCollapsed");
treePrint.printTree(tree);
```

When executed, we will get the following output. This is identical to the previous parse tree except that additional information is displayed:

```
(ROOT
  (S
  (NP (DT The) (NN old man))
  (VP (VBD sat)
  (PRT (RP down))
  (PP (IN beside)
  (NP (DT the) (NN tree))))
  (. .)))
det(old man-2, The-1)
nsubj(sat-3, old man-2)
root(ROOT-0, sat-3)
compound:prt(sat-3, down-4)
case(tree-7, beside-5)
det(tree-7, the-6)
nmod:beside(sat-3, tree-7
)
```

In the next set of code, we use the `xmlTree` format:

```
treePrint = new TreePrint("penn,xmlTree");
treePrint.printTree(tree);
```

This will display the following XML definition of the parse tree as shown next:

```
<node value="ROOT">
    <node value="S">
        <node value="NP">
            <node value="DT">
                <leaf value="The"/>
            </node>
            <node value="NN">
                <leaf value="old man"/>
            </node>
        </node>
        <node value="VP">
            <node value="VBD">
                <leaf value="sat"/>
            </node>
            <node value="PRT">
                <node value="RP">
                    <leaf value="down"/>
                </node>
            </node>
            <node value="PP">
                <node value="IN">
                    <leaf value="beside"/>
                </node>
                <node value="NP">
                    <node value="DT">
                        <leaf value="the"/>
                    </node>
                    <node value="NN">
                        <leaf value="tree"/>
                    </node>
                </node>
            </node>
        </node>
        <node value=".">
            <leaf value="."/>
        </node>
    </node>
</node>
```

See also

- The Stanford NLP API documentation is found at `https://nlp.stanford.edu/nlp/javadoc/javanlp/`

Using OpenNLP to generate a parse tree

In this recipe, we will use the OpenNLP API to generate a parse tree. We will use a previously created chunking model. We will demonstrate different parse trees that may be available for the same text and how to determine which of them have a higher probability of being correct.

Getting ready

To prepare, we need to do the following:

1. Create a new Maven project
2. Add the following dependency to the POM file:

```
<dependency>
    <groupId>org.apache.opennlp</groupId>
    <artifactId>opennlp-tools</artifactId>
    <version>1.9.0</version>
</dependency>
```

3. Download the file, `en-parser-chunking.bin`, from `http://opennlp.sourceforge.net/models-1.5/` and save it to the root directory of the project

How to do it...

The necessary steps include the following:

1. Add the following import statements to your project:

```
import java.io.FileInputStream;
import java.io.IOException;
import java.io.InputStream;
import opennlp.tools.cmdline.parser.ParserTool;
import opennlp.tools.parser.Parse;
import opennlp.tools.parser.Parser;
import opennlp.tools.parser.ParserFactory;
import opennlp.tools.parser.ParserModel;
```

2. Add the following `try` block to the `main` method. It creates the parser and defines a sentence string:

```
try (InputStream modelInputStream =
        new FileInputStream("en-parser-chunking.bin");) {
```

```
        ParserModel parserModel = new ParserModel(modelInputStream);
        Parser parser = ParserFactory.create(parserModel);
        String sentence = "The old man sat down beside the tree.";
        ...
} catch (IOException ex) {
    // Handle exceptions
}
```

3. Next, add the following code to the `try` block. The sentence is parsed and then the parse tree is displayed:

```
Parse parseTrees[] = ParserTool.parseLine(sentence, parser, 3);
int count = 1;
for (Parse parseTree : parseTrees) {
 System.out.println("Parse Tree " + count++);
 parseTree.show();
}
```

4. Execute the program. You will get the following output:

```
Parse Tree 1
(TOP (S (PP (S (S (NP (DT The) (JJ old) (NN man)) (VP (VBD sat)
(ADVP (RB down)))) (IN beside))) (PP (NP (DT the) (NN tree.)))))
Parse Tree 2
(TOP (S (S (NP (DT The) (JJ old) (NN man)) (VP (VBD sat) (ADVP (RB
down)))) (S (FRAG (PP (IN beside) (NP (DT the) (NN tree.)))))))
Parse Tree 3
(TOP (S (S (NP (DT The) (JJ old) (NN man)) (VP (VBD sat) (ADVP (RB
down)))) (FRAG (PP (IN beside) (NP (DT the) (NN tree.))))))
```

Multiple parse trees were generated since there are multiple ways of parsing the sentence.

How it works...

The `en-parser-chunking.bin` model was used to parse the sentence. The `ParserModel` class was instantiated using this model:

```
ParserModel parserModel = new ParserModel(modelInputStream);
Parser parser = ParserFactory.create(parserModel);
```

The `parseLine` method performed the parsing using three arguments:

- The first was the sentence to be parsed
- The second was the parser
- The third argument specified the number of parse tree variations to generate

The syntax is as follows:

```
Parse parseTrees[] = ParserTool.parseLine(sentence, parser, 3);
```

We used the `count` variable to track the variations and the `show` method displays the variations:

```
int count = 1;
for (Parse parseTree : parseTrees) {
    System.out.println("Parse Tree " + count++);
    parseTree.show();
}
```

There's more...

We can display more information about the parse tree and its elements. After the statement, `parseTree.show();`, add the following code. The `getChildren` method returns an array of `Parse` instances, which represent the sentence variations. In the `for` loop, we will display each variation on its own line:

```
System.out.println();
Parse children[] = parseTree.getChildren();
for (Parse child : children) {
    ...
}
System.out.println();
```

Add the following code to the body of the `for` loop. Here, we use the `getText` method to get the sentence. The `tagNodes` array holds information about each of the elements of the tree. For each of these tags, we get the word using the `tagNode` array `toString` method, its type using the `getType` method, and its probability using the `getProb` method:

```
System.out.println(child.getText());
Parse tagNodes[] = child.getTagNodes();
System.out.println("Tags");
for (Parse tagNode : tagNodes) {
    System.out.println("[" + tagNode + "]" + " Type: " + tagNode.getType()
        + " Probability: " + tagNode.getProb());
}
```

When this code is executed, we get the following output:

```
Parse Tree 1
(TOP (S (PP (S (S (NP (DT The) (JJ old) (NN man)) (VP (VBD sat) (ADVP (RB
down)))) (IN beside))) (PP (NP (DT the) (NN tree.)))))
```

```
The old man sat down beside the tree.
Tags
[The] Type: DT Probability: 0.9903294682064628
[old] Type: JJ Probability: 0.9930918395599688
[man] Type: NN Probability: 0.9967680852769704
[sat] Type: VBD Probability: 0.9899531760835939
[down] Type: RB Probability: 0.5400677393705835
[beside] Type: IN Probability: 0.9880135772452956
[the] Type: DT Probability: 0.9728459604220215
[tree.] Type: NN Probability: 0.8436682533087436
Parse Tree 2
(TOP (S (S (NP (DT The) (JJ old) (NN man)) (VP (VBD sat) (ADVP (RB down))))
(S (FRAG (PP (IN beside) (NP (DT the) (NN tree.)))))))
The old man sat down beside the tree.
Tags
[The] Type: DT Probability: 0.9903294682064628
[old] Type: JJ Probability: 0.9930918395599688
[man] Type: NN Probability: 0.9967680852769704
[sat] Type: VBD Probability: 0.9899531760835939
[down] Type: RB Probability: 0.5400677393705835
[beside] Type: IN Probability: 0.9880135772452956
[the] Type: DT Probability: 0.9728459604220215
[tree.] Type: NN Probability: 0.8436682533087436
Parse Tree 3
(TOP (S (S (NP (DT The) (JJ old) (NN man)) (VP (VBD sat) (ADVP (RB down))))
(FRAG (PP (IN beside) (NP (DT the) (NN tree.))))))
The old man sat down beside the tree.

Tags
[The] Type: DT Probability: 0.9903294682064628
[old] Type: JJ Probability: 0.9930918395599688
[man] Type: NN Probability: 0.9967680852769704
[sat] Type: VBD Probability: 0.9899531760835939
[down] Type: RB Probability: 0.5400677393705835
[beside] Type: IN Probability: 0.9880135772452956
[the] Type: DT Probability: 0.9728459604220215
[tree.] Type: NN Probability: 0.8436682533087436
```

See also

- The OpenNLP API documentation is found at `https://opennlp.apache.org/docs/1.9.0/apidocs/opennlp-tools/index.html`

Using the Google NLP API to parse text

In this recipe, we will use the Google NLP API to parse text. However, we can graphically display the tree. Using your browser, go to `https://cloud.google.com/natural-language/`. Near the bottom of the page, you will find a field labelled **Try the API**. Enter the string, `He walked to the store`. Next, press the **ANALYZE** button. Select the **Syntax** tab below the text field. You will see the parse tree as shown next:

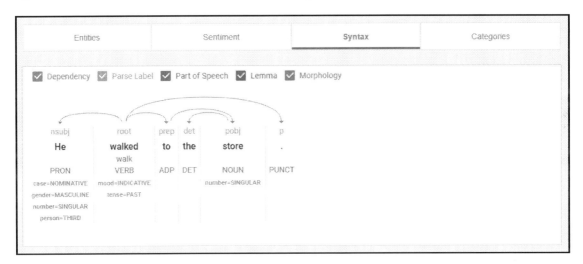

Getting ready

To prepare, we need to do the following:

1. Setup the GCP service and API key according to the recipe Getting ready to use the Google Cloud Platform in the `Appendix`, *Installation and Configuration*.

2. Create a new Maven project

3. Add the following dependencies to the POM file:

```
<dependency>
    <groupId>com.google.code.gson</groupId>
    <artifactId>gson</artifactId>
    <version>2.3.1</version>
</dependency>
<dependency>
    <groupId>com.google.cloud</groupId>
```

```
        <artifactId>google-cloud-language</artifactId>
        <version>1.40.0</version>
</dependency>
```

4. Add the environmental variable, GOOGLE_APPLICATION_CREDENTIALS, with a value that is the path to your API key, similar to C:\...\filename.json

How to do it...

The necessary steps include the following:

1. Add the following import statements to your project:

```
import java.io.IOException;
import java.util.Map;
import com.google.cloud.language.v1.AnalyzeSyntaxRequest;
import com.google.cloud.language.v1.AnalyzeSyntaxResponse;
import com.google.cloud.language.v1.Document;
import com.google.cloud.language.v1.Document.Type;
import com.google.cloud.language.v1.EncodingType;
import com.google.cloud.language.v1.LanguageServiceClient;
import com.google.cloud.language.v1.Token;
import com.google.protobuf.Descriptors.FieldDescriptor;
```

2. Add the following declaration and try-with-resources block to the main method of your project:

```
String text = "He walked to the store.";
try (LanguageServiceClient languageServiceClient =
        LanguageServiceClient.create()) {
    ...
} catch (IOException e) {
    // Handle exceptions
}
```

3. Insert the next code sequence to set up the server request and perform the parsing:

```
Document document = Document.newBuilder()
    .setContent(text)
    .setType(Type.PLAIN_TEXT)
    .build();
AnalyzeSyntaxRequest analyzeSyntaxRequest = AnalyzeSyntaxRequest
    .newBuilder()
    .setDocument(document)
    .setEncodingType(EncodingType.UTF16)
```

```
        .build();
AnalyzeSyntaxResponse analyzeSyntaxResponse = languageServiceClient
        .analyzeSyntax(analyzeSyntaxRequest);
```

4. Next, add the following code to display the results:

```
int count = 0;
for (Token token : analyzeSyntaxResponse.getTokensList()) {
    int headTokenIndex =
token.getDependencyEdge().getHeadTokenIndex();
        System.out.printf("%2d - ", count++);
        if (!"ROOT".equalsIgnoreCase(token
            .getDependencyEdge()
            .getLabel()
            .toString())) {
        for (int i = 0; i < headTokenIndex; i++) {
            System.out.printf(" ");
        }
    }
System.out.printf("'%s'", token.getText().getContent());
Map<FieldDescriptor, Object> fields =
token.getPartOfSpeech().getAllFields();
System.out.printf(" [");
for (FieldDescriptor fd : fields.keySet()) {
        String name = fd.getName();
        name = name.toUpperCase().substring(0, 1) +
        name.substring(1, name.length());
        System.out.printf("%s: %s, ", name,
token.getPartOfSpeech().getField(fd));
}
System.out.printf("] %d%n",headTokenIndex);
```

5. Execute the program. You will get the following output:

```
0 - 'He' [Tag: PRON, Case: NOMINATIVE, Gender: MASCULINE, Number:
SINGULAR, Person: THIRD, ] 1
  1 - 'walked' [Tag: VERB, Mood: INDICATIVE, Tense: PAST, ] 1
  2 - 'to' [Tag: ADP, ] 1
  3 - 'the' [Tag: DET, ] 4
  4 - 'store' [Tag: NOUN, Number: SINGULAR, ] 2
  5 - '.' [Tag: PUNCT, ] 1
```

How it works...

The LanguageServiceClient instance represents the client application, which connects to a Google server. The Document class encapsulates the text to be processed. The AnalyzeSyntaxRequest instance represents the request that was sent to the server. It used the document with a UTF-16 encoding. The analyzeSyntax method requested the analysis and returned a response contained in the AnalyzeSyntaxResponse instance:

```
Document document = Document.newBuilder()
        .setContent(text)
        .setType(Type.PLAIN_TEXT).build();
AnalyzeSyntaxRequest analyzeSyntaxRequest = AnalyzeSyntaxRequest
        .newBuilder()
        .setDocument(document)
        .setEncodingType(EncodingType.UTF16)
        .build();
AnalyzeSyntaxResponse analyzeSyntaxResponse = languageServiceClient
        .analyzeSyntax(analyzeSyntaxRequest);
```

The output processes each word, represented by the token variable, one at a time using the for loop. The count variable was used to label each word by its position in the sentence. This was used in conjunction with the headTokenIndex variable, which holds the index of the word it depends upon in the sentence:

```
int count = 0;
for (Token token : analyzeSyntaxResponse.getTokensList()) {
    int headTokenIndex = token.getDependencyEdge().getHeadTokenIndex();
    System.out.printf("%2d - ", count++);
    ...
}
```

The if statement was used to indent each word based upon its dependent word. The getDependencyEdge method returned a DependencyEdge instance, which contains information about what the current word is dependent upon. Its getLabel method returns the label for the word. If it is ROOT, then this is the highest level and is not indented. Otherwise, blanks are inserted based on the dependency level:

```
if
(!"ROOT".equalsIgnoreCase(token.getDependencyEdge().getLabel().toString()))
{
    for (int i = 0; i < headTokenIndex; i++) {
        System.out.printf(" ");
    }
}
```

The `getText` returns information regarding the token. To access the actual word, we used the `getContent` method:

```
System.out.printf("'%s'", token.getText().getContent());
```

For each token, there is a `FieldDescriptor` instance that contains POS information about each word. The `Map` instance was created and holds a `FieldDescriptor` instance for each field where the server was able to return relevant information. The `for` loop iterated through each of these descriptors, extracted the name of the field, and then displayed it with the first letter capitalized to make it more readable. The token instances `getPartOfSpeech` method was used in conjunction with the `getField` method to return the value associated with each field. The `headTokenIndex` value was displayed at the end of each line to show its dependent word:

```
Map<FieldDescriptor, Object> fields =
token.getPartOfSpeech().getAllFields();
System.out.printf(" [");
for (FieldDescriptor fd : fields.keySet()) {
    String name = fd.getName();
    name = name.toUpperCase().substring(0, 1) +
        name.substring(1, name.length());
    System.out.printf("%s: %s, ", name,
token.getPartOfSpeech().getField(fd));
}
System.out.printf("] %d%n",headTokenIndex);
```

The output, duplicated next, shows the words indented reflecting the dependencies. By comparing this to the earlier figure found at the beginning of this recipe, you can see how the words are related:

```
0 - 'He' [Tag: PRON, Case: NOMINATIVE, Gender: MASCULINE, Number: SINGULAR,
Person: THIRD, ] 1
  1 - 'walked' [Tag: VERB, Mood: INDICATIVE, Tense: PAST, ] 1
  2 - 'to' [Tag: ADP, ] 1
  3 - 'the' [Tag: DET, ] 4
  4 - 'store' [Tag: NOUN, Number: SINGULAR, ] 2
  5 - '.' [Tag: PUNCT, ] 1
```

There's more...

We can also process multiple sentences. Add the following assignment statement immediately after the declaration of the `text` variable:

```
text = "He walked to the store. Then, Jose bought a candy bar. "
    + "He ate all of it as he left the store.";
```

Next, insert the following code at the end of the `try` block:

```
for (Sentence sentence : analyzeSyntaxResponse.getSentencesList()) {
    System.out.println(sentence.getText().getContent());
    // Submit new request for each sentence
}
```

When this code is executed, you will see all of the sentences being processed and then the following three lines of output:

```
He walked to the store.
Then, Jose bought a candy bar.
He ate all of it as he left the store.
```

We can use the expression, `sentence.getText().getContent()`, to create a new request for each sentence. The request will return the parse tree for that sentence.

In addition, there are a number of other `Sentence` class methods that may be of interest. The `getPartOfSpeech` method returns an instance of the `PartOfSpeech` class. The methods of this class will provide descriptor-specific ways of accessing information regarding a word. For example, the `getTense` will return the tense of a noun being used. Also, the `Token` class has a `getLemma` method that will return the lemma of a word.

See also

- The GCP language detection API documentation is found at `https://developers.google.com/resources/api-libraries/documentation/language/v1/java/latest/index.html?com/google/api/services/language/v1/model/AnalyzeSyntaxRequest.html`

Identifying parent-child relationships in text

Parent-child relationships refer to dependencies between elements of a sentence. This can be subject-verb, adjective-noun, or similar type relationships. In this recipe, we will illustrate how these types of relationships can be found in text. We will use the Stanford NLP API to identify these relationships.

Getting ready

To prepare, we need to do the following:

1. Create a new Maven project
2. Add the following dependency to the POM file:

```
<dependency>
    <groupId>edu.stanford.nlp</groupId>
    <artifactId>stanford-corenlp</artifactId>
    <version>3.9.2</version>
</dependency>
```

In a browser, perform the following steps:

1. Navigate to `https://stanfordnlp.github.io/CoreNLP/#download`.
2. Select the download link for *English download 3.9.2*. This will download the file, `stanford-english-corenlp-2018-10-05-models.jar`.
3. Select a download directory. Extract the contents of this JAR file to a convenient location. In the directory, `...\stanford-english-corenlp-2018-10-05-models\edu\stanford\nlp\models\lexparser`, you will find the file, `stanford-corenlp-models-current.jar`.
4. Copy it to the root directory of your project.

How to do it...

The necessary steps include the following:

1. Add the following import statements to your project:

```
import java.io.StringReader;
import java.util.List;
import edu.stanford.nlp.ling.CoreLabel;
import edu.stanford.nlp.parser.lexparser.LexicalizedParser;
```

```
import edu.stanford.nlp.process.CoreLabelTokenFactory;
import edu.stanford.nlp.process.PTBTokenizer;
import edu.stanford.nlp.process.Tokenizer;
import edu.stanford.nlp.process.TokenizerFactory;
import edu.stanford.nlp.trees.GrammaticalStructure;
import edu.stanford.nlp.trees.GrammaticalStructureFactory;
import edu.stanford.nlp.trees.Tree;
import edu.stanford.nlp.trees.TreebankLanguagePack;
import edu.stanford.nlp.trees.TypedDependency;
```

2. Add the following to your `main` method to load the parser model and declare a sample sentence:

```
LexicalizedParser lexicalizedParser =
LexicalizedParser.loadModel("englishPCFG.ser.gz");
String sentence = "The old man sat down beside the tree.";
```

3. Next, add the following code to create the parse tree:

```
TokenizerFactory<CoreLabel> tokenizerFactory =
PTBTokenizer.factory(
    new CoreLabelTokenFactory(), "");
Tokenizer<CoreLabel> tokenizer = tokenizerFactory.getTokenizer(
    new StringReader(sentence));
List<CoreLabel> coreLabelList = tokenizer.tokenize();
Tree parseTree = lexicalizedParser.apply(coreLabelList);
```

4. To display a dependency list for the sentence, add the following code:

```
TreebankLanguagePack treebankLanguagePack =
    lexicalizedParser.treebankLanguagePack();
GrammaticalStructureFactory grammaticalStructureFactory =
    treebankLanguagePack.grammaticalStructureFactory();
GrammaticalStructure grammaticalStructure =
    grammaticalStructureFactory.newGrammaticalStructure(parseTree);
List<TypedDependency> typedDependencyList =
    grammaticalStructure.typedDependenciesCCprocessed();
System.out.println(typedDependencyList);
```

5. Execute the program. You will get the following output:

```
[det(man-3, The-1), amod(man-3, old-2), nsubj(sat-4, man-3),
root(ROOT-0, sat-4), compound:prt(sat-4, down-5), case(tree-8,
beside-6), det(tree-8, the-7), nmod:beside(sat-4, tree-8)]
```

How it works...

The `LexicalizedParser` class was used to generate the parse tree using the `apply` method. The method used a list of `CoreLabel` instances, each of which represents a word. This list was created using the tokenizer executed against the sentence:

```
LexicalizedParser lexicalizedParser =
LexicalizedParser.loadModel("englishPCFG.ser.gz");
String sentence = "The old man sat down beside the tree.";
TokenizerFactory<CoreLabel> tokenizerFactory =
    PTBTokenizer.factory(new CoreLabelTokenFactory(), "");
Tokenizer<CoreLabel> tokenizer =
    tokenizerFactory.getTokenizer(new StringReader(sentence));
List<CoreLabel> coreLabelList = tokenizer.tokenize();
Tree parseTree = lexicalizedParser.apply(coreLabelList);
```

A Treebank is created from a large corpus that have been annotated with POS tags. The `TreebankLanguagePack` class, by default, represents the English language. This Treebank was used to create an instance of the `GrammaticalStructureFactory` class. As its name implies, it is a factory object whose `newGrammaticalStructure` method created an instance of the `GrammaticalStructure` class appropriate for the parse tree:

```
TreebankLanguagePack treebankLanguagePack =
    lexicalizedParser.treebankLanguagePack();
GrammaticalStructureFactory grammaticalStructureFactory =
    treebankLanguagePack.grammaticalStructureFactory();
GrammaticalStructure grammaticalStructure =
    grammaticalStructureFactory.newGrammaticalStructure(parseTree);
```

The `typedDependenciesCCprocessed` method returned a list of the `TypedDependency` instances making up the parse tree. A simple form of the tree was then displayed:

```
List<TypedDependency> typedDependencyList =
grammaticalStructure.typedDependenciesCCprocessed();
System.out.println(typedDependencyList);
```

There's more...

We can use the `TypedDependency` list to provide more information about the tree. In the following `for` loop, we iterate over each dependency and display details about each one using the following methods:

- `dependency.gov()`: This returns the `governing` word. Its `originalText` method returns a string containing the word and its type. A `governing` word is one that frequently requires another word to complete its meaning.
- `dependency.reln()`: This returns the relationship between the `governing` word and the `dependent` word. The `getLongName` method returns the string representation of the relationship.
- `dependency.dep()`: This returns the `dependent` word and its type.

These methods are then used to display more meaning output. Add the following code to the end of the `main` method:

```
for (TypedDependency dependency : typedDependencyList) {
    System.out.println("Governor Word: [" + dependency.gov().originalText()
        + " - " + dependency.gov().tag()
        + "] Relation: [" + dependency.reln().getLongName()
        + "] Dependent Word: [" + dependency.dep()
        + "]");
}
```

When this code sequence is executed, you will get the following output:

```
Governor Word: [man - NN] Relation: [determiner] Dependent Word: [The/DT]
Governor Word: [man - NN] Relation: [adjectival modifier] Dependent Word:
[old/JJ]
Governor Word: [sat - VBD] Relation: [nominal subject] Dependent Word:
[man/NN]
Governor Word: [ - null] Relation: [root] Dependent Word: [sat/VBD]
Governor Word: [sat - VBD] Relation: [phrasal verb particle] Dependent
Word: [down/RP]
Governor Word: [tree - NN] Relation: [case marker] Dependent Word:
[beside/IN]
Governor Word: [tree - NN] Relation: [determiner] Dependent Word: [the/DT]
Governor Word: [sat - VBD] Relation: [nmod_preposition] Dependent Word:
[tree/NN]
```

The previous output contains the information needed to extract parent-child relationships. The actual relationships needed will vary depending on the problem. In the next code sequence, we demonstrate how to extract the subject-verb-object relationships between the words of the sentence.

We iterate through each dependency identifying the nouns, which use the NN tag. The `tag` method may return `null` so we need to check for that value before we get the actual tag. If we find a noun, we then iterate through the list again looking for those VBD tags, verbs, which have a nominal subject—that is, the likely subject—relation with the dependent element with the same name as the subject noun. If found, we will once again iterate through the dependency list looking for a governing tag of VBD, which has the relationship type of `nmod_preposition` with an object dependency noun matching the subject noun.

In other words, we find a noun that is dependent on a verb and then an object noun that is the same as the subject noun and is dependent on the verb. This is reflected by the following abbreviated output displayed earlier:

```
Governor Word: [man - NN] Relation: [determiner] Dependent Word: [The/DT]
Governor Word: [man - NN] Relation: [adjectival modifier] Dependent Word:
[old/JJ]
Governor Word: [sat - VBD] Relation: [nominal subject] Dependent Word:
[man/NN]
...
Governor Word: [sat - VBD] Relation: [nmod_preposition] Dependent Word:
[tree/NN]
```

Add the following code to the end of the `main` method:

```
for (TypedDependency subjectDependency : typedDependencyList) {
    if (subjectDependency.gov().tag() != null &&
            subjectDependency.gov().tag().equals("NN")) {
        for (TypedDependency verbDependency : typedDependencyList) {
            if (verbDependency.gov().tag() != null
                && verbDependency.gov().tag().equals("VBD")
                && verbDependency.reln().getLongName().equals("nominal
subject")
                && verbDependency.dep().originalText().equals(
                    subjectDependency.gov().originalText())) {
                for (TypedDependency objectDependency :
typedDependencyList) {
                    if (objectDependency.gov().tag() != null
                        && objectDependency.gov().tag().equals("VBD")
                        && objectDependency.reln().getLongName().equals(
                            "nmod_preposition")) {
System.out.println(subjectDependency.gov().originalText()
                        + " " + verbDependency.gov().originalText()
                        + " " +
objectDependency.dep().originalText());
                    }
                }
            }
        }
```

```
            }
        }
    }
```

When executed, you will get the following output. The relationship is duplicated because we have multiple occurrences of the tags:

```
man sat tree
man sat tree
```

Replace the `String sentence = "The old man sat down beside the tree.";` statement with the following statement:

```
String sentence = "The old man sat down beside the tree and read a book.";
```

This is a more complicated sentence and further illustrates the process. When the code is executed, you will get the following output:

```
[det(man-3, The-1), amod(man-3, old-2), nsubj(sat-4, man-3), nsubj(read-10,
man-3), root(ROOT-0, sat-4), compound:prt(sat-4, down-5), case(tree-8,
beside-6), det(tree-8, the-7), nmod:beside(sat-4, tree-8), cc(sat-4,
and-9), conj:and(sat-4, read-10), det(book-12, a-11), dobj(read-10,
book-12)]
```

```
Governor Word: [man/NN] Relation: [determiner] Dependent Word: [The/DT]
Governor Word: [man - {NN}] Relation: [determiner] Dependent Word: [The/DT]
Governor Word: [man/NN] Relation: [adjectival modifier] Dependent Word:
[old/JJ]
Governor Word: [man - {NN}] Relation: [adjectival modifier] Dependent Word:
[old/JJ]
Governor Word: [sat/VBD] Relation: [nominal subject] Dependent Word:
[man/NN]
Governor Word: [sat - {VBD}] Relation: [nominal subject] Dependent Word:
[man/NN]
Governor Word: [read/VBD] Relation: [nominal subject] Dependent Word:
[man/NN]
Governor Word: [read - {VBD}] Relation: [nominal subject] Dependent Word:
[man/NN]
Governor Word: [ROOT] Relation: [root] Dependent Word: [sat/VBD]
Governor Word: [ - {null}] Relation: [root] Dependent Word: [sat/VBD]
Governor Word: [sat/VBD] Relation: [phrasal verb particle] Dependent Word:
[down/RP]
Governor Word: [sat - {VBD}] Relation: [phrasal verb particle] Dependent
Word: [down/RP]
Governor Word: [tree/NN] Relation: [case marker] Dependent Word:
[beside/IN]
Governor Word: [tree - {NN}] Relation: [case marker] Dependent Word:
[beside/IN]
```

```
Governor Word: [tree/NN] Relation: [determiner] Dependent Word: [the/DT]
Governor Word: [tree - {NN}] Relation: [determiner] Dependent Word:
[the/DT]
Governor Word: [sat/VBD] Relation: [nmod_preposition] Dependent Word:
[tree/NN]
Governor Word: [sat - {VBD}] Relation: [nmod_preposition] Dependent Word:
[tree/NN]
Governor Word: [sat/VBD] Relation: [coordination] Dependent Word: [and/CC]
Governor Word: [sat - {VBD}] Relation: [coordination] Dependent Word:
[and/CC]
Governor Word: [sat/VBD] Relation: [conj_collapsed] Dependent Word:
[read/VBD]
Governor Word: [sat - {VBD}] Relation: [conj_collapsed] Dependent Word:
[read/VBD]
Governor Word: [book/NN] Relation: [determiner] Dependent Word: [a/DT]
Governor Word: [book - {NN}] Relation: [determiner] Dependent Word: [a/DT]
Governor Word: [read/VBD] Relation: [direct object] Dependent Word:
[book/NN]
Governor Word: [read - {VBD}] Relation: [direct object] Dependent Word:
[book/NN]

man sat tree
man read tree
man sat tree
man read tree
```

This output is incomplete as it is missing the direct object, book. This illustrates the
difficulty of extracting relationships. Let's see what happens if we replace the following
statement:

```
if (objectDependency.gov().tag() != null
        && objectDependency.gov().tag().equals("VBD")
        && objectDependency.reln().getLongName().equals(
            "nmod_preposition")) {
```

We will replace the preceding statements with the following code:

```
if (objectDependency.gov().tag() != null
        && objectDependency.gov().tag().equals("VBD")
        &&
(objectDependency.reln().getLongName().equals("nmod_preposition") ||
            objectDependency.reln().getLongName().equals("direct object")))
{
```

We will get better output, as shown next:

```
man sat tree
man sat book
```

```
man read tree
man read book
man sat tree
man sat book
man read tree
man read book
```

Ignoring the duplicate relationships, we still have a man who apparently sat on a book and read a tree. Certain NLP tasks can be difficult at times. The approach shown in this recipe provides a starting point for finding relationships. Sometimes, the problem is simplified to make the process easier. If we restrict the complexity of the sentence being processed, we can obtain better results.

See also

- The Stanford NLP API documentation is found at `https://nlp.stanford.edu/nlp/javadoc/javanlp/`

Finding co-references in a sentence

Co-reference is the term used to describe certain types of relationships between words of a document, for example, in the following sentence:

```
Tom was the tallest in his class. He was also the oldest.
```

There is a co-reference relationship between `Tom` and `He`. Both words refer to the same person. In this recipe, we will demonstrate how co-references can be identified within sentences using the Stanford NLP API.

Getting ready

To prepare, we need to do the following:

1. Create a new Maven project
2. Add the following dependency to the POM file:

```
<!--
https://mvnrepository.com/artifact/edu.stanford.nlp/stanford-corenl
p -->
<dependency>
    <groupId>edu.stanford.nlp</groupId>
```

```
        <artifactId>stanford-parser</artifactId>
        <version>3.9.2</version>
<dependency>
<dependency>
        <groupId>edu.stanford.nlp</groupId>
        <artifactId>stanford-corenlp</artifactId>
        <version>3.9.2</version>
</dependency>
<dependency>
        <groupId>edu.stanford.nlp</groupId>
        <artifactId>stanford-corenlp</artifactId>
        <version>3.9.2</version>
        <classifier>models</classifier>
</dependency>
```

You may need to increase the amount of space used by the **Java Virtual Machine (JVM)** for the program to execute. During the execution of the program, you might get the following exception:

```
StanfordCoreNLP Exception in thread "main" java.lang.OutOfMemoryError: Java
heap space
```

If so, you will need to increase the amount of memory used. This specifies how this is done as it varies by the Java development environment. However, most IDEs provide a means to modify the VM arguments of the JRE used. Using the argument, -Xmx4096M, will probably work. If not, try using a larger value.

How to do it...

The necessary steps include the following:

1. Add these import statements to your project:

```
import java.util.Iterator;
import java.util.List;
import java.util.Properties;import
edu.stanford.nlp.coref.CorefCoreAnnotations;
import edu.stanford.nlp.coref.data.CorefChain;
import edu.stanford.nlp.coref.data.CorefChain.CorefMention;
import edu.stanford.nlp.pipeline.Annotation;
import edu.stanford.nlp.pipeline.StanfordCoreNLP;
```

2. Add the following code sequence to the `main` method of your project. This defines sample sentences and a pipeline that will annotate the text:

```
Annotation sampleText = new Annotation(
    "He walked to the store. Then, Jose bought a candy bar. "
    + "He ate all of it as he left the store.");
Properties properties = new Properties();
properties.setProperty("annotators","tokenize,ssplit,pos,lemma,ner,
parse,coref");
StanfordCoreNLP pipeline = new StanfordCoreNLP(properties);
pipeline.annotate(sampleText);
```

3. Display the co-references using the next set of code:

```
for (CorefChain corefChain : sampleText.get (
        CorefCoreAnnotations.CorefChainAnnotation.class).values())
{
    System.out.println("CorefChain: " + corefChain);
    System.out.println("\tMention: " +
corefChain.getRepresentativeMention());
    System.out.println("\tMention Map: " +
corefChain.getMentionMap());
    System.out.println();
}
```

4. Execute the program. You will get the following output:

```
CorefChain: CHAIN2-["He" in sentence 1, "Jose" in sentence 2, "He"
in sentence 3, "he" in sentence 3]
 Mention: "Jose" in sentence 2
 Mention Map: {1 1=["He" in sentence 1], 3 1=["He" in sentence 3],
2 3=["Jose" in sentence 2], 3 7=["he" in sentence 3]}

CorefChain: CHAIN8-["a candy bar" in sentence 2, "it" in sentence
3]
 Mention: "a candy bar" in sentence 2
 Mention Map: {3 5=["it" in sentence 3], 2 7=["a candy bar" in
sentence 2]}
```

How it works...

The sample text consisted of three sentences and several co-references. A pipeline was created using several steps to process the sentences. The last step extracted the co-references. The `annotate` method invoked these steps against the sentences:

```
Annotation sampleText = new Annotation(
    "He walked to the store. Then, Jose bought a candy bar. "
    + "He ate all of it as he left the store.");
Properties properties = new Properties();
properties.setProperty("annotators",
tokenize,ssplit,pos,lemma,ner,parse,coref");
StanfordCoreNLP pipeline = new StanfordCoreNLP(properties);
pipeline.annotate(sampleText);
```

A `for` loop was used to display the results for each chain of references. For these sentences, there were two chains. An instance of the `CorefChain` class represents a set of co-references. We used the `toString` method to display the default representation. The `getRepresentativeMention` and `getMentionMap` methods returned the subject of a reference and the co-references respectively:

```
for (CorefChain corefChain : sampleText.get(
    CorefCoreAnnotations.CorefChainAnnotation.class).values()) {
    System.out.println("CorefChain: " + corefChain);
    System.out.println("\tMention: " +
corefChain.getRepresentativeMention());
    System.out.println("\tMention Map: " + corefChain.getMentionMap());
    System.out.println();
}
```

There's more...

We can obtain more detailed information about the co-references, which can be useful. The following set of code illustrates how this information is obtained. It can be added after the last `for` loop. The default representation is displayed first, as shown:

```
for (CorefChain corefChain : sampleText.get(
        CorefCoreAnnotations.CorefChainAnnotation.class).values()) {
    System.out.println("CorefChain: " + corefChain);
    ...
    System.out.println();
}
```

Add the following code to the loop, which displays the subject mention:

```
CorefMention corefMention = corefChain.getRepresentativeMention();
System.out.println("\tMention: " + corefMention + " Span: ["
    + corefMention.mentionSpan + "]");
    ...
```

Next, an instance of the `CorefMention` class is obtained to provide access to other methods. An iterator of `CorefMention` instances using the `getMentionsInTextualOrder` method and the `iterator` method:

```
List<CorefMention> mentionList = corefChain.getMentionsInTextualOrder();
Iterator<CorefMention> mentionIterator = mentionList.iterator();
    ...
```

Insert the following `while` loop to display the mentions. The span, gender, start, and end positions are displayed:

```
while (mentionIterator.hasNext()) {
    CorefMention nextCorefMention = mentionIterator.next();
    System.out.println("\t\tMention: " + nextCorefMention
        + " Span: [" + corefMention.mentionSpan + "]");
    System.out.print("\t\t\tType: " + nextCorefMention.mentionType
        + " Gender: " + nextCorefMention.gender);
    System.out.println(" Start: " + nextCorefMention.startIndex
        + " End: " + nextCorefMention.endIndex);
}
```

When this code is executed, you will get the following output. This additional information can be useful for many types of problems such as determining the relationships between text elements:

```
CorefChain: CHAIN2-["He" in sentence 1, "Jose" in sentence 2, "He" in
sentence 3, "he" in sentence 3]
 Mention: "Jose" in sentence 2 Span: [Jose]
 Mention: "He" in sentence 1 Span: [Jose]
 Type: PRONOMINAL Gender: MALE Start: 1 End: 2
 Mention: "Jose" in sentence 2 Span: [Jose]
 Type: PROPER Gender: MALE Start: 3 End: 4
 Mention: "He" in sentence 3 Span: [Jose]
 Type: PRONOMINAL Gender: MALE Start: 1 End: 2
 Mention: "he" in sentence 3 Span: [Jose]
 Type: PRONOMINAL Gender: MALE Start: 7 End: 8

CorefChain: CHAIN8-["a candy bar" in sentence 2, "it" in sentence 3]
 Mention: "a candy bar" in sentence 2 Span: [a candy bar]
 Mention: "a candy bar" in sentence 2 Span: [a candy bar]
```

```
Type: NOMINAL Gender: NEUTRAL Start: 5 End: 8
Mention: "it" in sentence 3 Span: [a candy bar]
Type: PRONOMINAL Gender: NEUTRAL Start: 5 End: 6
```

See also

- The Stanford NLP API documentation is found at `https://nlp.stanford.edu/nlp/javadoc/javanlp/`

Language Identification and Translation

7

Language processing is an important component of many applications. In this chapter, we will demonstrate how to determine the natural language in use, how to translate from one language to another, and how we can convert between text and speech.

There may be times when we are not sure which language we are dealing with. When this happens, we have several techniques that we can use. We will illustrate how this is done using LingPipe, Google, and Amazon libraries.

To translate between languages, we will use Google and Amazon; they both support a large number of languages and use a client/server approach. A client application will send a request to a server, which will respond with the translated text. These approaches require a bit more work than other approaches since we need to deal with communication and security.

Converting text to speech has a large number of applications, as does the inverse, that is, converting speech to text. We will use Google libraries to demonstrate these techniques.

In this chapter, we will cover the following recipes:

- Detecting the natural language in use using LingPipe
- Discovering supported languages using the Google API
- Detecting the natural language in use using the Google API
- Language translation using Google
- Language detection and translation using Amazon AWS
- Converting text to speech using the Google Cloud Text-to-Speech API
- Converting speech to text using the Google Cloud Speech-to-Text API

Technical requirements

In this chapter, you will need to install the following software, if they have not already been installed:

- Eclipse Photon 4.8.0
- Java JDK 8 or later

We will be using the following APIs, which you will be instructed to add for each recipe as appropriate:

- LingPipe 4.1.0
- Google NLP 1.40.0
- Google NLP 1.55.0
- AWS SDK for Java
- WS NLP API 1.11.475
- Google Cloud Text-to-Speech API 0.70.0-beta
- Google Cloud Speech API 0.61.0-beta
- Argparse4j 0.8.1

The code files for this chapter can be found at `https://github.com/PacktPublishing/Natural-Language-Processing-with-Java-Cookbook/tree/master/Chapter07`.

Detecting the natural language in use using LingPipe

LingPipe provides a technique for the identification of languages. It is based on a model that was derived from training data found in the Leipzig Corpora Collection (`http://corpora.uni-leipzig.de/en?corpusId=deu_newscrawl_2011`). In this recipe, we will demonstrate how this model can be used to identify the language used in a document.

Getting ready

To prepare, we need to follow these steps:

1. Create a new Maven project
2. Add the following dependency to the project's POM file:

```
<!-- https://mvnrepository.com/artifact/de.julielab/aliasi-lingpipe
-->
<dependency>
    <groupId>de.julielab</groupId>
    <artifactId>aliasi-lingpipe</artifactId>
    <version>4.1.0</version>
</dependency>
```

3. Download the complete version of LingPipe 4.1.2 from `http://alias-i.com/lingpipe/web/download.html`
4. Extract the `Lingpipe-4.1.2.tar` file from `Lingpipe-4.1.2.tar.gz`
5. Unzip the files from `Lingpipe-4.1.2.tar`
6. Copy the `...\Lingpipe-4.1.2-website\demos\models\langid-leipzig.classifier` file to the root of the project directory

How to do it...

The necessary steps include:

1. Add the following string declarations to the `main` method:

```
ArrayList<String> textList = new ArrayList<>();
textList.add("Language is a system that consists of the
development, "
        + "acquisition, maintenance and use of complex systems of "
        + "communication, particularly the human ability to do so;
"
        + "and a language is any specific example of such a
system.");
textList.add("Language ist ein Lied des US-amerikanischen DJs und "
        + "Musikproduzenten Porter Robinson, das von Heather Bright
"
        + "gesungen und am 10. April 2012 auf Beatport
veröffentlicht"
        + " wurde. Language kann dem Genre Electro House zugeordnet
"
        + "werden und hat 128 bpm. Die Vollversion war bereits ab "
```

```
        + "dem 26. März 2012 bei YouTube anhörbar. Der Track ist "
        + "unter anderem auch auf dem Soundtrack von Forza Horizon
enthalten.");
```

2. Insert a `try` block, which loads the model:

```
try {
    LMClassifier lmClassifier = (LMClassifier)
AbstractExternalizable
        .readObject(new File("langid-leipzig.classifier"));
    ...
} catch (IOException | ClassNotFoundException ex) {
    ex.printStackTrace();
}
```

3. Classify and display the language used for each text with the following for loop:

```
for (String text : textList) {
    Classification classification = lmClassifier.classify(text);
    System.out.println("Best Language: "
        + classification.bestCategory());
}
```

4. Execute the program. You will get the following output:

```
Best Language: en
Best Language: de
```

How it works...

We used the `AbstractExternalizable` class's static `readObject` method to read in the model, which was cast as an instance of the `LMClassifier` class:

```
LMClassifier lmClassifier = (LMClassifier) AbstractExternalizable
    .readObject(new File("langid-leipzig.classifier"));
```

We used the `classify` method to return a classification for each text entry in `ArrayList`. The `bestCategory` method was then applied to return the language code for the language identified, as shown:

```
for (String text : textList) {
    Classification classification = lmClassifier.classify(text);
    System.out.println("Best Language: "
        + classification.bestCategory());
}
```

There's more...

It would be better if we could display the language used instead of a language code. In the next code sequence, we create a `HashMap` that contains the codes and their corresponding language names. Add this code to a location before the for loop:

```
HashMap<String,String> languageEncodings = new HashMap();
languageEncodings.put("cat","Catalan");
languageEncodings.put("de","German");
languageEncodings.put("dk","Danish");
languageEncodings.put("ee","Estonian");
languageEncodings.put("en","English");
languageEncodings.put("fi","Finnish");
languageEncodings.put("fr","French");
languageEncodings.put("it","Italian");
languageEncodings.put("jp","Japanese");
languageEncodings.put("kr","Korean");
languageEncodings.put("nl","Dutch");
languageEncodings.put("no","Norwegian");
languageEncodings.put("se","Swedish");
languageEncodings.put("sorb","Sorbian");
languageEncodings.put("tr","Turkish");
```

Replace the `println` statement in the for loop with the following statement:

```
System.out.println("Best Language: " +
    languageEncodings.get(classification.bestCategory()));
```

When the code is executed, you will get the following output:

```
Best Language: English
Best Language: German
```

See also

- The LingPipe API documentation can be found at `http://alias-i.com/lingpipe/docs/api/index.html`.
- Further information about language identification using LingPipe is found in the *Language ID Tutorial* at `http://alias-i.com/lingpipe/demos/tutorial/langid/read-me.html`. This page also includes information about how to train a language-identification model for different natural languages.

Discovering supported languages using the Google API

The Google Translate API supports a number of languages. In this recipe, we will illustrate how we can programmatically determine which languages are supported. This is useful when we need to determine the two-letter code for a language, which is needed for some translation tasks. These two-letter codes generally conform to the ISO-639-1 identifiers, as documented at `https://en.wikipedia.org/wiki/ISO_639-1`.

In addition, we may need to be aware of any new languages that are supported. A list of currently-supported languages can be found at `https://cloud.google.com/translate/docs/languages`.

The **Google Cloud Platform (GCP)** Translate API supports **phrase-based machine translation (PBMT)** and **neural machine translation (NMT)** models. PBMT is a statistical approach that requires bilingual text and tries to predict how words should be translated. NMT models is a technique that uses deep learning techniques to perform a translation. These tend to be more accurate than the PBMT approach.

Getting ready

To prepare, we need to do the following:

1. Set up the GCP service and API key according to the *Getting ready to use the Google Cloud Platform* recipe in the `Appendix`, *Installation and Configuration*
2. Create a new Java Maven project
3. Add the following dependency to the POM:

```
<dependency>
    <groupId>com.google.cloud</groupId>
    <artifactId>google-cloud-translate</artifactId>
    <version>1.40.0</version>
</dependency>
```

4. Add the `GOOGLE_APPLICATION_CREDENTIALS` environmental variable with a value that is, the path to your API key similar to: `C:\...\filename.json`

How to do it...

The necessary steps include:

1. Add the following imports to the project:

```
import java.util.List;
import com.google.cloud.translate.Language;
import com.google.cloud.translate.Translate;
import com.google.cloud.translate.TranslateOptions;
```

2. Add the following code to the `main` method:

```
Translate translate =
    TranslateOptions.getDefaultInstance().getService();
List<Language> supportedLanguages =
translate.listSupportedLanguages();
for (Language language : supportedLanguages) {
    System.out.printf("%-20s Code: %3s\n", language.getName(),
        language.getCode());
}
```

3. Execute the program. You will get the following abbreviated output:

```
Afrikaans           Code:   af
Albanian            Code:   sq
Amharic             Code:   am
Arabic              Code:   ar
Armenian            Code:   hy
...
Xhosa               Code:   xh
Yiddish             Code:   yi
Yoruba              Code:   yo
Zulu                Code:   zu
```

How it works...

An instance of the `Translate` class was instantiated. This connects to the GCP Translate service. The `listSupportedLanguages` method returned a list of `Language` objects. The `getName` and `getCode` methods were used to display the currently-supported language names and their corresponding code:

```
Translate translate =
    TranslateOptions.getDefaultInstance().getService();
List<Language> supportedLanguages = translate.listSupportedLanguages();
```

```
for (Language language : supportedLanguages) {
    System.out.printf("%-20s Code: %3s\n", language.getName(),
        language.getCode());
}
```

See also

- The GCP Discovering Languages API documentation can be found at `https://cloud.google.com/translate/docs/discovering-supported-languages`

Detecting the natural language in use using the Google API

If the language being processed is unknown, we can use the GCP to determine the language. In this recipe, we will illustrate how to do this using the `Translate` class's `detect` method. To illustrate the process, we will use the first paragraph of the English and German Wikipedia web pages for the word *language*. These are shown next. The following shows the first paragraph of the English Wikipedia web page (`https://en.wikipedia.org/wiki/Language`):

"Language is a system that consists of the development, acquisition, maintenance and use of complex systems of communication, particularly the human ability to do so; and a language is any specific example of such a system."

The following shows the first paragraph of the German Wikipedia web page (`https://de.wikipedia.org/wiki/Language`):

"Language ist ein Lied des US-amerikanischen DJs und Musikproduzenten Porter Robinson, das von Heather Bright gesungen und am 10. April 2012 auf Beatport veröffentlicht wurde. Language kann dem Genre Electro House zugeordnet werden und hat 128 bpm. Die Vollversion war bereits ab dem 26. März 2012 bei YouTube anhörbar. Der Track ist unter anderem auch auf dem Soundtrack von Forza Horizon enthalten."

We will also examine how well GCP works with sentences that contain words from multiple languages.

Getting ready

To prepare, we need to follow these steps:

1. Create a new Java Maven project
2. Add the following dependency to the POM:

```
<dependency>
    <groupId>com.google.cloud</groupId>
    <artifactId>google-cloud-translate</artifactId>
    <version>1.55.0</version>
</dependency>
```

3. Add the GOOGLE_APPLICATION_CREDENTIALS environment variable with a value that is, the path to your API key similar to: C:\...\filename.json

How to do it...

The necessary steps include:

1. Add the following imports to your project:

```
import java.util.ArrayList;
import java.util.List;
import com.google.cloud.translate.Detection;
import com.google.cloud.translate.Language;
import com.google.cloud.translate.Translate;
import com.google.cloud.translate.TranslateOptions;
```

2. Insert the following code into the main method. These statements create an instance of the Translate class and define sample sentences:

```
Translate translate =
TranslateOptions.getDefaultInstance().getService();

ArrayList<String> textList = new ArrayList<>();
textList.add("Language is a system that consists of the
development, "
        + "acquisition, maintenance and use of complex systems of "
        + "communication, particularly the human ability to do so;
"
        + "and a language is any specific example of such a
system.");
textList.add("Language ist ein Lied des US-amerikanischen DJs und "
        + "Musikproduzenten Porter Robinson, das von Heather Bright
```

```
"
        + "gesungen und am 10. April 2012 auf Beatport
veröffentlicht"
        + " wurde. Language kann dem Genre Electro House zugeordnet
"
        + "werden und hat 128 bpm. Die Vollversion war bereits ab "
        + "dem 26. März 2012 bei YouTube anhörbar. Der Track ist "
        + "unter anderem auch auf dem Soundtrack von Forza Horizon
enthalten.");
```

3. Add the following code sequence to detect the languages in use and display the results:

```
List<Detection> detectionList = translate.detect(textList);

List<Language> supportedLanguages =
translate.listSupportedLanguages();
int count = 0;
for (Detection detection : detectionList) {
    for (Language language : supportedLanguages) {
        if (language.getCode().equals(detection.getLanguage())) {
            System.out.printf(
                "Text: \"%-16s\"   Code: %2s   Language: %-12s
Confidence: %5.3f\n",
                textList.get(count).substring(0, Math.min(16,
                    textList.get(count).length())),
                language.getCode(), language.getName(),
                detection.getConfidence());
            count++;
        }
    }
}
```

4. Execute the program. You will get the following output:

```
Text: "Language is a sy"   Code: en   Language: English
Confidence: 1.000
Text: "Language ist ein"   Code: de   Language: German
Confidence: 1.000
```

How it works...

The `detect` method returned a list of `Detection` instances, each representing information about each entry in the text list:

```
List<Detection> detectionList = translate.detect(textList);
```

We used the `listSupportedLanguages` method, described in the *Discovering supported languages using the Google API* recipe, to make it possible to display the language name:

```
List<Language> supportedLanguages = translate.listSupportedLanguages();
```

The nested for loops were used in conjunction with the `count` variable to display the results. The `Language` class's `getCode` method and the `Detection` class's `getLanguage` both returned a two-character code for a language. When the if statement is true, we used the `Language` class's `getName` method to return a more friendly form of the language code. The `count` variable was used to obtain the original text. The `Detection` class's `getConfidence` method returned the likelihood that the correct language was identified.

For these two text samples, we obtained good results, as shown:

```
int count = 0;
for (Detection detection : detectionList) {
    for (Language language : supportedLanguages) {
        if (language.getCode().equals(detection.getLanguage())) {
            System.out.printf(
                "Text: \"%-16s\"  Code: %2s  Language: %-12s Confidence:
%5.3f\n",
            textList.get(count).substring(0, Math.min(16,
                textList.get(count).length())),
            language.getCode(), language.getName(),
detection.getConfidence());
            count++;
        }
    }
}
```

There's more...

The GCP works well for shortened text sequences. Add the following statements after the two earlier `add` methods. These strings are the first part of the previous English and German samples:

```
textList.add("Language is");
textList.add("Language ist");
```

When the code is executed, you will get the following output:

```
Text: "Language is      "  Code: en  Language: English      Confidence:
1.000
Text: "Language ist     "  Code: de  Language: German       Confidence:
1.000
```

It is not uncommon to find sentences that contain foreign words or phrases. In the next example, we used sentences found at `https://ask.metafilter.com/126800/Same-sentence-different-language-still-makes-sense`. Add the following two statements after the previous `add` method insertions:

```
textList.add("The French for 'what's up' is 'Quoi de neuf?'");
textList.add("menin aeide thea Peleiadeo Achileos\" becomes \"Men in "
        + "Aida, they appeal, eh? A day, O Achilles!'");
```

When the code is executed, you will get the following output:

```
Text: "The French for '"   Code: en   Language: English   Confidence:
1.000
Text: "menin aeide thea"   Code: en   Language: English   Confidence:
0.987
```

See also

- The GCP Language Detection API documentation can be found at `https://cloud.google.com/translate/docs/detecting-language`

Language translation using Google

The GCP provides an API for the translation of text from one language to another. In this recipe, we will demonstrate how this is done. When translation is performed, it uses the NMT model by default. However, if the model is not supported for the languages used, it will use the PBMT model.

The PBMT approach uses a statistical, predictive technique for language translation. The NMT usually does a better job in translation for larger and more complex text occurrences since it is based on a neural network.

Getting ready

To prepare, we need to follow these steps:

1. Create a new Java Maven project
2. Add the following dependencies to the POM:

```
<dependency>
    <groupId>com.google.cloud</groupId>
    <artifactId>google-cloud-translate</artifactId>
    <version>1.55.0</version>
</dependency>
```

3. Add the GOOGLE_APPLICATION_CREDENTIALS environment variable with a value that is, the path to your API key similar to: C:\...\filename.json

How to do it...

The necessary steps include:

1. Add the following imports to your project:

```
import java.util.ArrayList;
import java.util.List;
import com.google.cloud.translate.Translate;
import com.google.cloud.translate.TranslateOptions;
import com.google.cloud.translate.Translation;
```

2. Add the following statement to the main method. This will create an instance of the Translate class, which will perform the translations:

```
Translate translate =
TranslateOptions.getDefaultInstance().getService();
```

3. Add the following code sequence to define a Greek string, perform the translation, and display the result:

```
String text = "Αυτοκινητόδρομος";
Translation translation = translate.translate(text);
System.out.printf("%-16s Translation: %s\n", text,
translation.getTranslatedText());
```

4. Execute the program. You will get the following output:

```
Αυτοκινητόδρομος Translation: Highway
```

How it works...

The `TranslateOptions` class's `getDefaultInstance` method returns an instance of the `TranslateOptions` class. The `getService` method was used to obtain an instance of the `Translate` class:

```
Translate translate = TranslateOptions.getDefaultInstance().getService();
```

A string was declared for the Greek word meaning highway. The `translate` method was executed, which returned a `Translation` instance that represents the translated text. The original text was displayed followed by its default translation to English, as shown:

```
String text = "Αυτοκινητόδρομος";
Translation translation = translate.translate(text);
System.out.printf("%s Translation: %s\n", text,
translation.getTranslatedText());
```

There's more...

The `translate` method is overloaded, providing various translation options to be applied using the `TranslateOption` class. These methods are listed here:

- `sourceLanguage`: Takes a language code that specifies the language being translated.
- `targetLanguage`: Takes a language code that specifies the language being translated to.
- `model`: Specifies the model to use. The model used can be specified using the `model` method, as shown next
  (`Translate.TranslateOption.model("nmt")`). The `nmt` and `base` strings are used for the NMT and PBMT models, respectively.

Add the following code to the `main` method. The code demonstrates the use of these methods. The first sequence specifies a target language of German using the NMT model. The second sequence uses the PBMT model, as shown:

```
translation = translate.translate(text,
Translate.TranslateOption.sourceLanguage("el"),
    Translate.TranslateOption.targetLanguage("de"),
Translate.TranslateOption.model("nmt"));
System.out.printf("%s Translation: %s\n", text,
translation.getTranslatedText());

translation = translate.translate(text,
```

```
Translate.TranslateOption.sourceLanguage("el"),
    Translate.TranslateOption.targetLanguage("de"),
Translate.TranslateOption.model("base"));
System.out.printf("%s Translation: %s\n", text,
translation.getTranslatedText());
```

Execute the program. You will get the following output:

```
Αυτοκινητόδρομος Translation: Autobahn
Αυτοκινητόδρομος Translation: Autobahn
```

We can also translate a list of text. To illustrate this process, we will use text found in Wikipedia for the German, Korean, and Portuguese languages that discuss the Big Bang theory. For the following references, we used their first sentence:

```
Language: German
Web page: https://de.wikipedia.org/wiki/Urknall
Text: Als Urknall wird in der Kosmologie der Beginn des Universums, also der Anfangspunkt der
Entstehung von Materie, Raum und Zeit bezeichnet.

Language: Korean
Web page: https://ko.wikipedia.org/wiki/%EB%8C%80%ED%8F%AD%EB%B0%9C
Text: 대폭발(大爆發, 영어: Big Bang 빅뱅[*])[1] 은 천문학 또는 물리학에서, 우주의 처음을 설명하는 우주론
모형으로, 매우 높은 에너지를 가진 작은 물질과 공간이 약 137억 년 전의 거대한 폭발을 통해 우주가 되었다고
보는 이론이다.

Language: Portuguese
Web page: https://pt.wikipedia.org/wiki/Big_Bang
Text: Big Bang ou Grande Expansão[1] é a teoria cosmológica dominante sobre o desenvolvimento
inicial do universo.
```

Add the following declaration of a list to the application:

```
List<String> translationList = new ArrayList<>();
```

Next, add the text from the preceding sources:

```
translationList.add(
    "Als Urknall wird in der Kosmologie der Beginn des Universums, also "
    + "der Anfangspunkt der Entstehung von Materie, Raum und Zeit bezeichnet.");
translationList.add(
    "대폭발(大爆發, 영어: Big Bang 빅뱅[^])[1] 은 천문학 또는 물리학에서, 우주의 "
    + "처음을 설명하는 우주론 모형으로, 매우 높은 에너지를 가진 작은 물질과 공간이 약 137억 년 전의 거대
한 "
    + "폭발을 통해 우주가 되었다고 보는 이론이다.");
translationList.add(
    "Big Bang ou Grande Expansão[1] é a teoria cosmológica dominante "
    + "sobre o desenvolvimento inicial do universo.");
```

Use the `translate` method with the list that specifies a target language of English. The method returns a list of `Translation` objects:

```
List<Translation> translations = translate.translate(translationList,
    Translate.TranslateOption.targetLanguage("en"));
```

Display the translations as shown next. Only the first 32 characters of the original source is displayed, along with the name of the source language and the translation:

```
for(int i=0; i< translationList.size(); i++) {
    System.out.printf("\n%-32s \nSource Langue Code: %-32s\n\tTranslation:
%s\n",
        translationList.get(i).substring(0, Math.min(32,
        translationList.get(i).length())),
        translations.get(i).getSourceLanguage(),
        translations.get(i).getTranslatedText());
}
```

When this code sequence is executed, you will get the following output:

```
Als Urknall wird in der Kosmolog
Source Language Code: de
 Translation: In cosmology, the big bang is the beginning of the universe, that is, the beginning
of the formation of matter, space, and time.


대폭발(大爆發, 영어: Big Bang 빅뱅[*])[1]
Source Language Code: ko
 Translation: Big Bang Big Bang [1] is a cosmological model that explains the beginnings of the
universe in astronomy or physics, in which small matter and space with very high energies form
huge explosions about 13.7 billion years ago It is the theory that the universe has become
through.


Big Bang ou Grande Expansào[1] é
Source Language Code: pt
 Translation: Big Bang or Great Expansion [1] is the dominant cosmological theory about the early
development of the universe.
```

We can also translate text that contains HTML markup. The markup is retained in the translated text, unchanged. To illustrate this capability, we will use the HTML for the first paragraph of a web page, found at `https://en.wikipedia.org/wiki/Language`, as shown next:

```
<p><b>Language</b> is a system that consists of the development,
acquisition, maintenance and use of complex systems of <a
href="/wiki/Communication" title="Communication">communication</a>,
particularly the <a href="/wiki/Human" title="Human">human</a> ability to
do so; and <b>a language</b> is any specific example of such a system.
</p>
```

Add the following statements to declare the text and apply the `translate` method:

```
text = "<p><b>Language</b> is a system that consists of the development, "
    + "acquisition, maintenance and use of complex systems of "
    + "<a href=\"/wiki/Communication\" title=\"Communication\">"
    + "communication</a>, particularly the <a href=\"/wiki/Human\" "
    + "title=\"Human\">human</a> ability to do so; and <b>a language</b> "
    + "is any specific example of such a system.\r\n</p>";
translation = translate.translate(text,
Translate.TranslateOption.targetLanguage("es"));
System.out.printf("%-32s \nTranslation: %s\n", text.substring(0, 32),
    translation.getTranslatedText());
```

When the code is executed, you will get the following output:

```
<p><b>Language</b> is a system t
Translation: <p> <b>El lenguaje</b> es un sistema que consiste en el
desarrollo, adquisición, mantenimiento y uso de sistemas complejos de <a
href="/wiki/Communication" title="Comunicación">comunicación</a> ,
particularmente la capacidad <a href="/wiki/Human"
title="Humano">humana</a> para hacerlo; y <b>un lenguaje</b> es cualquier
ejemplo específico de tal sistema. </p>
```

See also

- The GCP translation documentation can be found at `https://cloud.google.com/translate/docs/translating-text`

Language detection and translation using Amazon AWS

In this recipe, we will examine how to detect the language in use and how to translate text between languages using the Amazon Translate API. The process of translating is easy to use once an Amazon account has been set up. There is an AWS SDK for Java Version 1.0 and 2.X. We will be using the 2.X version. Support for the earlier version is being dropped.

Getting ready

To prepare, we need to follow these steps:

1. Create a new Maven project
2. Add the following dependencies to the POM file:

```
<!--
https://mvnrepository.com/artifact/com.amazonaws/aws-java-sdk-core
-->
<dependency>
    <groupId>com.amazonaws</groupId>
    <artifactId>aws-java-sdk-core</artifactId>
    <version>1.11.475</version>
</dependency>

<!--
https://mvnrepository.com/artifact/com.amazonaws/aws-java-sdk-trans
late -->
<dependency>
    <groupId>com.amazonaws</groupId>
    <artifactId>aws-java-sdk-translate</artifactId>
    <version>1.11.475</version>
</dependency>
```

How to do it...

The necessary steps include:

1. Add the following imports to the project:

```
import java.util.ArrayList;
import java.util.HashMap;
import com.amazonaws.auth.AWSCredentialsProvider;
import com.amazonaws.auth.DefaultAWSCredentialsProviderChain;
import com.amazonaws.services.translate.AmazonTranslate;
import com.amazonaws.services.translate.AmazonTranslateClient;
import com.amazonaws.services.translate.model.TranslateTextRequest;
import com.amazonaws.services.translate.model.TranslateTextResult;
```

2. Add the following statements to the `main` method, which will declare the text to be translated:

```
ArrayList<String> textList = new ArrayList<>();
textList.add("Language is a system that consists of the
development, "
    + "acquisition, maintenance and use of complex systems of "
    + "communication, particularly the human ability to do so; "
    + "and a language is any specific example of such a system.");
textList.add("Language ist ein Lied des US-amerikanischen DJs und "
    + "Musikproduzenten Porter Robinson, das von Heather Bright "
    + "gesungen und am 10. April 2012 auf Beatport veröffentlicht"
    + " wurde. Language kann dem Genre Electro House zugeordnet "
    + "werden und hat 128 bpm. Die Vollversion war bereits ab "
    + "dem 26. März 2012 bei YouTube anhörbar. Der Track ist "
    + "unter anderem auch auf dem Soundtrack von Forza Horizon
enthalten.");
```

3. Follow the previous statements with code to access the Amazon credentials and set up a translation request as follows:

```
AWSCredentialsProvider awsCredentialsProvider =
    DefaultAWSCredentialsProviderChain.getInstance();
AmazonTranslate amazonTranslate = AmazonTranslateClient.builder()
    .withCredentials(awsCredentialsProvider)
    .withRegion("us-east-2")
    .build();
TranslateTextRequest translateTextRequest = new
TranslateTextRequest()
    .withText(textList.get(0))
    .withSourceLanguageCode("en")
    .withTargetLanguageCode("es");
```

4. Add the following code to perform the translation and display the results:

```
TranslateTextResult translateTextResult =
    amazonTranslate.translateText(translateTextRequest);
System.out.println(translateTextResult.getTranslatedText());
System.out.println();
```

5. Execute the program. You will get the following output:

```
El lenguaje es un sistema que consiste en el desarrollo,
adquisición, mantenimiento y uso de sistemas complejos de
comunicación, en particular la capacidad humana para hacerlo; y un
lenguaje es cualquier ejemplo específico de tal sistema.
```

How it works...

The `DefaultAWSCredentialsProviderChain`'s `getInstance` method was used to access the credentials for your Amazon account. An instance of the `AmazonTranslate` class was then created using the `AmazonTranslateClient` class based on the credentials and `us-east-2` region. You may need to change the region based on your location. A list of regions can be found at `https://docs.aws.amazon.com/AWSEC2/latest/UserGuide/using-regions-availability-zones.html`. We can change the region using the following code:

```
AWSCredentialsProvider awsCredentialsProvider =
    DefaultAWSCredentialsProviderChain.getInstance();
AmazonTranslate amazonTranslate = AmazonTranslateClient.builder()
    .withCredentials(awsCredentialsProvider)
    .withRegion("us-east-2")
    .build();
```

An instance of the `TranslateTextRequest` class is used to hold the translation request parameters. We used the first text entry in the `textList ArrayList` instance, and specified a source language of English and a target language of Spanish, as shown in the following:

```
TranslateTextRequest translateTextRequest = new TranslateTextRequest()
    .withText(textList.get(0))
    .withSourceLanguageCode("en")
    .withTargetLanguageCode("es");
```

The `translateText` method performs the actual translation. It sends a request to the Amazon server, which returned an instance of the `TranslateTextResult` class. We used the `getTranslatedText` method to display the translated text:

```
TranslateTextResult translateTextResult =
    amazonTranslate.translateText(translateTextRequest);
System.out.println(translateTextResult.getTranslatedText());
System.out.println();
```

There's more...

If the source language is not known, we can use the `auto` string as the source language code, as shown next. We use the `getSourceLanguageCode` and `getTargetLanguageCode` methods to return these respective languages. The for loop iterates through the `ArrayList` and translates each entry:

```
for (String text : textList) {
    translateTextRequest = new TranslateTextRequest()
        .withText(text)
        .withSourceLanguageCode("auto")
        .withTargetLanguageCode("es");
    translateTextResult =
amazonTranslate.translateText(translateTextRequest);
    System.out.println(
        "Source Language: " + translateTextResult.getSourceLanguageCode() +
        "\nTarget language: " + translateTextResult.getTargetLanguageCode()
+
        "\nTranslation: " + translateTextResult.getTranslatedText());
    System.out.println();
}
```

When this code is executed, you will get the following output:

```
Source Language: en
Target language: es
Translation: El lenguaje es un sistema que consiste en el desarrollo,
adquisición, mantenimiento y uso de sistemas complejos de comunicación, en
particular la capacidad humana para hacerlo; y un lenguaje es cualquier
ejemplo específico de tal sistema.

Source Language: de
Target language: es
Translation: Language es una canción del DJ y productor musical
estadounidense Porter Robinson, cantada por Heather Bright y lanzada en
Beatport el 10 de abril de 2012. El idioma se puede asignar al género
Electro House y tiene 128 bpm. La versión completa estaba disponible en
YouTube a partir del 26 de marzo de 2012. La pista también está incluida en
la banda sonora de Forza Horizon.
```

The current language codes are found at `https://docs.aws.amazon.com/translate/latest/dg/how-it-works.html#how-to-auto`. The valid language codes as of 1/1/2019 are listed as follows:

Language	Code
Arabic	ar
Chinese (Simplified)	zh
Chinese (Traditional)	zh-TW
Czech	cs
Danish	da
Dutch	nl
English	en
Finnish	fi
French	fr
German	de
Hebrew	he
Indonesian	id
Italian	it
Japanese	ja
Korean	ko
Polish	pl
Portuguese	pt
Russian	ru
Spanish	es
Swedish	sv
Turkish	tr

The codes used to represent a language may not always be intuitive. The next code sequence creates a `HashMap` instance that we can use to provide more readable language names. The language code is used as the key and the more user-friendly language name is stored as the value:

```
HashMap<String,String> languageEncodings = new HashMap();
languageEncodings.put("ar","Arabic");
languageEncodings.put("zh","Chinese (Simplified)");
languageEncodings.put("zh-TW","Chinese (Traditional)");
languageEncodings.put("cs","Czech");
languageEncodings.put("da","Danish");
languageEncodings.put("nl","Dutch");
languageEncodings.put("en","English");
languageEncodings.put("fi","Finnish");
languageEncodings.put("de","German");
```

```
languageEncodings.put("he","Hebrew");
languageEncodings.put("id","Indonesian");
languageEncodings.put("it","Italian");
languageEncodings.put("ja","Japanese");
languageEncodings.put("ko","Korean");
languageEncodings.put("pl","Polish");
languageEncodings.put("pt","Portuguese");
languageEncodings.put("ru","Russian");
languageEncodings.put("es","Spanish");
languageEncodings.put("sv","Swedish");
languageEncodings.put("tr","Turkish");
```

Replacing the previous `println` method with the next statement makes the output more readable:

```
System.out.println(
    "Source Language: "
    + languageEncodings.get(translateTextResult.getSourceLanguageCode())
    + "\nTarget language: "
    + languageEncodings.get(translateTextResult.getTargetLanguageCode())
    + "\nTranslation: " + translateTextResult.getTranslatedText());
```

When this code is executed, you will get the following output:

```
Source Language: English
Target language: Spanish
Translation: El lenguaje es un sistema que consiste en el desarrollo,
adquisición, mantenimiento y uso de sistemas complejos de comunicación, en
particular la capacidad humana para hacerlo; y un lenguaje es cualquier
ejemplo específico de tal sistema.

Source Language: German
Target language: Spanish
Translation: Language es una canción del DJ y productor musical
estadounidense Porter Robinson, cantada por Heather Bright y lanzada en
Beatport el 10 de abril de 2012. El idioma se puede asignar al género
Electro House y tiene 128 bpm. La versión completa estaba disponible en
YouTube a partir del 26 de marzo de 2012. La pista también está incluida en
la banda sonora de Forza Horizon.
```

See also

- The Amazon Translate page can be found at `https://aws.amazon.com/translate/`
- The Java API documentation can be found at `https://sdk.amazonaws.com/java/api/latest/software/amazon/awssdk/services/translate/package-summary.html`

Converting text to speech using the Google Cloud Text-to-Speech API

In this recipe, we will use the Google Cloud Text-to-Speech API to convert a string into an audio file. We will use a client to send requests to a Google server for processing. We will use the audio file as input to the *Converting speech to text Using the Google Cloud Speech-to-Text API* recipe.

Getting ready

To prepare, we need to follow these steps:

1. Create a new Java Maven project
2. Add the following dependencies to the POM:

```
<dependency>
    <groupId>com.google.cloud</groupId>
    <artifactId>google-cloud-texttospeech</artifactId>
    <version>0.70.0-beta</version>
</dependency>
<dependency>
    <groupId>net.sourceforge.argparse4j</groupId>
    <artifactId>argparse4j</artifactId>
    <version>0.8.1</version>
</dependency>
```

3. Add the `GOOGLE_APPLICATION_CREDENTIALS` environment variable with a value that is, the path to your API key similar to: `C:\...\filename.json`

How to do it...

The necessary steps include:

1. Add the following imports to your project:

```
import java.io.FileNotFoundException;
import java.io.FileOutputStream;
import java.io.IOException;
import java.io.OutputStream;
import com.google.cloud.texttospeech.v1.AudioConfig;
import com.google.cloud.texttospeech.v1.AudioEncoding;
import com.google.cloud.texttospeech.v1.SsmlVoiceGender;
import com.google.cloud.texttospeech.v1.SynthesisInput;
import com.google.cloud.texttospeech.v1.SynthesizeSpeechResponse;
import com.google.cloud.texttospeech.v1.TextToSpeechClient;
import com.google.cloud.texttospeech.v1.VoiceSelectionParams;
import com.google.protobuf.ByteString;
```

2. Add the following declarations to the `main` method:

```
String text = "Now is the time for all good men to come to the aid
of their country.";
String fileName = "audio.linear16";
SsmlVoiceGender ssmlVoiceGender = SsmlVoiceGender.NEUTRAL;
AudioEncoding audioEncoding = AudioEncoding.LINEAR16;
String languageCode = "en-US";
```

3. Insert the following try-with-resources block to create a client that will interact with the Google server:

```
try (TextToSpeechClient textToSpeechClient =
TextToSpeechClient.create()) {
    ...
} catch (IOException ex) {
    // Handle exceptions
}
```

4. Insert the following code to create an input source:

```
SynthesisInput synthesisInput = SynthesisInput
    .newBuilder()
    .setText(text)
    .build();
```

5. Add the next code sequence to set up the conversion parameters:

```
VoiceSelectionParams voiceSelectionParams = VoiceSelectionParams
    .newBuilder()
    .setLanguageCode(languageCode)
    .setSsmlGender(ssmlVoiceGender)
    .build();
```

6. Add the following code to configure the audio file:

```
AudioConfig audioConfig = AudioConfig
    .newBuilder()
    .setAudioEncoding(audioEncoding)
    .build();
```

7. Insert the next code sequence to perform the conversion:

```
SynthesizeSpeechResponse synthesizeSpeechResponse =
        synthesisInput, voiceSelectionParams, audioConfig);
ByteString audioContents =
synthesizeSpeechResponse.getAudioContent();
```

8. Use the following code to save the audio to a file:

```
try (OutputStream outputStream = new FileOutputStream(fileName)) {
    outputStream.write(audioContents.toByteArray());
} catch (FileNotFoundException ex) {
    // Handle exceptions
} catch (IOException ex) {
    // Handle exceptions
}
```

9. Execute the program. Other than a few warnings, you will not see any output. The `audio.linear16` file will be found in your project's root directory.

How it works...

Several declarations are used to configure the conversion process. We used a simple string to demonstrate the process. We can specify the gender of the voice. In the example, a gender-neutral voice was used. Other audio encoding schemes could be used. We used `AudioEncoding.LINEAR16` to make the next recipe, *Converting speech to text using the Google Cloud Speech-to-Text API*, easier to use:

```
String text = "Now is the time for all good men to come to the aid of their
country.";
String fileName = "audio.linear16";
```

```
SsmlVoiceGender ssmlVoiceGender = SsmlVoiceGender.NEUTRAL;
AudioEncoding audioEncoding = AudioEncoding.LINEAR16;
String languageCode = "en-US";
```

The `TextToSpeechClient` instance represents a client that connected to and used the Google Text-to-Speech server. The `SynthesisInput` class held the text to be converted:

```
SynthesisInput synthesisInput = SynthesisInput
    .newBuilder()
    .setText(text)
    .build();
```

The `VoiceSelectionParams` instance configured the conversion process based upon the previously-defined variables. The `AudioConfig` instance used the `audioEncoding` variable to specify the audio file type:

```
VoiceSelectionParams voiceSelectionParams = VoiceSelectionParams
    .newBuilder()
    .setLanguageCode(languageCode)
    .setSsmlGender(ssmlVoiceGender)
    .build();
AudioConfig audioConfig = AudioConfig
    .newBuilder()
    .setAudioEncoding(audioEncoding)
    .build();
```

The `synthesizeSpeech` method sent the request to the server using the input text and configurations. It returned an instance of the `SynthesizeSpeechResponse` class that holds the audio. The `getAudioContent` method returned a `ByteString` instance that represents the audio. This was written to the file:

```
SynthesizeSpeechResponse synthesizeSpeechResponse =
    textToSpeechClient.synthesizeSpeech(
        synthesisInput, voiceSelectionParams, audioConfig);
ByteString audioContents = synthesizeSpeechResponse.getAudioContent();

try (OutputStream outputStream = new FileOutputStream(fileName)) {
    outputStream.write(audioContents.toByteArray());
} catch (FileNotFoundException ex) {
    // Handle exceptions
} catch (IOException ex) {
    // Handle exceptions
}
```

See also

- The Google Text-to-Speech main page can be found at `https://cloud.google.com/text-to-speech/`
- The Google Text-to-Speech API can be found at `https://googleapis.github.io/google-cloud-java/google-cloud-clients/apidocs/index.html`

Converting speech to text using the Google Cloud Speech-to-Text API

In this recipe, we will demonstrate how to read in an audio file and convert it to speech. We will use the `audio.linear16` audio file created in the *Converting text to speech using the Google Cloud Text-to- Speech API* recipe as input to the example.

Getting ready

To prepare, we need to follow these steps:

1. Create a new Java Maven project
2. Add the following dependency to the POM:

```
<dependency>
    <groupId>com.google.cloud</groupId>
    <artifactId>google-cloud-speech</artifactId>
    <version>0.61.0-beta</version>
</dependency>
```

3. Add the `GOOGLE_APPLICATION_CREDENTIALS` environmental variable with a value that, is the path to your API key similar to: `C:\...\filename.json`

How to do it...

The necessary steps include:

1. Add the following imports to your project:

```java
import java.io.File;
import java.io.IOException;
import java.nio.file.Files;
import java.util.List;
import com.google.cloud.speech.v1.RecognitionAudio;
import com.google.cloud.speech.v1.RecognitionConfig;
import com.google.cloud.speech.v1.RecognitionConfig.AudioEncoding;
import com.google.cloud.speech.v1.RecognizeResponse;
import com.google.cloud.speech.v1.SpeechClient;
import com.google.cloud.speech.v1.SpeechRecognitionAlternative;
import com.google.cloud.speech.v1.SpeechRecognitionResult;
import com.google.protobuf.ByteString;
```

2. Insert the following try-with-resources block to the `main` method:

```java
try (SpeechClient speechClient = SpeechClient.create()) {
    ...
} catch (IOException ex) {
    // Handle exceptions
}
```

3. Add the following declarations to the `try` block to configure the conversion process:

```java
String fileName = "audio.linear16";
int sampleRateHertz = 24000;
AudioEncoding audioEncoding = AudioEncoding.LINEAR16;
String languageCode = "en-US";
```

4. Add the next code sequence to read in the audio file and convert it into a `ByteString` instance:

```java
File file = new File(fileName);
byte[] dataByteArray = Files.readAllBytes(file.toPath());
ByteString audioByteString = ByteString.copyFrom(dataByteArray);
```

5. Insert the next set of code to configure the conversion:

```java
RecognitionConfig recognitionConfig = RecognitionConfig
    .newBuilder()
    .setEncoding(audioEncoding)
    .setSampleRateHertz(sampleRateHertz)
```

```
.setLanguageCode(languageCode)
.build();
```

6. Add the following statements, which prepare the audio and call the server:

```
RecognitionAudio recognitionAudio = RecognitionAudio
    .newBuilder()
    .setContent(audioByteString)
    .build();
RecognizeResponse recognizeResponse = speechClient.recognize(
    recognitionConfig, recognitionAudio);
```

7. Add the following sequence to get and display the converted text:

```
SpeechRecognitionResult result = recognizeResponse.getResults(0);
SpeechRecognitionAlternative transcription =
result.getAlternatives(0);
System.out.printf("Transcription: %s%nConfidence: %5.3f%n",
    transcription.getTranscript(),
    transcription.getConfidence());
```

8. Execute the program. You will get the following output:

```
Transcription: now is the time for all good men to come to the aid
of their country
Confidence: 0.988
```

You may receive a few warnings, which can be ignored.

How it works...

The initial declarations specified the audio file name along with various audio parameters. These would need to be changed if a different audio file format was used:

```
String fileName = "audio.linear16";
int sampleRateHertz = 24000;
AudioEncoding audioEncoding = AudioEncoding.LINEAR16;
String languageCode = "en-US";
```

A `ByteString` instance was created before it was sent to the server. The `RecognitionConfig` instance was used to configure the conversion:

```
File file = new File(fileName);
byte[] dataByteArray = Files.readAllBytes(file.toPath());
ByteString audioByteString = ByteString.copyFrom(dataByteArray);
RecognitionConfig recognitionConfig = RecognitionConfig
    .newBuilder()
    .setEncoding(audioEncoding)
    .setSampleRateHertz(sampleRateHertz)
    .setLanguageCode(languageCode)
    .build();
```

The `RecognitionAudio` instance combined the configuration with the audio and was sent to the server using the `recognize` method, as shown:

```
RecognitionAudio recognitionAudio = RecognitionAudio
    .newBuilder()
    .setContent(audioByteString)
    .build();
RecognizeResponse recognizeResponse = speechClient.recognize(
    recognitionConfig, recognitionAudio);
```

When the server responded, we obtained the first result and its first version of the translation. The `getTranscript` and `getConfidence` methods returned the translation and the degree of confidence of the translation, respectively:

```
SpeechRecognitionResult result = recognizeResponse.getResults(0);
SpeechRecognitionAlternative transcription = result.getAlternatives(0);
System.out.printf("Transcription: %s%nConfidence: %5.3f%n",
    transcription.getTranscript(),
    transcription.getConfidence());
```

There's more...

There may be more than one possible translation available. When this is a possibility, we can use the following code sequence to display all of these variations. It is similar to the previous code sequence:

```
List<SpeechRecognitionResult> resultsList =
recognizeResponse.getResultsList();
for (SpeechRecognitionResult speechRecognitionResult : resultsList) {
    List<SpeechRecognitionAlternative> alternativeList =
        speechRecognitionResult.getAlternativesList();
    for (SpeechRecognitionAlternative alternative : alternativeList) {
```

```
System.out.printf("Transcription: %s%nConfidence: %5.3f%n",
    alternative.getTranscript(),
    alternative.getConfidence());
    }
}
```

If you replace the last code sequence in the previous section with this code, you will get the following output when executed:

```
Transcription: now is the time for all good men to come to the aid of their
country
Confidence: 0.988
```

See also

- The Google Speech-to-Text main page can be found at `https://cloud.google.com/speech-to-text/`
- The Google Speech-to-Text API can be found at `http://googleapis.github.io/googleapis/java/all/latest/apidocs/index.html?com/google/cloud/speech/v1beta1/SpeechRecognitionResultOrBuilder.html`

Identifying Semantic Similarities within Text

8

Semantic similarity refers to how closely related two or more different texts are to each other. That is, how much two words, sentences, or other text entities are alike. Finding similarities is useful as a classification technique and has been used by applications such as spelling and plagiarism checkers.

We can assess the similarity between two words using a number of techniques. At a simplistic level, we can identify how much change is required to convert one word into another word using a sequence of insertion, deletion, and/or substitution operations.

At a deeper level, we can examine the meaning of words to determine their similarity. For example, the words *teaching* and *instructing* are spelled very differently, but they convey the same basic concept. Stemming and lemmatization can be useful in making these types of comparisons.

The Apache Commons Text library possesses a number of classes in the `org.apache.commons.text.similarity` package, and supports similarity between strings. In this chapter, we will demonstrate a number of these classes and methods.

The algorithms that will be illustrated include the following:

- Cosine similarity
- Hamming distance
- Levenshtein distance

In this chapter, we will cover the following recipes:

- Finding the cosine similarity of the text
- Finding the distance between text
- Finding differences between plaintext instances
- Finding hyponyms and antonyms

Technical requirements

In this chapter, you will need to install the following software, if they haven't already been installed:

- Eclipse Photon 4.8.0
- Java JDK 8 or later

We will be using the following APIs, which you will be instructed to add for each recipe as appropriate:

- Apache Commons Text Library 1.6
- java-diff-utils 4.0
- **Java API for WordNet Searching (JAWS)** API 1.3.1

The code files for this chapter can be found at `https://github.com/PacktPublishing/Natural-Language-Processing-with-Java-Cookbook/tree/master/Chapter08`.

Finding the cosine similarity of the text

Cosine similarity measures the distance between two vectors. This technique creates a vector that represents the number of elements found in a string.

The Apache Commons Text library's `CosineSimilarity` class supports this measurement. The class has a single default constructor and a single `CosineSimilarity` method. The method accepts two `Map` instances, representing the vectors. It returns a `Double`, representing their similarity.

More detailed explanations of cosine similarity can be found at `https://en.wikipedia.org/wiki/Cosine_similarity` and `https://stackoverflow.com/questions/1746501/can-someone-give-an-example-of-cosine-similarity-in-a-very-simple-graphical-wa`.

Getting ready

To prepare for this recipe, we need to do the following:

1. Create a new Maven project.
2. Add the following dependency to the project's POM file:

```
<!--
https://mvnrepository.com/artifact/org.apache.commons/commons-text
-->
<dependency>
    <groupId>org.apache.commons</groupId>
    <artifactId>commons-text</artifactId>
    <version>1.6</version>
</dependency>
```

How to do it...

Here are the necessary steps:

1. Add the following `import` statements to the project:

```
import java.util.Arrays;
import java.util.HashMap;
import java.util.Map;
import java.util.stream.Collectors;
import org.apache.commons.text.similarity.CosineSimilarity;
```

2. Add the following code sequence to the `main` method:

```
CosineSimilarity cosineSimilarity = new CosineSimilarity();
String firstSample = "A simple sentence";
String secondSample = "One simple sentence";
```

3. Add these statements to create vectors for processing:

```
Map<CharSequence, Integer> vectorA = Arrays
    .stream(firstSample.split(""))
    .collect(Collectors.toMap(
        character -> character, character -> 1, Integer::sum));
Map<CharSequence, Integer> vectorB = Arrays
    .stream(secondSample.split(""))
    .collect(Collectors.toMap(
        character -> character, character -> 1, Integer::sum));
```

4. Add the next statement to compute and display the cosine similarities:

```
System.out.printf("%5.4f\n",cosineSimilarity.cosineSimilarity(vecto
rA, vectorB));
```

5. Execute the program. You will get the following output:

```
0.9659
```

How it works...

An instance of the `CosineSimilarity` class was created, followed by the declaration of two sample strings. Next, a lambda expression was used to create the `Map` instance that represents the string vectors. The sample strings were split into individual characters. These characters were summed and added to the `Map` instance using the character as the key. These map instances represent the two sentences as numeric vectors:

```
Map<CharSequence, Integer> vectorA = Arrays
    .stream(firstSample.split(""))
    .collect(Collectors.toMap(
        character -> character, character -> 1, Integer::sum));
Map<CharSequence, Integer> vectorB = Arrays
    .stream(secondSample.split(""))
    .collect(Collectors.toMap(
        character -> character, character -> 1, Integer::sum));
```

The `cosineSimilarity` method was then used to compute and display the cosine similarities:

```
System.out.printf("%5.4f\n",cosineSimilarity.cosineSimilarity(vectorA,
vectorB));
```

Since the two strings were very similar, the value that was returned was very close to 1.0. Dissimilar strings result in a value closer to 0.0.

There's more...

Instead of using a lambda expression to create the vectors, we can use a more verbose approach, as shown here. In the following code sequence, we will create a new Map instance and use a ternary operator to handle null return values from the get method. This operator uses less code than an equivalent if statement. Since the HashMap uses CharSequence as the key, it is necessary to convert the character into a string for the get and put operations:

```
HashMap<CharSequence, Integer> vectorC = new HashMap<>();
for (char character : secondSample.toCharArray()) {
    int count = (vectorC.get(character + "") == null) ? 0 :
vectorC.get(character + "");
    vectorC.put(character + "", count + 1);
}
```

Use the following statement to test the new vector:

```
System.out.printf("%5.4f\n",cosineSimilarity.cosineSimilarity(vectorA,
vectorC));
```

When executed, you will get the same value of 0.9659.

This example splits the strings into individual characters. If we split the strings into words instead, we will get a different value for the cosine similarity. The following code sequence uses a split method argument of a single blank. This will split the strings into words:

```
vectorA = Arrays
    .stream(firstSample.split(" "))
    .collect(Collectors.toMap(word -> word, word -> 1, Integer::sum));
vectorB = Arrays
    .stream(secondSample.split(" "))
    .collect(Collectors.toMap(word -> word, word -> 1, Integer::sum));
```

We will use the same cosineSimilarity statement to compute the cosine similarity:

```
System.out.printf("%5.4f\n",cosineSimilarity.cosineSimilarity(vectorA,
vectorB));
```

When this code is executed, we will get the following output:

```
0.6667
```

The cosine similarity value is significantly smaller when we use this element type for the sample vectors.

See also

- The documentation for the Apache Commons Text similarity package can be found at `https://commons.apache.org/proper/commons-text/javadocs/api-release/org/apache/commons/text/similarity/package-summary.html`

Finding the distance between text

There are several ways to measure the distance between two strings. In this recipe, we will demonstrate how to use the Apache Commons Text library to compute the Hamming and Levenshtein distances.

Distance is concerned with the number of operations needed to convert one string into another string. These operations can be either single-character deletion, insertion, or substitution.

The Hamming distance algorithm works on strings of equal length, which may limit its utility in some situations. It simply measures the number of positions in the two strings that differ. It is case-sensitive.

The `HammingDistance` class possesses a single default constructor and an `apply` method, which takes two strings as its arguments. The method returns the distance between the strings.

A more detailed Hamming distance explanation can be found at `http://en.wikipedia.org/wiki/Hamming_distance`.

There are three classes that support the computation of the Levenshtein distance:

- `LevenshteinResults`: A class that holds information about the number of character insertions, deletions, and/or substitutions needed to change one string into another
- `LevenshteinDistance`: Provides a simple measurement of the distance between strings
- `LevenshteinDetailedDistance`: Uses the `LevenshteinResults` class to provide more information about the differences between strings

Getting ready

To prepare for this recipe, we need to do the following:

1. Create a new Maven project.
2. Add the following dependency to the project's POM file:

```
<!--
https://mvnrepository.com/artifact/org.apache.commons/commons-text
-->
<dependency>
    <groupId>org.apache.commons</groupId>
    <artifactId>commons-text</artifactId>
    <version>1.6</version>
</dependency>
```

How to do it...

Here are the necessary steps:

1. Add the following `import` statements to the project:

```
import org.apache.commons.text.similarity.HammingDistance;
import
org.apache.commons.text.similarity.LevenshteinDetailedDistance;
import org.apache.commons.text.similarity.LevenshteinDistance;
import org.apache.commons.text.similarity.LevenshteinResults;
```

2. Add the following code sequence, to compute the Hamming distance, to the `main` method:

```
HammingDistance hammingDistance = new HammingDistance();
System.out.println("Hamming Distance: " +
hammingDistance.apply("bat", "bat"));
System.out.println("Hamming Distance: " +
hammingDistance.apply("bat", "cat"));
System.out.println("Hamming Distance: " +
hammingDistance.apply("bat", "rut"));
```

3. Insert the following sequence to compute the Levenshtein distance:

```
LevenshteinDistance levenshteinDistance = new
LevenshteinDistance();
System.out.println("Levenshtein Distance: "
    + levenshteinDistance.apply("bat", "bat"));
System.out.println("Levenshtein Distance: "
    + levenshteinDistance.apply("bat", "rat"));
System.out.println("Levenshtein Distance: "
    + levenshteinDistance.apply("bat", "rut"));
System.out.println("Levenshtein Distance: "
    + levenshteinDistance.apply("bat", "battle"));
```

4. Add the following sequence to get more information about the Levenshtein distance:

```
LevenshteinDetailedDistance levenshteinDetailedDistance =
    new LevenshteinDetailedDistance();
LevenshteinResults levenshteinResults =
    levenshteinDetailedDistance.apply("similar", "simulator");
System.out.println("Number of deletions: "
    + levenshteinResults.getDeleteCount());
System.out.println("Number of insertions: "
    + levenshteinResults.getInsertCount());
System.out.println("Number of substitutions: "
    + levenshteinResults.getSubstituteCount());
```

5. Execute the program. You will get the following output:

```
Hamming Distance: 0
Hamming Distance: 1
Hamming Distance: 2

Levenshtein Distance: 0
Levenshtein Distance: 1
Levenshtein Distance: 2
Levenshtein Distance: 3

Number of deletions: 0
Number of insertions: 2
Number of substitutions: 1
```

To change the word *similar* to *simulator*, the second letter, i, is replaced (substituted) with the letter u. The two letters, to, are inserted before the letter r.

How it works...

These classes and methods are easy to use and understand. The `apply` method was used with each class to obtain an integer that represents the distance between two strings. The `LevenshteinDetailedDistance` class' `apply` method is different and returns an instance of the `LevenshteinResults` class. This class possesses three methods that return the number of deletions, insertions, and substitutions needed to convert the first string into the second string.

See also

- The documentation for the Apache Commons Text similarity package can be found at `https://commons.apache.org/proper/commons-text/javadocs/api-release/org/apache/commons/text/similarity/package-summary.html`

Finding differences between plaintext instances

While the distance measurements illustrated in the *Finding the distance between text* recipe are useful, we are often interested in the differences between two different versions of text that consist of multiple sentences. The Diff Match Patch library provides support for this task.

In this recipe, we will illustrate how to find the differences between two sentences and then between a series of sentences. After that, we will demonstrate how to find differences between text files.

Getting ready

For preparing this recipe, we need to do the following:

1. Create a new Maven project.
2. Add the following dependency to the project's POM file:

```
<dependency>
    <groupId>io.github.java-diff-utils</groupId>
    <artifactId>java-diff-utils</artifactId>
    <version>4.0</version>
</dependency>
```

How to do it...

Here are the necessary steps:

1. Add the following `import` statements to the project:

```
import java.util.Arrays;
import java.util.List;
import java.nio.file.Files;
import java.nio.file.Path;
import java.io.File;
import java.io.IOException;
import com.github.difflib.DiffUtils;
import com.github.difflib.UnifiedDiffUtils;
import com.github.difflib.algorithm.DiffException;
import com.github.difflib.patch.AbstractDelta;
import com.github.difflib.patch.Patch;
import com.github.difflib.text.DiffRow;
import com.github.difflib.text.DiffRowGenerator;
```

2. Add the following code sequence to the `main` method. It creates an instance of the `DiffRowGenerator` class, which set ups the generator:

```
DiffRowGenerator diffRowGenerator = DiffRowGenerator
    .create()
    .showInlineDiffs(true)
    .mergeOriginalRevised(true)
    .inlineDiffByWord(true)
    .oldTag(f -> "-")
    .newTag(f -> "^")
    .build();
```

3. Add the following sequence, which generates a list of differences between two sentences:

```
try {
    List<DiffRow> diffRowList = diffRowGenerator
        .generateDiffRows(Arrays.asList("A simple sentence."),
            Arrays.asList("Also, a simple sentence."));
        System.out.println(diffRowList.get(0).getOldLine());
} catch (DiffException e) {
    // Handle exceptions
}
```

4. Execute the program. You will get the following output:

```
-A-^Also,^ ^a ^simple sentence.
```

The dashes surround the words to delete, and the caret symbols indicate which words to add.

How it works...

Several methods were used with a fluent style of programming to build an instance of the `DiffRowGenerator` class. Each of these methods configured the instance in difference ways, as detailed here:

- `create`: Returns an instance of the `DiffRowGenerator.Builder` class
- `showInlineDiffs`: Specifies that differences between text will be shown
- `mergeOriginalRevised`: Specifies that the differences will be merged with the original text
- `inlineDiffByWord`: Indicates that the differences will be by word
- `oldTag`: The markup tag to reflect deleted text
- `newTag`: The markup tag to reflect additions
- `build`: Creates an instance of `DiffRowGenerator`

The following statement instantiated the `DiffRowGenerator` instance to specify the deleted text and added text tags:

```
DiffRowGenerator diffRowGenerator = DiffRowGenerator
    .create()
    .showInlineDiffs(true)
    .mergeOriginalRevised(true)
    .inlineDiffByWord(true)
    .oldTag(f -> "-")
```

```
    .newTag(f -> "^")
    .build();
```

The `generateDiffRows` method takes two lists of words and returns a list of `DiffRow` elements. These elements contain the markups and words of the text. The `get` method used an argument of 0 to get the first `DiffRow` instance. Since there is only one instance, this will be sufficient. The `getOldLine` method returns the lines with the markups:

```
try {
    List<DiffRow> diffRowList = diffRowGenerator.generateDiffRows(
        Arrays.asList("A simple sentence."),
        Arrays.asList("Also, a simple sentence."));
    System.out.println(diffRowList.get(0).getOldLine());
} catch (DiffException e) {
    // Handle exceptions
}
```

There's more...

We can also use multiple lines, as shown in the following code sequence. In this case, we need to iterate through the `DiffRow` list using a loop. We used the `getOldLine` and `getNewLine` methods to show what changes were applied:

```
try {
    List<DiffRow> diffRowList = diffRowGenerator.generateDiffRows(
        Arrays.asList("Start with a clean pot.", "Add the good
ingredients."),
        Arrays.asList("Start with a clean pot.", "Add the best
ingredients.",
        "Don't forget to stir."));

    for (DiffRow diffRow : diffRowList) {
        System.out.println("Old Line: " + diffRow.getOldLine());
        System.out.println("New Line:" + diffRow.getNewLine());
        System.out.println();
    }
} catch (DiffException e) {
    // Handle exceptions
}
```

Executing the preceding code sequence will give you the following output. No changes are needed for the first line. The second line required several modifications. The third line is a single insertion since the first list of words did not have a third line:

```
Old Line: Start with a clean pot.
New Line:Start with a clean pot.

Old Line: Add the -good-^best^ ingredients.
New Line:Add the best ingredients.

Old Line: ^Don't forget to stir.^
New Line:Don't forget to stir.
```

It is also possible to process text found in files. In this example, we created two files to be added to the project's root directory. The first file is called `File1.txt` and is shown here:

```
Start with a pot. Add the good ingredients.
Don't forget to stir.
```

The second file is called `File2.txt` and contains the following code:

```
Start with a clean pot. Add the best ingredients.
Don't forget to stir!
```

Insert a `try` block, as shown here, to create two lists based on the contents of the files:

```
try {
    List<String> file1List = Files.readAllLines(
        new File("File1.txt").toPath());
    List<String> file2List = Files.readAllLines(
        new File("File2.txt").toPath());
    ...
} catch (IOException ex) {
    // Handle exceptions
} catch (DiffException ex) {
    // Handle exceptions
}
```

Add the following sequence of code to the `try` block. The `for` loop will display one line at a time with the changes. The delta type refers to the type of change that's made. There are three delta types available: change, delete, and insert. The source shows where a change is needed in the first sequence. The target shows where in the resulting sentences a change is applied:

```
for (int i = 0; i < file1List.size(); i++) {
    Patch<String> stringPatch = DiffUtils.diffInline(
        file1List.get(i), file2List.get(i));
```

```
        System.out.println("Line: " + (i + 1));
        for (AbstractDelta<String> stringDelta : stringPatch.getDeltas()) {
        System.out.println("\tDelta Type: " + stringDelta.getType()
            + "\n\t\tSource - "
            + stringDelta.getSource() + "\n\t\tTarget - " +
    stringDelta.getTarget());
    }
}
```

When this code is executed, you will get the following output:

```
Line: 1
 Delta Type: INSERT
 Source - [position: 13, size: 0, lines: []]
 Target - [position: 13, size: 1, lines: [clean ]]
 Delta Type: CHANGE
 Source - [position: 26, size: 1, lines: [good]]
 Target - [position: 32, size: 1, lines: [best]]
 Delta Type: INSERT
 Source - [position: 43, size: 0, lines: []]
 Target - [position: 49, size: 1, lines: [ ]]
Line: 2
 Delta Type: CHANGE
 Source - [position: 20, size: 1, lines: [.]]
 Target - [position: 20, size: 1, lines: [!]]
```

See also

- The Diff Match Patch library can be found at `https://github.com/google/diff-match-patch/`

Finding hyponyms and antonyms

Hyponyms and antonyms can be useful in identifying similar words. In this recipe, we will use the JAWS API to perform this task. This API uses the WordNet database as the source of words and their usage.

 A hyponym is a word that is similar, but more precise, in meaning to another word. An antonym of a word is a word that has the opposite meaning. For example, the word *sailor* is a hyponym of *person*, and *buy* is an antonym for *sell*.

Getting ready

To prepare for this recipe, we need to do the following:

1. Create a new Maven project.
2. Add the following repository to the project's POM file:

```
<repository>
    <id>jitpack.io</id>
    <name>jitpack</name>
    <url>https://jitpack.io</url>
</repository>
```

3. Add the following dependency to the project's POM file:

```
<dependency>
    <groupId>com.github.jaytaylor</groupId>
    <artifactId>jaws</artifactId>
    <version>1.3.1</version>
</dependency>
```

4. Download the `WordNet-3.0.tar.gz` file from `https://wordnet.princeton.edu/download/current-version`.
5. Extract the `WordNet-3.0.tar` file to a convenient location. Then, extract the TAR file. This will create a directory named `WordNet-3.0`.

How to do it...

Here are the necessary steps:

1. Add the following `import` statements to the project:

```
import edu.smu.tspell.wordnet.AdjectiveSynset;
import edu.smu.tspell.wordnet.NounSynset;
import edu.smu.tspell.wordnet.Synset;
import edu.smu.tspell.wordnet.SynsetType;
import edu.smu.tspell.wordnet.WordNetDatabase;
import edu.smu.tspell.wordnet.WordSense;
```

2. Add the following statements to the `main` method to set up the WordNet data, where the ellipses are replaced by the path to the `WordNet-3.0` directory. We extracted this directory earlier, in the *Getting ready* section:

```
System.setProperty("wordnet.database.dir", ".../WordNet-3.0/dict");
WordNetDatabase wordNetDatabase =
WordNetDatabase.getFileInstance();
```

3. Add the following code sequence to extract the hyponyms for a sample noun:

```
String noun = "horse";
Synset[] synsets = wordNetDatabase.getSynsets(noun,
SynsetType.NOUN);
for (int i = 0; i < synsets.length; i++) {
    NounSynset nounSynset = (NounSynset) (synsets[i]);
    NounSynset[] hyponyms = nounSynset.getHyponyms();
    ...
}
```

4. Insert the following set of statements to display the hyponyms and antonyms:

```
System.out.println(nounSynset.getWordForms()[0] + " - "
    + nounSynset.getDefinition());
if (hyponyms.length > 0) {
    System.out.println(" Hyponyms");
    for (NounSynset hyponym : hyponyms) {
        System.out.println("\t" + hyponym.getWordForms()[0]);
    }
}

WordSense[] antonyms = nounSynset.getAntonyms(noun);
if (antonyms.length > 0) {
    System.out.println(" Antonyms");
    for (WordSense antonym : antonyms) {
        System.out.println("\t" + antonym.getWordForm());
    }
}
System.out.println();
```

5. Execute the code. You will get the following output:

```
horse - solid-hoofed herbivorous quadruped domesticated since
prehistoric times
 Hyponyms
 roan
 stablemate
 gee-gee
 eohippus
```

```
mesohippus
protohippus
male horse
mare
saddle horse
pony
polo pony
wild horse
hack
hack
pony
racehorse
steeplechaser
stalking-horse
harness horse
workhorse
post horse
pacer
stepper
chestnut
liver chestnut
bay
sorrel
palomino
pinto
```

horse - a padded gymnastic apparatus on legs
  Hyponyms
  pommel horse
  vaulting horse

cavalry - troops trained to fight on horseback

sawhorse - a framework for holding wood that is being sawed
  Hyponyms
  trestle

knight - a chessman shaped to resemble the head of a horse; can move two squares horizontally and one vertically (or vice versa)

How it works...

The JAWS library requires the location of the WordNet files to be specified with the `wordnet.database.dir` property, as shown here. An instance of the `WordNetDatabase` was then created:

```
System.setProperty("wordnet.database.dir", ".../WordNet-3.0/dict");
WordNetDatabase wordNetDatabase = WordNetDatabase.getFileInstance();
```

We used the word *horse* as the sample text for this recipe. It can be changed to any other noun. The `Synset` interface represents a collection of words and phrases, all of which have a similar meaning. The `getSynsets` method returned an array of `Synnet` objects for the sample word:

```
String noun = "horse";
Synset[] synsets = wordNetDatabase.getSynsets(noun, SynsetType.NOUN);
```

Next, we used a `for` loop to iterate through the array and created an array of `NounSynset` instances that represent a `Synset` for a noun. A given noun, such as *horse,* may have multiple meanings with multiple hyponyms. The `for` loop processed each one:

```
for (int i = 0; i < synsets.length; i++) {
    NounSynset nounSynset = (NounSynset) (synsets[i]);
    NounSynset[] hyponyms = nounSynset.getHyponyms();
    ...
}
```

The `NounSynset` interface's `getWordForms` method returns an array of strings that contains the variations of the word. We were only interested in the first one, so the subscript of 0 was used. The `getDefinition` method returned the definition of the word that was found in the WordNet database:

```
System.out.println(nounSynset.getWordForms()[0] + " - " +
    nounSynset.getDefinition());
```

The previous statement displays the following, the first time it is called:

```
horse - solid-hoofed herbivorous quadruped domesticated since prehistoric
times
```

The following two loops displayed the hyponyms and antonyms for the sample word. The two code sequences are very similar to each other, except the first uses the `getWordForms` method and the second uses the `getWordForm` method. The first returned multiple pieces of information. Only the first sequence was used in this example:

```
if (hyponyms.length > 0) {
    System.out.println(" Hyponyms");
    for (NounSynset hyponym : hyponyms) {
        System.out.println("\t" + hyponym.getWordForms()[0]);
    }
}

WordSense[] antonyms = nounSynset.getAntonyms(noun);
if (antonyms.length > 0) {
    System.out.println(" Antonyms");
    for (WordSense antonym : antonyms) {
        System.out.println("\t" + antonym.getWordForm());
    }
}
System.out.println();
```

There's more...

The JAWS API can handle more than just nouns. It can also handle verbs, adjectives, and adverbs. In the following sequence, we will illustrate how to handle adjectives. Notice that the type of word is specified by a `SynsetType` enumeration. For an adjective, we used `SynsetType.ADJECTIVE`.

Other differences include the use of `AdjectiveSynset` instead of `NounSynset` and the use of the `getSimilar` method instead of the `getHyponyms` method. Otherwise, the code follows the noun version very closely:

```
String adjective = "big";
synsets = wordNetDatabase.getSynsets(adjective, SynsetType.ADJECTIVE);
for (int i = 0; i < synsets.length; i++) {
    AdjectiveSynset adjectiveSynset = (AdjectiveSynset) (synsets[i]);
    AdjectiveSynset[] similars = adjectiveSynset.getSimilar();

System.out.println(adjectiveSynset.getWordForms()[0] + " - "
    + adjectiveSynset.getDefinition());
if (similars.length > 0) {
    System.out.println(" Similar");
    for (AdjectiveSynset similar : similars) {
        System.out.println("\t" + similar.getWordForms()[0]);
    }
}
```

```
    }

    WordSense[] antonyms = adjectiveSynset.getAntonyms(adjective);
    if (antonyms.length > 0) {
        System.out.println(" Antonyms");
        for (WordSense antonym : antonyms) {
            System.out.println("\t" + antonym.getWordForm());
        }
    }
    System.out.println();
```

When this sequence is executed, you will get the following output:

```
large - above average in size or number or quantity or magnitude or extent
 Similar
 ample
 astronomic
 bear-sized
 bigger
 biggish
 blown-up
 bouffant
 broad
 bulky
 capacious
 colossal
 deep
 double
 enormous
 cosmic
 elephantine
 epic
 extensive
 gigantic
 great
 grand
 huge
 hulking
 humongous
 king-size
 large-mouthed
 large-scale
 large-scale
 life-size
 macroscopic
 macro
 man-sized
 massive
```

```
massive
medium-large
monstrous
mountainous
outsize
overlarge
plumping
queen-size
rangy
super
titanic
volumed
voluminous
whacking
wide-ranging
Antonyms
little
```

See also

- The JAWS API documentation can be found at `http://mind.cs.byu.edu/ projects/DARCI/source_code/source_code/LanguageAnalysis/doc/edu/smu/ tspell/wordnet/package-summary.html`

9
Common Text Processing and Generation Tasks

Randomness is important in many areas of **natural language processing** (**NLP**). It is useful in assisting learning algorithms, making better predictions, and generating more accurate models. Randomness is found in the data used to train and evaluate models.

We will use the LanguageTool API to demonstrate how to perform the spell-checking and grammar- checking of a document. Both of these tasks can be useful for NLP activities. LanguageTool supports several languages.

With the very significant amount of data being generated, it is useful to have a way of summarizing text. We will illustrate one approach for performing this task utilizing the summarizer API found at `https://github.com/piravp/auto-summarizer`.

Dictionaries, as supported by the MAP interface, are used for many NLP tasks. We will illustrate how they can be inverted using POS data as the basis of the example. Support for this process is found within the Java SDK and other libraries.

In this chapter, we will cover the following recipes:

- Generating random numbers
- Spell-checking using the LanguageTool API
- Checking grammar using the LanguageTool API
- Summarizing text in a document
- Creating, inverting, and using dictionaries

Technical requirements

In this chapter, you will need to install the following software, if it has not already been installed:

- Eclipse Photon 4.8.0
- Java JDK 8 or later

We will be using the following APIs, which you will be instructed to add for each recipe as appropriate:

- Apache Commons RNG Library 1.2
- LanguageTool 4.4
- Summarizer API
- Guava: Google core libraries for Java API 27.0.1-jre

The code files for this chapter can be found at `https://github.com/PacktPublishing/Natural-Language-Processing-with-Java-Cookbook/tree/master/Chapter09`.

Generating random numbers

Random number generation is supported in several ways by the Java **SDK (Software Development Kit)**. In addition, there is some Apache support found in the Commons RNG library. In this recipe, we will demonstrate many of these techniques. We start with the use of the `Random` class and how it can be used to generate numbers beginning with a specified range. This is followed by an examination of the `Math.random` method and the `ThreadLocalRandom` class. In additon, Java 8 provides additional stream techniques for generating random numbers.

We will conclude this section with a demonstration of the Apache Commons **RNG: Random Numbers Generators** project. This API supports the generation of random numbers with the intent of providing more flexibility, speed, and higher quality results. This may prove to be a better choice for many developers. The rationale for the project and the shortcomings of the core Java `Random` class is elaborated upon at `http://commons.` `apache.org/proper/commons-rng/userguide/why_not_java_random.html`.

Getting ready

To prepare this recipe, we need to do the following:

1. Create a new Maven project
2. Add the following dependency to the project's POM file:

```
<!--
https://mvnrepository.com/artifact/org.apache.commons/commons-rng-s
imple -->
<dependency>
    <groupId>org.apache.commons</groupId>
    <artifactId>commons-rng-simple</artifactId>
    <version>1.2</version>
</dependency>
```

How to do it...

Follow these steps:

1. Add the following import statements to the project:

```
import java.util.Random;
import java.util.concurrent.ThreadLocalRandom;
import org.apache.commons.rng.UniformRandomProvider;
import org.apache.commons.rng.simple.RandomSource;
```

2. In the `main` method, add the following code sequence to create an instance of the `Random` class and generate a series of random numbers:

```
Random random = new Random();
System.out.println("Random Integer Numbers");
for(int i=0; i<5; i++) {
    System.out.println(random.nextInt());
}
```

3. Next, add the following to demonstrate how to generate a range of numbers:

```
System.out.println("Random Numbers from 0 (Inclusive) to 500
(Exclusive)");
for(int i=0; i<5; i++) {
    System.out.println(random.nextInt(500));
}
System.out.println("Random Numbers from 10 (Inclusive) to 20
(Exclusive)");
for(int i=0; i<5; i++) {
    System.out.println(random.nextInt(10)+10);
}
```

4. Add the following code sequence to the `main` method to demonstrate various random- number generation techniques:

```
System.out.println("Random double: " + Math.random());
System.out.println(ThreadLocalRandom.current().nextInt());
System.out.println(ThreadLocalRandom.current().nextDouble(10.0,
20.0));

random = new Random();
System.out.println("Random Integer Numbers Using a Stream");
for (int i = 0; i < 5; i++) {
    System.out.println(random.ints(10, 20).findFirst().getAsInt());
}

System.out.println("Random Integer Numbers Using a Stream");
random.ints(5, 10, 20).forEach(num -> System.out.println(num));
```

5. Execute the program and you will get the following output:

```
Random Integer Numbers
-1637144090
2050835838
836402032
-1577729467
544120621
```

```
Random Numbers from 0 (Inclusive) to 500 (Exclusive)
363
30
406
132
473

Random Numbers from 10 (Inclusive) to 20 (Exclusive)
11
18
15
14
10
Random double: 0.5867305663207172
-271461573
10.508849601348473
Random Integer Numbers Using a Stream
16
12
11
17
12
Random Integer Numbers Using a Stream
10
10
18
15
11
6
```

How it works...

An instance of the `Random` class was created followed by a `for` loop that was used in the `nextInt` method against the object. This generated 5 random integers as shown in the code:

```
System.out.println("Random Integer Numbers");
for(int i=0; i<5; i++) {
    System.out.println(random.nextInt());
}
```

The next two `for` loops used overloaded versions of the `nextInt` method to control the range of numbers generated. The first example used an argument of `500`. This resulted in random integers between `0` (inclusive) to `500` (exclusive) being returned. The second example used an argument of `10` but also added `10` to the generated number. This resulted in a number from `10` (inclusive) to `20` (exclusive) being displayed:

```
System.out.println("Random Numbers from 0 (Inclusive) to 500 (Exclusive)");
for(int i=0; i<5; i++) {
    System.out.println(random.nextInt(500));
}
System.out.println("Random Numbers from 10 (Inclusive) to 20 (Exclusive)");
for(int i=0; i<5; i++) {
    System.out.println(random.nextInt(10)+10);
}
```

The `Math.random` method returns a positive double value ranging from `0.0` to a value less than `1.0`. This method uses the `java.util.Random` class `nextDouble` method to generate its values. The first time it is invoked, a new instance of the `Random` class is created. The seed used by this method cannot be set. Add the next statement to the `main` method:

```
System.out.println("Random double: " + Math.random());
```

In a multi-threaded environment, there will be contention problems when the same `Random` object is used and is synchronized. This can be avoided using the `java.util.concurrent` package's `ThreadLocalRandom` class.

This class possesses essentially the same methods as the `Random` class. The class is explained as shown:

```
ThreadLocalRandom.current().someMethod
```

This prevents the accidental usage of the same instance across multiple threads. It is not possible to set the seed for this class. The following shows how the `nextInt` method is used:

```
System.out.println(ThreadLocalRandom.current().nextInt());
```

There is also a variation that uses two arguments for many of the class methods. The first argument is the lower bound of the range (inclusive). The second argument is the upper bound (exclusive). The following shows the use of the method for double numbers:

```
System.out.println(ThreadLocalRandom.current().nextDouble(10.0,20.0));
```

We can also take advantage of the `Stream` class introduced in Java 8. There are several methods that have been added to the `Random` class to support streams. In the next code sequence, we duplicate the random-number example that displays integers from 10 to 20, but we use streams instead.

The `ints` method returns an `IntStream` instance that generates the numbers. The `findFirst` method returns an `OptionalInt` value. This object can handle null values in a safer fashion than was possible before Java 8. The `getAsInt` method returns the actual integer as shown:

```
random = new Random();
System.out.println("Random Integer Numbers Using a Stream");
for (int i = 0; i < 5; i++) {
    System.out.println(random
        .ints(10, 20)
        .findFirst()
        .getAsInt());
}
```

The overloaded `ints` method that takes three arguments is shown next. The first two are for the lower and upper range of the numbers respectively. The last argument specifies how many random numbers are to be generated. This allows us to use the `forEach` method along with a lambda expression to display the numbers as shown in the following code:

```
System.out.println("Random Integer Numbers Using a Stream");
random.ints(5, 10, 20).forEach(num->System.out.println(num));
```

There's more...

The Apache Commons **RNG: Random Numbers Generators**, provides a greater selection of random-number generators. The `UniformRandomProvider` class possesses a number of methods for generating numbers. It is instantiated by using the `create` method of the `RandomSource` class. This method's argument specifies the random-number generator to use.

In the next code sequence, we used the KISS random generator, which is a port from the Marsaglia's KISS algorithm (http://www.cse.yorku.ca/~oz/marsaglia-rng.html). As before, an argument of 500 results in the generation of integers from 0 (inclusive) to 500 (exclusive):

```
UniformRandomProvider uniformRandomProvider =
    RandomSource.create(RandomSource.KISS);
System.out.println(uniformRandomProvider.nextInt(500));
```

When executed, you will get output similar to the following:

```
361
```

The `RandomSource` enumeration documentation is found at `http://commons.apache.org/proper/commons-rng/commons-rng-simple/apidocs/org/apache/commons/rng/simple/RandomSource.html`. There, you will find several other generator options.

See also

- Documentation for the `Random` class is found at `https://docs.oracle.com/javase/10/docs/api/java/util/Random.html`
- An overview of the Apache Commons RNG is found at `http://commons.apache.org/proper/commons-rng/`

Spell-checking using the LanguageTool API

LanguageTool is a tool used to check spelling and grammar within text. It is free to use as long as no more than 20,000 characters are submitted at a time. Details regarding pricing is found at `https://languagetool.org/`. In this recipe, we will demonstrate how to spell-check text.

Getting ready

To prepare this recipe, we need to do the following:

1. Create a new Maven project
2. Add the following dependency to the POM file:

```
<dependency>
    <groupId>org.languagetool</groupId>
    <artifactId>language-en</artifactId>
    <version>4.4</version>
</dependency>
```

How to do it...

Follow these steps:

1. Add the following import statements to the project:

```
import java.io.IOException;
import java.util.List;
import org.languagetool.JLanguageTool;
import org.languagetool.language.AmericanEnglish;
import org.languagetool.rules.Rule;
import org.languagetool.rules.RuleMatch;
```

2. In the `main` method, add the following code:

```
JLanguageTool jLanguageTool = new JLanguageTool(new
AmericanEnglish());
try {
    ...
} catch (IOException ex) {
    // Handle exceptions
}
```

3. LanguageTool will check for more than just spelling problems. To disable all checking except for spelling, add the following code to the `try` block:

```
for (Rule rule : jLanguageTool.getAllRules()) {
    if (!rule.isDictionaryBasedSpellingRule()) {
        jLanguageTool.disableRule(rule.getId());
    }
}
```

4. Next, add the following code to declare a test string and perform the check:

```
String text= "He dissapeared with nott even a trace. It was rong.";
List<RuleMatch> ruleMatchList = jLanguageTool.check(text);
```

5. Add the next code sequence to display the errors found:

```
for (RuleMatch ruleMatch : ruleMatchList) {
    System.out.println("Spelling problem in the sentence: ["
        + ruleMatch.getSentence().getText() + "]");
    System.out.println("'" + text.substring(
        ruleMatch.getFromPos(), ruleMatch.getToPos()) + "'"
            + " At Position: [" + ruleMatch.getFromPos() + "-"
            + ruleMatch.getToPos() + "]");
    int count = 1;
    System.out.println("--- Possible Corrections ---");
```

```
        for (String replacement : ruleMatch.getSuggestedReplacements())
{
        System.out.println("Correction " + count++ + ": " +
replacement);
    }
    System.out.println();
}
```

6. Execute the program. You will get the following output:

```
Spelling problem in the sentence: [He dissapeared with nott even a
trace. ]
'dissapeared' At Position: [3-14]
--- Possible Corrections ---
Correction 1: disappeared

Spelling problem in the sentence: [He dissapeared with nott even a
trace. ]
'nott' At Position: [20-24]
--- Possible Corrections ---
Correction 1: not
Correction 2: note
Correction 3: Mott
Correction 4: Lott
Correction 5: NLTT
Correction 6: nowt
Correction 7: not t

Spelling problem in the sentence: [It was rong.]
'rong' At Position: [46-50]
--- Possible Corrections ---
Correction 1: long
Correction 2: ring
Correction 3: song
Correction 4: Kong
Correction 5: Long
Correction 6: wrong
Correction 7: Wong
Correction 8: rang
Correction 9: Cong
Correction 10: Yong
Correction 11: gong
Correction 12: pong
Correction 13: rung
Correction 14: bong
Correction 15: prong
Correction 16: tong
Correction 17: RNG
```

```
Correction 18: Ron
Correction 19: Hong
Correction 20: ONG
Correction 21: Roeg
Correction 22: dong
```

How it works...

An instance of the `JLanguageTool` class is created based on the language being checked. For this example, we choose American English. The available languages are found in the `org.languagetool.language` package:

```
JLanguageTool jLanguageTool = new JLanguageTool(new AmericanEnglish());
```

We used the first `for` loop to disable all checking except for spelling. The `getAllRules` method returns the rules currently used by the `JLanguageTool` instance. In the `if` statement, we check each rule and if it is not a spelling rule, we use the `disableRule` method to disable it:

```
for (Rule rule : jLanguageTool.getAllRules()) {
    if (!rule.isDictionaryBasedSpellingRule()) {
        jLanguageTool.disableRule(rule.getId());
    }
}
```

We choose a simple sentence with three spelling errors. The `check` method was executed against this string, which returned a list of `RuleMatch` instances. These objects contain information about the error:

```
String text= "He dissapeared with nott even a trace. It was rong.";
List<RuleMatch> ruleMatchList = jLanguageTool.check(text);
```

We iterated through each error and displayed appropriate information about it. We started by displaying the sentence in which the error occurred. The `getMessage` method returns a detailed description of the error. A `getShortMessage` method exists, but it does not always provide a useful description of the potential error.

The `getFromPos` and `getToPos` methods return the character index from the beginning and ending of the string respectively, which is seen in the following code:

```
for (RuleMatch ruleMatch : ruleMatchList) {
    System.out.println("Spelling problem in the sentence: ["
        + ruleMatch.getSentence().getText() + "]");
    System.out.println("'" + text.substring(
```

```
                    ruleMatch.getFromPos(), ruleMatch.getToPos()) + "'"
                   +" At Position: [" + ruleMatch.getFromPos() + "-"
                   + ruleMatch.getToPos() + "]");
       ...
     }
```

The last `for` loop lists the possible words that might be appropriate to replace the misspelling. It does this by using the `getSuggestedReplacements` method:

```
int count = 1;
System.out.println("--- Possible Corrections ---");
for (String replacement : ruleMatch.getSuggestedReplacements()) {
    System.out.println("Correction " + count++ + ": " + replacement);
}
System.out.println();
```

Notice that the output often lists a large number of possible corrections. This is especially true for shorter words. For the misspelled word, *nott*, it suggested *nowt*. This is tested for *It's nowt to do with me*. The correct replacement is context dependent.

See also

- The LanguageTool Java API is found at `https://languagetool.org/development/api/index.html?org/languagetool/JLanguageTool.html`
- In the next recipe, *Checking grammar using the LanguageTool API*, we will demonstrate how to perform a grammar check

Checking grammar using the LanguageTool API

LanguageTool is a tool used to check spelling and grammar within text. It is free to use as long as no more than 20,000 characters are submitted at a time. Details regarding pricing is found at `https://languagetool.org/#Price`.

In the *Spell-checking using the LanguageTool API* recipe, we demonstrated how to perform spell-checking. In this recipe, we will demonstrate how to check the grammar of a text.

Getting ready

To prepare this recipe, we need to do the following:

1. Create a new Maven project
2. Add the following dependency to the POM file:

```
<dependency>
    <groupId>org.languagetool</groupId>
    <artifactId>language-en</artifactId>
    <version>4.4</version>
</dependency>
```

How to do it...

Follow these steps:

1. Add the following `import` statements to your project:

```
import java.io.IOException;
import java.util.List;
import org.languagetool.JLanguageTool;
import org.languagetool.language.BritishEnglish;
import org.languagetool.rules.RuleMatch;
```

2. Add the following code to your `main` method:

```
JLanguageTool jLanguageTool = new JLanguageTool(new
BritishEnglish());
try {
    String test = "This is is not good. "
        + "The boy hit ball. "
        + "He go to the school and I taught him. "
        + "Sue and Albert are married and she has been working for
a long time. "
        + "Hit ball. "
        + "He don't want no excuse.";
    List<RuleMatch> ruleMatchList = jLanguageTool.check(test);
    ...
} catch (IOException ex) {
    // Handle exceptions
}
```

3. Insert the following code segment into the `try` block:

```
for (RuleMatch ruleMatch : ruleMatchList) {
    System.out.println("Grammar problem in the sentence: ["
        + ruleMatch.getSentence().getText() + "]");
    System.out.println(ruleMatch.getMessage() + "'");
    System.out.println("At Position: [" + ruleMatch.getFromPos() +
"_"
        + ruleMatch.getToPos() + "]");
    System.out.println("Problem description: " +
        ruleMatch.getRule().getDescription());
    int count = 1;
    System.out.println("--- Possible Corrections ---");
    for (String replacement : ruleMatch.getSuggestedReplacements())
{
        System.out.println("Correction " + count++ + ": " +
replacement);
    }
    System.out.println();
}
```

4. Execute the program. You will get the following output:

```
Grammar problem in the sentence: [This is is not good. ]
Possible typo: you repeated a word'
At Position: [5-10]
Problem description: Word repetition (e.g. 'will will')
--- Possible Corrections ---
Correction 1: is

Grammar problem in the sentence: [He go to the school and I taught
him. ]
The pronoun 'He' is usually used with a third-person or a past
tense verb: <suggestion>goes</suggestion>,
<suggestion>went</suggestion>.'
At Position: [42-44]
Problem description: Agreement error: Non-third person/past tense
verb with 'he/she/it' or a pronoun
--- Possible Corrections ---
Correction 1: goes
Correction 2: went

Grammar problem in the sentence: [Sue and Albert are married and
she has been working for a long time. ]
Use a comma before 'and' if it connects two independent clauses
(unless they are closely connected and short).'
At Position: [96-107]
Problem description: comma between independent clauses
```

```
--- Possible Corrections ---
Correction 1: married, and

Grammar problem in the sentence: [He don't want no excuse.]
Double negatives are discouraged in standard English. Can you
reformulate this phrase or is a comma missing?'
At Position: [163-172]
Problem description: Double negative (example, 'not... nothing'
instead of 'not... anything')
--- Possible Corrections ---
```

How it works...

An instance of the JLanguageTool class was created based on the language being checked. For this example, we choose British English. The available languages are found in the org.languagetool.language package. The first string consisted of several sentences, some containing potential grammatical errors:

```
JLanguageTool jLanguageTool = new JLanguageTool(new BritishEnglish());
String test = "This is is not good. "
    + "The boy hit ball. "
    + "He go to the school and I taught him. "
    + "Sue and Albert are married and she has been working for a long time.
"
    + "Hit ball. "
    + "He don't want no excuse.";
```

The check method performed the actual checking and returned a list of RuleMatch instances, each containing information about an error:

```
List<RuleMatch> ruleMatchList = jLanguageTool.check(test);
```

We iterated through the list and displayed information about each error. We used the getSentence then the getText method to display the sentence containing the error. The getMessage method returns a detailed description of the error. A getShortMessage method exists, but it does not always provide a useful description.

The getFromPos and getToPos methods returned the character index from the beginning and the end of the string, respectively. The getDescription differs from the getMessage method in that it provides a more generic description of the problem:

```
for (RuleMatch ruleMatch : ruleMatchList) {
    System.out.println("Grammar problem in the sentence: ["
        + ruleMatch.getSentence().getText() + "]");
    System.out.println(ruleMatch.getMessage() + "'");
```

```
      System.out.println("At Position: [" + ruleMatch.getFromPos() + "-"
          + ruleMatch.getToPos() + "]");
      System.out.println("Problem description: " +
          ruleMatch.getRule().getDescription());
      ...
  }
```

The last sequence displays suggested corrections to the problem. Notice that, with the last error, there were no suggestions:

```
int count = 1;
System.out.println("--- Possible Corrections ---");
for (String replacement : ruleMatch.getSuggestedReplacements()) {
    System.out.println("Correction " + count++ + ": " + replacement);
}
System.out.println();
```

See also

- The LanguageTool Java API is found at `https://languagetool.org/development/api/index.html?org/languagetool/JLanguageTool.html`

Summarizing text in a document

The automatic summarization of a document can be a useful feature for many applications. In this recipe, we will examine how this can be done using code found at `https://github.com/piravp/auto-summarizer`. We will show you how to use the techniques supported by the project and explain how the summary is performed.

Getting ready

To prepare this recipe, we need to do the following:

1. Create a new Java project
2. Rename your package `main.java`
3. Download the files from `https://github.com/piravp/auto-summarizer`
4. Extract the files to a convenient location
5. Copy the source files from the directory `C:\...\auto-summarizer-master\src\main\java` and add them to the `main.java` package

6. Create a directory called `files` off the root level of your project
7. Copy the files `file-medium_en.txt` and `stopwords-en.txt` from the files subdirectory in the extracted directory, and save it in the `files` directory

How to do it...

Follow these steps:

1. Add the following `import` statement to your project:

   ```
   import java.util.ArrayList;
   ```

2. In the `main` method, add this:

   ```
   String filePath = "files/file-medium_en.txt";
   String languageCode = "EN";
   int lengthOfSummary = 5;
   ```

3. Next, insert the following code into the `main` method:

   ```
   SentenceBuilder sentenceBuilder = new SentenceBuilder(languageCode,
   filePath);
   WordBuilder wordBuilder = new WordBuilder();
   wordBuilder.getWords(languageCode, filePath);
   wordBuilder.removeStopWords(languageCode);
   wordBuilder.doCount(WordBuilder.getCleanWordObjects());
   wordBuilder.findTopNWords(lengthOfSummary);
   ```

4. Add the next code sequence to display the summary:

   ```
   ArrayList<Sentence> sentenceList =
   sentenceBuilder.getSentenceObjects();
   ArrayList<Word> wordList = WordBuilder.getMaxWordList();
   StringBuilder textSummary = new StringBuilder();
   for (int i = 0; i < wordList.size(); i++) {
       int index = wordList.get(i).getBelongingSentenceNo();
       textSummary.append(sentenceList.get(index).getText() + " ");
   }
   System.out.println(textSummary);
   ```

5. Execute the program. You will get the following output:

   ```
   In this report, the reader will be presented a life-cycle
   assessment on the iPhone 6 manufactured by Apple. While in use, the
   phone will require energy for recharging. A way to avoid
   unnecessary emissions caused from this could be by offering a new
   ```

```
pair of earplugs only to users whom have never owned an iPhone
before. The reader will be presented both positive and negative
aspects of the product. The phone is equipped with modern features,
both hardware and design wise, yet at what cost.
```

How it works...

We used the `file-medium_en.txt` though most other files that need to be summarized can be used. These files contain texts of varying length describing the iPhone 6 development. A language code of EN was used to specify English, and the summary length was set to 5. This restricts the number of sentences in the summary to 5. The only other language supported is **Norwegian (NO)**:

```
String filePath = "files/file-medium_en.txt";
String languageCode = "EN";
int lengthOfSummary = 5;
```

An instance of the `SentenceBuilder` class was created based on the language code and file. The `SentenceBuilder` class will create an internal `ArrayList` of `Sentence` objects based on the contents of the file. A `Sentence` object is a simple representation of a sentence:

```
SentenceBuilder sentenceBuilder = new SentenceBuilder(languageCode,
filePath);
```

Next, an instance of the `WordBuilder` class was instantiated. This class effectively splits sentences into `Word` objects that contain information about individual words. The following methods were invoked:

- `getWords`: Returns a list of `Word` objects based on the language code and the file supplied as arguments to the method.
- `removeStopWords`: Returns a list of `Word` objects based on the language code with the stop words removed. The stop words are found in the `files` directory. For English, it uses the `stopwords-en.txt` file.
- `doCount`: Computes the occurrence frequency for the words being processed.
- `findTopNWords`: Builds an internal list of the top *N* words where *N* is specified by the `lengthOfSummary` variable.

The code for the `WordBuilder` class is seen as follows:

```
WordBuilder wordBuilder = new WordBuilder();
wordBuilder.getWords(languageCode, filePath);
wordBuilder.removeStopWords(languageCode);
wordBuilder.doCount(WordBuilder.getCleanWordObjects());
wordBuilder.findTopNWords(lengthOfSummary);
```

The `getSentenceObjects` method was invoked next, which returns an `ArrayList` of `Sentence` objects:

```
ArrayList<Sentence> sentenceList = sentenceBuilder.getSentenceObjects();
```

The `getMaxWordList` was then called, which returned an `ArrayList` of `Word` objects. This simply returned the list of `Words` created by the `findTopNWords` method. An instance of the `StringBuilder` class was created to build the summary text. For each word found in the `Word` list, the text for any sentence containing that word is appended to the summary text. The summary text was then displayed:

```
ArrayList<Word> wordList = WordBuilder.getMaxWordList();
StringBuilder textSummary = new StringBuilder();
for (int i = 0; i < wordList.size(); i++) {
    int index = wordList.get(i).getBelongingSentenceNo();
    textSummary.append(sentenceList.get(index).getText() + " ");
}
System.out.println(textSummary);
```

This is a fairly straightforward approach to summarizing text, but it will suffice for many problem domains.

There's more...

There are a number of auxiliary methods available to provide different ways of displaying the summary and to provide additional information about the analysis. The `Summarizer` class's `createSummary` method is a quick way of displaying the summary as demonstrated next:

```
Summarizer summarizer = new Summarizer();
summarizer.createSummary();
```

When this code is executed, you will get the following output. However, it is not as easy to read as the previous example:

```
No. 0 Text: In this report, the reader will be presented a life-cycle
assessment on the iPhone 6 manufactured by Apple.
No. 15 Text: While in use, the phone will require energy for recharging.
No. 24 Text: A way to avoid unnecessary emissions caused from this could be
by offering a new pair of earplugs only to users whom have never owned an
iPhone before.
No. 1 Text: The reader will be presented both positive and negative aspects
of the product.
No. 8 Text: The phone is equipped with modern features, both hardware and
design wise, yet at what cost.
```

A `DebugClass` class supports numerous types of analysis. The `printInfo` method generates a rather lengthy list of information about the analysis:

```
DebugClass.printInfo();
```

When this statement is executed, you will get the following abbreviated output:

```
--------------Raw lines from file---------------
In this report, the reader will be presented a life-cycle assessment on the
iPhone 6 manufactured by Apple. The reader will be presented both positive
and negative aspects of the product.
Considering the different aspects, there will be a discussion on
improvements needed in order to improve the sustainability of the product.
...
With a big company like Apple there will be consequences connected to the
environment both in terms of the energy use and in terms of the gas
emissions. Fortunately, Apple has been aware of their negative impact on
the nature and has taken visible action. Despite of this, as this report
points out, they have areas they can improve on. They should specifically
focus on encouraging suppliers and other partners to use renewable forms of
energy.
With a company like Apple, even the smallest change can pose a big
difference on a bigger scale and over a longer period.

----------Tree Map showing every sentence-----------
No. 0 Text: In this report, the reader will be presented a life-cycle
assessment on the iPhone 6 manufactured by Apple.
No. 1 Text: The reader will be presented both positive and negative aspects
of the product.
No. 2 Text: Considering the different aspects, there will be a discussion
on improvements needed in order to improve the sustainability of the
product.
...
No. 50 Text: Despite of this, as this report points out, they have areas
```

```
they can improve on.
No. 51 Text: They should specifically focus on encouraging suppliers and
other partners to use renewable forms of energy.
No. 52 Text: With a company like Apple, even the smallest change can pose a
big difference on a bigger scale and over a longer period.

----------Word list(dirty)-----------
0 in ...belongs to sentence 0
1 this ...belongs to sentence 0
2 report ...belongs to sentence 0
...
915 a ...belongs to sentence 52
916 longer ...belongs to sentence 52
917 period ...belongs to sentence 52

----------Word list after removing stop words(clean)-----------
0 report ...belongs to sentence 0
1 reader ...belongs to sentence 0
2 will ...belongs to sentence 0
3 presented ...belongs to sentence 0
...
429 scale ...belongs to sentence 52
430 longer ...belongs to sentence 52
431 period ...belongs to sentence 52
```

The `printFreqMap` method displays how often each word appears in the text:

```
DebugClass.printFreqMap();
```

The following abbreviated output will be displayed when the statement is executed:

```
----------Each word and number of occurrences-----------
Word: report Occurrences: 2 ...belongs to sentence 0
Word: reader Occurrences: 2 ...belongs to sentence 0
Word: will Occurrences: 6 ...belongs to sentence 0
...
Word: scale Occurrences: 1 ...belongs to sentence 52
Word: longer Occurrences: 1 ...belongs to sentence 52
Word: period Occurrences: 1 ...belongs to sentence 52
Size of keyset is 271
```

A shorter set of statistical output is displayed by the `printStats` method:

```
DebugClass.printStats();
```

When this statement is executed, you will get the following output:

```
----------------Stats--------------------
Number of lines: 23
```

```
Number of sentences: 53
Number of words: 918
Number of stop-words removed: 486
Number of words without stop-words: 432
Number of unique words w/o stop-words: 271
```

The top *N* words and information regarding these words is provided by the following code:

```
summarizer.sortTopNWordList();
DebugClass.printTopNWords();
```

When these statements are executed, you will get the following output:

```
------------------Top N words------------------
'apple' is max with 17 occurrences. It belongs to sentence 0.
'product' is max with 7 occurrences. It belongs to sentence 1.
'phone' is max with 5 occurrences. It belongs to sentence 8.
'energy' is max with 10 occurrences. It belongs to sentence 15.
'emissions' is max with 8 occurrences. It belongs to sentence 24.
```

See also

The API documentation for this library can be found in the extracted `docs` sub-directory. Open the `index.html` file in a browser to bring up the main Javadoc page.

Creating, inverting, and using dictionaries

Dictionaries hold key-value pairs where the key is the index. An inverted dictionary is one where the values become the keys and the keys becomes the values. Dictionaries are frequently used to support many NLP tasks. For example, in the previous recipe, *Summarizing text in a document*, the `LinkedHashMap` class was used internally to maintain the word frequency with respect to the number of occurrences for text.

In this recipe, we will explore how dictionaries and inverted dictionaries are handled in Java. We will use the Java core SDK and the Guava (Google core libraries for Java and API for our libraries). The Guava website is found at `https://github.com/google/guava`.

Problems can arise when the values are not unique. We will use the Java 8 Streams to address these issues.

Getting ready

To prepare this recipe, we need to do the following:

1. Create a new Maven project
2. Add the following dependency to your project:

```
<dependency>
    <groupId>com.google.guava</groupId>
    <artifactId>guava</artifactId>
    <version>27.0.1-jre</version>
</dependency>
```

How to do it...

Follow these steps:

1. Add the following imports to your project:

```
import java.util.HashMap;
import java.util.List;
import java.util.Map;
import java.util.stream.Collectors;
import com.google.common.collect.BiMap;
import com.google.common.collect.HashBiMap;
```

2. Add the following declaration to the `main` method:

```
Map<String, String> initalHashMap = new HashMap<>();
```

3. Insert the following code to populate a `HashMap` and invert it:

```
initalHashMap.put("The", "DT");
initalHashMap.put("dog", "NN");
initalHashMap.put("eats", "VBZ");
initalHashMap.put("regularly", "RB");
Map<String, String> invertedHashMap = new HashMap<>();
for(Map.Entry<String, String> entry : initalHashMap.entrySet()){
    invertedHashMap.put(entry.getValue(), entry.getKey());
}
```

4. Next, add the next code sequence to display the results:

```
System.out.println(initalHashMap);
System.out.println(invertedHashMap);
System.out.println();
```

5. Execute the program. You will get the following output:

```
{The=DT, regularly=RB, eats=VBZ, dog=NN}
{DT=The, RB=regularly, NN=dog, VBZ=eats}
```

How it works...

We created an `HashMap` instance where both the key and the values are strings.

```
Map<String, String> initalHashMap = new HashMap<>();
```

We used the sentence *The dog eats everything* to demonstrate the process. The POS tags for these words are initialized with the `put` methods:

```
initalHashMap.put("The", "DT");
initalHashMap.put("dog", "NN");
initalHashMap.put("eats", "VBZ");
initalHashMap.put("regularly", "RB");
```

The inverted `HashMap` was then created using a `for-each` loop. Each entry is processed one at a time with the key and value reversed:

```
Map<String, String> invertedHashMap = new HashMap<>();
for(Map.Entry<String, String> entry : initalHashMap.entrySet()) {
    invertedHashMap.put(entry.getValue(), entry.getKey());
}
```

The two maps were then displayed.

There's more...

The Guava API also provides a simple way of inverting dictionaries. In the code that follows, we use the `BiMap` class to hold the POS tags. This class automatically maintains the inverse mapping. The class's name is short for *bidirectional map*. The `put` method adds the initial mappings:

```
BiMap<String, String> initialBiMap = HashBiMap.create();
initialBiMap.put("The", "DT");
initialBiMap.put("dog", "NN");
initialBiMap.put("eats", "VBZ");
initialBiMap.put("regularly", "RB");
```

The inverse is readily available through the `inverse` method as shown next. The two mappings are then displayed:

```
BiMap<String, String> invertedBiMap = initialBiMap.inverse();
System.out.println(initialBiMap);
System.out.println(invertedBiMap);
System.out.println();
```

When this code is executed, you will get the following output:

```
{The=DT, dog=NN, eats=VBZ, regularly=RB}
{DT=The, NN=dog, VBZ=eats, RB=regularly}
```

Yet another technique for creating an inverse is explained using a Java 8 stream. We reused the `initalHashMap` HashMap and created a `Stream` instance using the `entrySet` and `stream` methods. The `collect` method reduces the stream using the `Collectors` class's `toMap` method. This method accumulates elements of the stream using its function arguments. `Function` is a functional interface whose `apply` method accepts a single argument and returns a single value. The `getValue` and `getKey` methods match this signature and create the inverse `Map` instance by using the initial value as the key and the initial key as the value:

```
Map<String, String> mapInversed = initalHashMap.entrySet()
    .stream()
    .collect(Collectors.toMap(
Map.Entry::getValue,
Map.Entry::getKey));
System.out.println(initalHashMap);
System.out.println(mapInversed);
System.out.println();
```

When this code is executed, you will get the following output:

```
{The=DT, regularly=RB, eats=VBZ, dog=NN}
{DT=The, RB=regularly, NN=dog, VBZ=eats}
```

When the values of a dictionary are not unique, we need to use a different technique to invert it. In the next example, we add multiple POS tags for the sentence *Time flies like an arrow*. This sentence is ambiguous and has several different potential meanings (https://www.google.com/search?q=nlp+pos+Time+flies+like+an+arrow.&rlz=1C1CHBF_
enUS810US810&tbm=isch&source=iu&ictx=1&fir=E0bp39EiRt1sZM%253A%252Cqcb2YiHxVV0q
CM%252C_&usg=AI4_-
kR6VyTKC69iCWUoGRn9WCL5PRn0Qw&sa=X&ved=2ahUKEwictpGy2ubfAhVLmK0KHaOXDMwQ9QEwCno
ECAQQBg#imgrc=E0bp39EiRt1sZM).

In the next set of code, we set up the `initalHashMap` using the possible POS tags for the sentence. We have used simple one-letter tags where each grouping of `put` operations reflects a different set of POS tags that could describe the sentence:

```
initalHashMap = new HashMap<>();
initalHashMap.put("Time", "N");
initalHashMap.put("flies", "V");
initalHashMap.put("like", "P");
initalHashMap.put("an", "D");
initalHashMap.put("arrow", "N");

initalHashMap.put("Time", "V");
initalHashMap.put("flies", "N");
initalHashMap.put("like", "P");
initalHashMap.put("an", "D");
initalHashMap.put("arrow", "N");

initalHashMap.put("Time", "N");
initalHashMap.put("flies", "N");
initalHashMap.put("like", "V");
initalHashMap.put("an", "D");
initalHashMap.put("arrow", "N");

initalHashMap.put("Time", "V");
initalHashMap.put("flies", "V");
initalHashMap.put("like", "V");
initalHashMap.put("an", "D");
initalHashMap.put("arrow", "N");
```

Next, we use a similar process to that used in the previous example. A stream and the `Collectors` class is used to generate the inverse map. One difference is that we use the `Collectors` class's `mapping` method as the second argument of a `groupingBy` method to add multiple keys as values:

```
Map<String, List<String>> invertedMap = initalHashMap.entrySet()
    .stream()
    .collect(Collectors.groupingBy(Map.Entry::getValue,
Collectors.mapping(Map.Entry::getKey, Collectors.toList())));
System.out.println(initalHashMap);
System.out.println(invertedMap);
```

When this code is executed, you will get the following output:

```
{flies=V, like=V, arrow=N, Time=V, an=D}
{D=[an], V=[flies, like, Time], N=[arrow]}
```

See also

- The `java.base` module for the `java.util.stream` package is found at `https:/ /docs.oracle.com/javase/10/docs/api/index.html?java/util/package- summary.html`. You will find the documentation of the `MAP` interface there.
- The `com.google.common.collect` package documentation is found at `https:/ /google.github.io/guava/releases/19.0/api/docs/index.html?com/google/ common/collect/package-summary.html`.

Extracting Data for Use in NLP Analysis

10

Most NLP tasks are concerned with the analysis of data. In this chapter, we will illustrate several approaches to acquiring data from multiple sources. This includes processing data from an HTML page and PDF, Word, and Excel documents. Each of these techniques involves connecting to a data source and then extracting the data from that source. For complex documents, such as Wikipedia articles or a Word document, we will be faced with choices in terms of what type of data we want to retrieve.

For example, with an HTML document, we may be interested in the actual text and possibly the HTML markup. For a document containing a table of contents, we may want to process that information separately. To extract text form a Wikipedia article, we treat it as an HTML document.

These recipes are an introduction to the topic. Most of these data sources can be quite complex. We will only be able to provide an introduction to the approach and provide links to resources where you can find additional information.

In this chapter we will cover the following recipes:

- Connecting to an HTML page
- Extracting text and metadata from an HTML page
- Extracting text from a PDF document
- Extracting metadata from a PDF document
- Extracting text from a Word document
- Extracting metadata from a Word document
- Extracting text from a spreadsheet
- Extracting metadata from a spreadsheet

Technical requirements

In this chapter, you will need to install the following software, if it has not already been installed:

- Eclipse Photon 4.8.0
- Java JDK 8 or later

We will be using the following APIs, which you will be instructed to add for each recipe as appropriate:

- Jsoup 1.8.3
- Apache PDFBox API 2.0.13

The code files for this chapter can be found at `https://github.com/PacktPublishing/Natural-Language-Processing-with-Java-Cookbook/tree/master/Chapter10`.

Connecting to an HTML page

Sometimes, the data we need to process is located in one or more web pages. In this recipe, we will demonstrate how to connect to a web page. In addition, we will extract the contents of that page.

Getting ready

To prepare, we need to create a new Java project.

How to do it...

Follow these steps:

1. Insert the following `import` statements to the project:

```java
import java.io.BufferedReader;
import java.io.IOException;
import java.io.InputStream;
import java.io.InputStreamReader;
import java.net.HttpURLConnection;
import java.net.MalformedURLException;
import java.net.URL;
import java.util.Date;
```

2. In the `main` method, add the following `try` block:

```java
try {
    ...
} catch (MalformedURLException ex) {
    // Handle exceptions
} catch (IOException ex) {
    // Handle exceptions
}
```

3. Insert the next code sequence to establish a connection to the web page:

```java
URL url = new URL("https://en.wikipedia.org/wiki/HTML");
    HttpURLConnection httpURLConnection = (HttpURLConnection)
url.openConnection();
httpURLConnection.setRequestMethod("GET");
httpURLConnection.connect();
```

4. Next, add the following code to read in the contents of the page and display it:

```java
InputStreamReader inputStreamReader =
    new InputStreamReader((InputStream)
httpURLConnection.getContent());
BufferedReader bufferedReader = new
BufferedReader(inputStreamReader);
StringBuilder stringBuilder = new StringBuilder();
String line = "";
while (line != null) {
    line = bufferedReader.readLine();
    stringBuilder.append(line + "\n");
}
System.out.println(stringBuilder.toString());
```

5. Execute the program. You will get the following abbreviated output:

```
<div role="navigation" class="navbox" aria-
labelledby="ISO_standards_by_standard_number" ...
...
<ul><li><a href="/wiki/ISO_1" title="ISO 1">1</a></li>
<li><a href="/wiki/ISO_2" title="ISO 2">2</a></li>
<li><a href="/wiki/Renard_series" title="Renard series">3</a></li>
...
<script>(window.RLQ=window.RLQ||[]).push(function(){mw.config.set({
"wgBackendResponseTime":114,"wgHostname":"mw1333"});});</script>
    </body>
</html>
```

How it works...

The URL class represents a URL for a page. In this case, we used Wikipedia's HTML page. The openConnection method returns an instance of an HttpURLConnection class. This class is a wrapper around a socket that represents a connection to the Wikipedia server. The setRequestMethod is an HTTP command that requests the data for an HTML page. The connect method establishes a connection to the server:

```
URL url = new URL("https://en.wikipedia.org/wiki/HTML");
HttpURLConnection httpURLConnection = (HttpURLConnection)
url.openConnection();
httpURLConnection.setRequestMethod("GET");
httpURLConnection.connect();
```

With connect, the getContent method returns an InputStreamReader instance that permitted us to read the contents of the page. We buffered the input using the BufferedReader class. An instance of the StringBuilder class was used to build up the contents of the page one line at a time. The contents were then displayed:

```
InputStreamReader inputStreamReader = new InputStreamReader(
    (InputStream) httpURLConnection.getContent());
BufferedReader bufferedReader = new BufferedReader(inputStreamReader);
StringBuilder stringBuilder = new StringBuilder();
String line = "";
while (line != null) {
    line = bufferedReader.readLine();
    stringBuilder.append(line + "\n");
}
System.out.println(stringBuilder.toString());
```

There's more...

There are numerous other methods that provide additional information regarding the connection and page. The following are a few that may be of interest:

- getContentLength: Returns the length of the data being transferred
- getContentType: Returns the content type
- getDate: Returns the date of the page
- getExpiration: Indicates when the page will no longer be considered valid
- getLastModified: Shows when the page was last modified

Add the following code to the main function to illustrate these functions for the page. The Date class is used to convert the integer date returned by the last three methods into a more readable form:

```
System.out.println(httpURLConnection.getContentLength());
System.out.println(httpURLConnection.getContentType());
System.out.println(new Date(httpURLConnection.getDate()));
System.out.println(new Date(httpURLConnection.getExpiration()));
System.out.println(new Date(httpURLConnection.getLastModified()));
```

When this code is executed, you will get output similar to the following:

```
349370
text/html; charset=UTF-8
Wed Jan 16 20:50:58 CST 2019
Wed Dec 31 18:00:00 CST 1969
Mon Jan 14 13:01:07 CST 2019
```

See also

- The Javadoc for the HttpURLConnection class is found at https://docs.oracle.com/javase/10/docs/api/java/net/HttpURLConnection.html

Extracting text and metadata from an HTML page

We will use **Jsoup** to access the contents of an HTML page. Jsoup (`https://jsoup.org/`) is an API that works with HTML. It provides numerous classes and methods to access HTML pages. The **Document Object Model (DOM)** represents the contents of a web page.

It allows access to the contents of a web page and can be used from multiple languages. Jsoup provides access to DOM through Java methods.

Metadata is data about an entity. For a web page, this may include information such as the character encoding used for the page. We will also illustrate how this type of information can be obtained using Jsoup.

Getting ready

To prepare this recipe, we need to do the following:

1. Create a new Maven project
2. Add the following dependency to the project:

```
<!-- https://mvnrepository.com/artifact/org.jsoup/jsoup -->
<dependency>
    <groupId>org.jsoup</groupId>
    <artifactId>jsoup</artifactId>
    <version>1.8.3</version>
</dependency>
```

3. Create a file called `page.html`, and add the following to the file:

```
<!DOCTYPE html>
<html>
    <head>
        <title>A title</title>
        <meta charset="UTF-8">
    </head>
    <body>
        <div id="div1">Interesting text</div>
        <img src="somepicture.jpg" alt="Picture 1" width="500px"
height="600px">
        <img src="someotherpicture.jpg" alt="Picture 2">
        <a href="https://www.somepage.com">Visit Us!</a>
        <a href="https://www.someotherpage.com">Visit Them!</a>
```

```
        </body>
    </html>
```

4. Save it in the project's root directory

How to do it...

Follow these steps:

1. Add the following imports to the project:

```
import java.io.File;
import java.io.IOException;
import org.jsoup.Jsoup;
import org.jsoup.nodes.Document;
import org.jsoup.nodes.Element;
import org.jsoup.select.Elements;
```

2. Add the following try block to the main method:

```
try {
    String htmlText =
Jsoup.connect("https://en.wikipedia.org/wiki/Language").get().html(
);
    System.out.println(htmlText.substring(0, 100));
    System.out.println();
} catch (IOException e) {
    // Handle exceptions
}
```

3. Execute the program. You will get the following output:

```
<!doctype html>
<html class="client-nojs" lang="en" dir="ltr">
 <head>
  <meta charset="UTF-8">
```

How it works...

The `Jsoup` class's `connect` method is connected to the Wikipedia language web page. It returned a `Connection` object. The `get` method was applied and returned a `Document` object representing the page. The `html` method returned the text for the page:

```
String htmlText = Jsoup.connect(
    "https://en.wikipedia.org/wiki/Language").get().html();
```

The text was then displayed using only the first 100 characters of the page to minimize the output for this example:

```
System.out.println(htmlText.substring(0, 100));
```

Removing the `substring` method will display the HTML code for the entire page.

There's more...

To illustrate how other `Jsoup` methods work, we will use a smaller web page: `page.html`. Insert the following statement at the end of the `try` block. The `parse` method will create a `Document` object representing the contents of the HTML file. The method takes two arguments. The first is a `File` object for the file and the second is the encoding format for the file:

```
Document document = Jsoup.parse(new File("page.html"), "utf-8");
```

Insert the following code to display the contents of the page. The `html` method returns the text:

```
String data = document.html();
System.out.println(data);
```

When this code is executed, you will get the following output:

```
<!doctype html>
<html>
 <head>
  <title>A title</title>
  <meta charset="UTF-8">
 </head>
 <body>
  <div id="div1">
   Interesting text
  </div>
  <img src="somepicture.jpg" alt="Picture 1" width="500px" height="600px">
```

```
<img src="someotherpicture.jpg" alt="Picture 2">
<a href="https://www.somepage.com">Visit Us!</a>
<a href="https://www.someotherpage.com">Visit Them!</a>
</body>
</html>
```

We can also return just the contents of the body tag using the body method as shown here:

```
System.out.println(document.body());
```

When this code is executed, you will get the following output:

```
<body>
<div id="div1">
 Interesting text
</div>
<img src="somepicture.jpg" alt="Picture 1" width="500px" height="600px">
<img src="someotherpicture.jpg" alt="Picture 2">
<a href="https://www.somepage.com">Visit Us!</a>
<a href="https://www.someotherpage.com">Visit Them!</a>
</body>
```

If we are only interested in the text that makes up the page, and not the HTML tags, we can use the body method to return a Document object and then use the text method to return just the text as shown here:

```
htmlText = document.body().text();
System.out.println("Body Text: [" + htmlText + "]");
```

You will get the following output:

```
Body Text: [Interesting text Visit Us! Visit Them!]
```

Metadata about a page can be obtained using a variety of Document methods. In the example code sequence, we return the title of the page:

```
String title = document.title();
System.out.printf("Title: %s%n", title);
```

When executed, we will get the following:

```
Title: A title
```

The charset method returns the value for the character encoding and the location method returns the location of the file as shown next:

```
String charsetName = document.charset().name();
String location = document.location();
```

```
System.out.println("Charset: " + charsetName);
System.out.println("Location: " + location);
```

We will obtain the following output when the code is executed where the location is dependent on where the file is found:

```
Charset: UTF-8
Location: ...\page.html
```

HTML links are common to web pages. The `select` method, shown next, will return an `Elements` object representing the elements specified by the argument of the method's single argument. In this example we used, `a[href]`, which specifies the links HTML tag:

```
Elements links = document.select("a[href]");
```

The `for` loop iterates through these links displaying one at a time:

```
for (Element link : links) {
    System.out.println("Link: " + link.attr("href")
        + "   Text : " + link.text());
}
```

This code will give us the following output:

```
Link: https://www.somepage.com   Text : Visit Us!
Link: https://www.someotherpage.com   Text : Visit Them!
```

We can display a list of the images used in the page using a similar approach. As shown next, we used a regular expression to specify possible file extensions as the argument of the `select` method:

```
Elements images = document.select("img[src~=(?i)\\.(png|jpe?g|gif)]");
for (Element image : images) {
    System.out.println("Source File Name : " + image.attr("src"));
    System.out.println("Height : " + image.attr("height"));
    System.out.println("Width : " + image.attr("width"));
    System.out.println("Alternate Text : " + image.attr("alt"));
    System.out.println();
}
```

The output of this code follows. The second image did not have a height or width specified, so that information is left empty:

```
Source File Name : somepicture.jpg
Height : 600px
Width : 500px
Alternate Text : Picture 1
```

```
Source File Name : someotherpicture.jpg
Height :
Width :
Alternate Text : Picture 2
```

See also

- The API documentation for Jsoup is found at `https://jsoup.org/apidocs/overview-summary.html`

Extracting text from a PDF document

In this recipe, we will learn how to extract text and images from a PDF document. The process of extracting metadata from a PDF document is found in the next recipe: *Extracting metadata from a PDF document*.

We will use the **Apache PDFBox API** to illustrate this process. This API is fairly complex. While we will only show how to extract text and images, more detailed information can be extracted. This API provides a series of classes and methods to identify and manipulate the structure and contents of PDF documents. To create a sample PDF document, we will use Microsoft Word. However, there are other ways of creating PDF documents, including **PDFBox**.

Getting ready

To prepare this recipe, we need to do the following:

1. Create a new Maven project.
2. Add the following dependency to the project's POM file:

```
<dependency>
    <groupId>org.apache.pdfbox</groupId>
    <artifactId>pdfbox</artifactId>
    <version>2.0.13</version>
</dependency>
```

3. Create the following Word file and name it `PDFFile`. Notice that there is a page break before the text, `Start of second page`, that is not shown here. You can use any image files for the images:

```
A simple PDF document:
Bullet 1
Bullet 2
Bullet 3
```

```
Image 1
```

```
Image 2
End of first page.
Start of second page
```

```
Image 3
The end of the document.
```

4. Modify the document properties as shown next. How you edit the document properties depends on the version of Word you are using. The following screenshot shows the properties for the document:

Properties ˅	
Size	29.2KB
Pages	2
Words	31
Total Editing Time	1193 Minutes
Title	The Ttile
Tags	sample java
Comments	This is a comment
Template	Normal.dotm
Status	In work
Categories	NLP
Subject	The subject
Hyperlink Base	Add text
Company	My Company

Related Dates

Last Modified	Today, 1:14 PM
Created	Yesterday, 5:27 PM
Last Printed	Today, 1:14 PM

5. Save the file in the root directory of the project.
6. Export the file as a PDF document. You can also create the PDF file using any other technique that is available to you.

How to do it...

Follow these steps:

1. Add the following imports to the project:

```
import java.awt.image.BufferedImage;
import java.awt.image.RenderedImage;
import java.io.File;
import java.io.IOException;
import java.util.ArrayList;
import java.util.List;
import javax.imageio.ImageIO;
import org.apache.pdfbox.cos.COSName;
import org.apache.pdfbox.pdmodel.PDDocument;
import org.apache.pdfbox.pdmodel.PDPage;
```

```
import org.apache.pdfbox.pdmodel.PDResources;
import org.apache.pdfbox.pdmodel.graphics.PDXObject;
import org.apache.pdfbox.pdmodel.graphics.form.PDFormXObject;
import org.apache.pdfbox.pdmodel.graphics.image.PDImageXObject;
import org.apache.pdfbox.rendering.PDFRenderer;
import org.apache.pdfbox.text.PDFTextStripper;
```

2. Add the following `try` block to the `main` method:

```
try {
    File file = new File("PDFFile.pdf");
    PDDocument pdDocument = PDDocument.load(file);
    ...
    pdDocument.close();
} catch (IOException ex) {
    // Handle exceptions
    ex.printStackTrace();
}
```

3. Insert the next code sequence to extract and display the document's text:

```
PDFTextStripper pdfTextStripper = new PDFTextStripper();
String documentText = pdfTextStripper.getText(pdDocument);
System.out.println(documentText);
```

4. Execute the program. You will get the following output:

```
The Sample Document

A simple PF document.
• Bullet 1
• Bullet 2
• Bullet 3

Image 1

Image 2
End of first page.
Start of second page

Image 3
The end of the document.
```

How it works...

A File object was created representing the PDFFile.pdf. The PDDocument class's static load method created an instance of PDDocument that holds the contents of the file. The close method was used to close the PDDocument once we were through with it:

```
File file = new File("PDFFile.pdf");
PDDocument pdDocument = PDDocument.load(file);
```

The PDFTextStripper class extracted the text from the document. The text was then displayed:

```
PDFTextStripper pdfTextStripper = new PDFTextStripper();
String documentText = pdfTextStripper.getText(pdDocument);
System.out.println(documentText);
```

There's more...

Other information can be obtained from the document. The following code illustrates how we can extract the images from the document. We start by creating an instance of the PDFRenderer class:

```
PDFRenderer pdfRenderer = new PDFRenderer(pdDocument);
```

Add the following code to extract each image and save it to a file. Each RenderedImage instance represents an image. The ImageIO class's write method will write each image out to the project's root directory. This method takes three arguments: the RenderedImage instance, the file type as a string, and a File for the file to be created:

```
System.out.println("Images");
List<RenderedImage> renderedImages = getImagesFromPDF(pdDocument);
for (int i = 0; i < renderedImages.size(); i++) {
    RenderedImage renderedImage = renderedImages.get(i);
    String imageFileName = "image" + i + ".jpg";
    System.out.println(imageFileName);
    ImageIO.write(renderedImage, "PNG", new File(imageFileName));
}
```

The following methods, `getImagesFromPDF` and `getImagesFromResources`, were adapted from https://stackoverflow.com/questions/8705163/extract-images-from-pdf-using-pdfbox.

The `getImagesFromPDF` method creates a list of the `RenderedImage` instances contained in the document. The `PDDocument` class's `getPages` method returned a `PDPage` instance that corresponds to a page of the document. Its `getResources` method returns that page's resources including the images. The `getImagesFromResources` was invoked to get these images:

```
public static List<RenderedImage> getImagesFromPDF(PDDocument pdDocument) {
    List<RenderedImage> renderedImages = new ArrayList<>();
    try {
        for (PDPage pdPage : pdDocument.getPages()) {
renderedImages.addAll(
                getImagesFromResources(pdPage.getResources()));
        }
    } catch (IOException ex) {
        // Handle exceptions
    }
    return renderedImages;
}
```

The `getImagesFromResources` method, which follows, is a recursive method. It builds a list of `RenderedImage` instances from the page's resources. A PDF document can have nested resources. The recursive nature of this method will capture all of the page's images by delving into these nested resources.

The `for` loop iterates through the `COSName` instances that make up the resources. These instances represent the names of the resource elements. The `getXObject` method returns the actual object. If this object is of the `PDFormXObject` type, the method is called recursively. If the object is of the `PDImageXObject` type, then it is an image, and is added to the list. All other types are ignored:

```
private static List<RenderedImage> getImagesFromResources(
        PDResources pdResources) throws IOException {
    List<RenderedImage> renderedImages = new ArrayList<>();
    for (COSName cosNames : pdResources.getXObjectNames()) {
        PDXObject pdxObject = pdResources.getXObject(cosNames);
        if (pdxObject instanceof PDFormXObject) {
            renderedImages.addAll(
                getImagesFromResources(((PDFormXObject)
                pdxObject).getResources()));
        } else if (pdxObject instanceof PDImageXObject) {
            renderedImages.add(((PDImageXObject)
```

```
                    pdxObject).getImage());
            }
        }
    return renderedImages;
}
```

You will get the following output when this code is executed:

```
Images
image0.png
image1.png
image2.png
```

The files will be found in the project's root directory. To extract an entire page as an image, use the following code. It differs from the previous technique as it uses the `PDFRenderer` class's `renderImage` method to create a `BufferedImage` instance that is used as the first argument of the `ImageIO` class's `write` method:

```
BufferedImage bufferedImage = pdfRenderer.renderImage(0);
System.out.println("Page Image. png ");
ImageIO.write(bufferedImage, "PNG", new File("Page Image.png"));
```

When this code is executed, you will get the following output with the file being placed in the project's root directory:

```
Page Image.png
```

See also

We can use the following references for extracting text from a PDF document:

- The Apache PDFBox main page is found at `https://pdfbox.apache.org/`
- The JavaDocs for Apache PDFBox is found at `https://pdfbox.apache.org/docs/2.0.13/javadocs`

Extracting metadata from a PDF document

Metatdata, in this recipe, refers to the information about a PDF document. In this recipe, we will illustrate how to use the Apache PDFBox API to extract metadata. This information includes the document's title, subject, author, and creation dates, among other things. It will reuse some of the steps found in the *Extracting text from a PDF document* recipe.

Getting ready

To prepare this recipe, we need to do the following:

1. Create a new Maven project
2. Add the following dependency to the project's POM file:

```
<dependency>
    <groupId>org.apache.pdfbox</groupId>
    <artifactId>pdfbox</artifactId>
    <version>2.0.13</version>
</dependency>
```

3. Use the PDF document created in the recipe, *Extracting text from a PDF document,* and save it in the root directory of this project

How to do it...

Follow these steps:

1. Add the following imports to the project:

```
import java.io.File;
import java.io.IOException;
import java.util.Set;
import org.apache.pdfbox.pdmodel.PDDocument;
import org.apache.pdfbox.pdmodel.PDDocumentInformation;
```

2. Add the following `try` block to the `main` method. It will load `PDFDocument`:

```
try {
    File file = new File("PDFFile.pdf");
    PDDocument pdDocument = PDDocument.load(file);
    ...
    pdDocument.close();
} catch (IOException ex) {
    // Handle exceptions
}
```

3. Next, insert the next code sequence to obtain and display the metadata:

```
PDDocumentInformation pdDocumentInformation =
    pdDocument.getDocumentInformation();
Set<String> metaDataKeys = pdDocumentInformation.getMetadataKeys();
for (String key : metaDataKeys) {
    System.out.println(key + ": "
```

```
            + pdDocumentInformation.getPropertyStringValue(key));
    }
```

4. Execute the program. You will get the following output:

```
Author: Author's name
CreationDate: D:20190120133027-06'00'
Creator: Microsoft® Word 2016
Keywords: sample java
ModDate: D:20190120133027-06'00'
Producer: Microsoft® Word 2016
Subject: The subject
Title: The Title
```

How it works...

A `File` object was created representing the `PDFFile.pdf`. The `PDDocument` class's static `load` method created an instance of `PDDocument` that holds the contents of the file. The `close` method was used to close the `PDDocument` once we were through with it:

```
File file = new File("PDFFile.pdf");
PDDocument pdDocument = PDDocument.load(file);
```

The `PDDocumentInformation` represents the metadata for the PDF document. The `getMetadataKeys` method returns a set of keys for this information. In the `for` loop, we iterated through the set and displayed the corresponding key's values:

```
PDDocumentInformation pdDocumentInformation =
pdDocument.getDocumentInformation();
Set<String> metaDataKeys = pdDocumentInformation.getMetadataKeys();
for (String key : metaDataKeys) {
    System.out.println(key + ": "
        + pdDocumentInformation.getPropertyStringValue(key));
}
```

There's more...

The output of the previous example is not as user-friendly as it could be. In the next set of code, we used methods to access specific properties of the document. This approach will allow us to display this information in a more controlled fashion:

```
System.out.println("Author: " + pdDocumentInformation.getAuthor());
System.out.println("Creator: " + pdDocumentInformation.getCreator());
System.out.println("Keywords: " + pdDocumentInformation.getKeywords());
```

```
System.out.println("Subject: " + pdDocumentInformation.getSubject());
System.out.println("Title: " + pdDocumentInformation.getTitle());
System.out.println("Creation Date: " +
pdDocumentInformation.getCreationDate().getTime());
System.out.println("Last Modified Date: " +
pdDocumentInformation.getModificationDate().getTime());
System.out.println();
```

When this code is executed, you will get the following output:

```
Author: Author's name
Creator: Microsoft® Word 2016
Keywords: sample java
Subject: The subject
Title: The Title
Creation Date: Sun Jan 20 13:30:27 CST 2019
Last Modified Date: Sun Jan 20 13:30:27 CST 2019
```

If any of the return values are empty, then we would have to add `test` to avoid displaying empty results.

See also

We can use the following references for extracting metadata from a PDF document:

- The Apache PDFBox main page is found at `https://pdfbox.apache.org/`
- The JavaDocs for Apache PDFBox is found at `https://pdfbox.apache.org/docs/2.0.13/javadocs/`

Extracting text from a Word document

There is a large amount of text found in Word documents. In this recipe, we will illustrate how to obtain this text using the Apache PDFBox API. We will reuse the Word document created in the *Extracting text from a PDF document* recipe

Getting ready

To prepare the recipe, we need to do the following:

1. Create a new Maven project.
2. Add the following dependency to the project's POM file:

```
<dependency>
    <groupId>org.apache.pdfbox</groupId>
    <artifactId>pdfbox</artifactId>
    <version>2.0.13</version>
</dependency>
```

3. Use the Word document created in the *Extracting text from a PDF document* recipe. Save it in the root directory of this project.

How to do it...

Follow these steps:

1. Add the following imports to the project:

```
import java.awt.image.BufferedImage;
import java.io.ByteArrayInputStream;
import java.io.File;
import java.io.FileInputStream;
import java.io.IOException;
import java.util.List;
import javax.imageio.ImageIO;
import org.apache.poi.xwpf.extractor.XWPFWordExtractor;
import org.apache.poi.xwpf.usermodel.XWPFDocument;
import org.apache.poi.xwpf.usermodel.XWPFParagraph;
import org.apache.poi.xwpf.usermodel.XWPFPictureData;
```

2. Insert the following `try` block to the `main` method:

```
try {
    String fileName = "PDFFile.docx";
    XWPFDocument xwpfDocument = new XWPFDocument(
        new FileInputStream(fileName));
    ...
} catch (IOException e) {
    // Handle exceptions
}
```

3. Insert the next code sequence into the `try` block:

```
XWPFWordExtractor xwpfWordExtractor = new
XWPFWordExtractor(xwpfDocument);
System.out.println(xwpfWordExtractor.getText());
xwpfWordExtractor.close();
```

4. Execute the program. You will get the following output:

```
The Sample Document

A simple PF document.
Bullet 1
Bullet 2
Bullet 3

Image 1

Image 2
End of first page.


Start of second page

Image 3
The end of the document.
```

How it works...

The XWPFDocument class represents the Word document. An instance of the class was created based on the File object provided in its constructor:

```
String fileName = "PDFFile.docx";
XWPFDocument xwpfDocument = new XWPFDocument(
    new FileInputStream(fileName));
```

An instance of the XWPFWordExtractor class was then created based upon the XWPFDocument instance. The XWPFWordExtractor class's getText method returned the text for the document which was then displayed. The XWPFWordExtractor class instance was then closed:

```
XWPFWordExtractor xwpfWordExtractor = new XWPFWordExtractor(xwpfDocument);
System.out.println(xwpfWordExtractor.getText());
xwpfWordExtractor.close();
```

There's more...

We can also obtain the text for each paragraph. The XWPFDocument class's getParagraphs returns a list of XWPFParagraph instance, each representing a paragraph of the document. In the following sequence, the text for each paragraph is displayed:

```
List<XWPFParagraph> xwpfParagraphs = xwpfDocument.getParagraphs();
for (XWPFParagraph paragraph : xwpfParagraphs) {
    System.out.println("[" + paragraph.getText() + "]");
}
```

When this code is executed, you will get the following output. Brackets were added to more clearly see what text constitutes a paragraph. Blank paragraphs were displayed, since the original document had empty paragraphs:

```
[The Sample Document]
[]
[A simple PF document.]
[Bullet 1]
[Bullet 2]
[Bullet 3]
[]
[Image 1]
[]
[Image 2]
[End of first page.]
[
]
[Start of second page]
[]
[Image 3]
[The end of the document.]
```

We can also extract and save the images contained within a document. The XWPFDocument class's getAllPictures method returns a list of XWPFPictureData instances. Each instance represents an image found in the document:

```
List<XWPFPictureData> images = xwpfDocument.getAllPictures();
```

In the following for loop, a byte array is obtained using the XWPFPictureData class get method. The ImageIO class's read and write methods are used to create and write out a BufferedImage instance containing the image. The image is written to a file with the that same name as used by the Word document:

```
for (int i = 0; i < images.size(); i++) {
    System.out.println("Saving: " + images.get(i));
```

```
        byte[] byteArray = images.get(i).getData();
        BufferedImage bufferedImage = ImageIO.read(
            new ByteArrayInputStream(byteArray));
        ImageIO.write(bufferedImage, "PNG",
            new File(images.get(i).getFileName()));
    }
```

When executed, you will get the following output. The image files will also appear in the project's root directory:

```
Saving: Name: /word/media/image1.png - Content Type: image/png
Saving: Name: /word/media/image2.png - Content Type: image/png
Saving: Name: /word/media/image3.png - Content Type: image/png
```

See also

We can use the following references for extracting text from a Word document:

- The Apache PDFBox main page is found at `https://pdfbox.apache.org/`
- The JavaDocs for Apache PDFBox is found at `https://pdfbox.apache.org/docs/2.0.13/javadocs/`

Extracting metadata from a Word document

Metadata found in a Word document can be extracted using the **Apache PDFBox API**. We will demonstrate how this is performed using the Word document created in the recipe, *Extracting text from a PDF document*. While there are numerous properties available, we will only illustrate how a small subset can be obtained.

Getting ready

To prepare this recipe, we need to do the following:

1. Create a new Maven project.
2. Add the following dependency to the project's POM file:

```
<dependency>
    <groupId>org.apache.pdfbox</groupId>
    <artifactId>pdfbox</artifactId>
    <version>2.0.13</version>
</dependency>
```

3. Use the Word document created in the recipe. Extract text from a PDF document, and save it in the root directory of this project.

How to do it...

Follow these steps:

1. Add the following imports into the project:

```
import java.io.FileInputStream;
import java.io.IOException;
import org.apache.poi.ooxml.POIXMLProperties.CoreProperties;
import org.apache.poi.ooxml.POIXMLProperties.ExtendedProperties;
import org.apache.poi.xwpf.extractor.XWPFWordExtractor;
import org.apache.poi.xwpf.usermodel.XWPFDocument;
```

2. Add the following `try` block to the `main` method:

```
try {
    String fileName = "PDFFile.docx";
    XWPFDocument xwpfDocument = new XWPFDocument(
        new FileInputStream(fileName));
    XWPFWordExtractor xwpfWordExtractor =
        new XWPFWordExtractor(xwpfDocument);

    ...
    xwpfWordExtractor.close();
} catch (IOException e) {
    // Handle exceptions
}
```

3. Insert the following statements into the `try` block:

```
CoreProperties coreProperties =
xwpfWordExtractor.getCoreProperties();
System.out.println("Creator: " + coreProperties.getCreator());
System.out.println("Keywords: " + coreProperties.getKeywords());
System.out.println("Subject: " + coreProperties.getSubject());
System.out.println("Title: " + coreProperties.getTitle());
System.out.println("Creation Date: " +
coreProperties.getCreated());
System.out.println("Last Modified Date: " +
coreProperties.getModified());
```

4. Execute the program. You will get the following output:

```
Creator: Author's name
Keywords: sample java
Subject: The subject
Title: The Title
Creation Date: Sat Jan 19 17:27:00 CST 2019
Last Modified Date: Sun Jan 20 13:30:00 CST 2019
```

How it works...

The XWPFDocument class represents the Word document. An instance of the class was created based on the File object provided in its constructor:

```
String fileName = "PDFFile.docx";
XWPFDocument xwpfDocument = new XWPFDocument(
    new FileInputStream(fileName));
```

An instance of the XWPFWordExtractor class was then created based upon the XWPFDocument instance, which was closed when it was no longer needed. We used its getCoreProperties method to obtain an instance of the CoreProperties class. This class provided us with access to many useful properties. The accessor methods used were self-explanatory:

```
CoreProperties coreProperties = xwpfWordExtractor.getCoreProperties();
```

There's more...

There are other extended properties that may be useful. We obtain an instance of the ExtendedProperties, which represents these properties, using the XWPFWordExtractor class's getMetadataTextExtractor method:

```
ExtendedProperties extendedProperties =
xwpfWordExtractor.getMetadataTextExtractor().getExtendedProperties();
```

The following methods in this code block illustrate how many of the extended properties can be obtained and displayed:

```
System.out.println("Number of Pages: " + extendedProperties.getPages());
System.out.println("Number of Words: " + extendedProperties.getWords());
System.out.println("Number of Characters: " +
    extendedProperties.getCharacters());
System.out.println("Application Version: " +
```

```
extendedProperties.getAppVersion());
System.out.println("Company: " + extendedProperties.getCompany());
```

When this code is executed, you will get the following output:

```
Number of Pages: 2
Number of Words: 24
Number of Characters: 143
Application Version: 16.0000
Company: My Company
```

See also

We can use the following references for extracting metadata from a Word document:

- The Apache PDFBox main page is found at `https://pdfbox.apache.org/`
- The JavaDocs for Apache PDFBox is found at `https://pdfbox.apache.org/docs/2.0.13/javadocs/`

Extracting text from a spreadsheet

There is a lot of useful data found in spreadsheets. In this recipe, we will illustrate how to extract text from an Excel spreadsheet using the Apache PDFBox API. We will create a sample spreadsheet for the examples to work against.

Getting ready

To prepare this recipe, we need to do the following:

1. Create a new Maven project.
2. Add the following dependency to the project's POM file:

```
<dependency>
    <groupId>org.apache.pdfbox</groupId>
    <artifactId>pdfbox</artifactId>
    <version>2.0.13</version>
</dependency>
```

3. Create a new Excel spreadsheet that appears as follows. The last cell entry contains a hyperlink to `www.weather.com`:

	A	B	C	D	E	F
1	1/25/2019	Monday	Tuesday	Wednesd	Thursday	Friday
2	8	43	45	23	33	41
3	9	45	48	25	36	44
4	10	55	57	27	42	53
5	11	59	63	33	45	57
6	12	62	65	38	48	62
7	1	66	68	42	52	64
8	2	69	72	43	54	66
9	3	72	74	43	57	68
10	4	74	75	45	60	64
11	5	73	73	42	60	61
12	Weather Site					

4. Modify the spreadsheet's properties as shown next. How you edit the document properties depends on the version of Excel you are using:

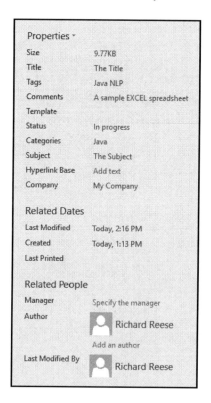

Properties ▾

Size	9.77KB
Title	The Title
Tags	Java NLP
Comments	A sample EXCEL spreadsheet
Template	
Status	In progress
Categories	Java
Subject	The Subject
Hyperlink Base	Add text
Company	My Company

Related Dates

Last Modified	Today, 2:16 PM
Created	Today, 1:13 PM
Last Printed	

Related People

Manager	Specify the manager
Author	Richard Reese
	Add an author
Last Modified By	Richard Reese

5. Save the spreadsheet in the root directory of the project.

How to do it...

Follow these steps:

1. Insert the following imports:

```
import java.io.FileInputStream;
import java.io.FileNotFoundException;
import java.io.IOException;
import org.apache.poi.ss.usermodel.Cell;
import org.apache.poi.ss.usermodel.Row;
import org.apache.poi.ss.usermodel.Sheet;
import org.apache.poi.ss.usermodel.Workbook;
import org.apache.poi.xssf.usermodel.XSSFWorkbook;
```

2. Add the following `try` block to the `main` method:

```
try (FileInputStream fileInputStream = new
FileInputStream("Temperatures.xlsx")) {
    Workbook workBook = new XSSFWorkbook(fileInputStream);
    ...
    workBook.close();
} catch (FileNotFoundException e) {
    // Handle exceptions
} catch (IOException e) {
    // Handle exceptions
}
```

3. Insert the next code sequence into the `try` block:

```
for (int i = 0; i < workBook.getNumberOfSheets(); i++) {
    Sheet sheet = workBook.getSheetAt(i);
    for (Row row : sheet) {
        System.out.printf("Row: - %2d", row.getRowNum());
        for (Cell cell : row) {
            System.out.printf("\t%3s", cell);
        }
        System.out.println();
    }
    System.out.println();
}
```

4. Execute the program. You will get the following output:

```
Row: - 0 25-Jan-2019 Monday Tuesday Wednesday Thursday Friday
Row: - 1 8.0 43.0 45.0 23.0 33.0 41.0
Row: - 2 9.0 45.0 48.0 25.0 36.0 44.0
Row: - 3 10.0 55.0 57.0 27.0 42.0 53.0
```

```
Row: -  4 11.0 59.0 63.0 33.0 45.0 57.0
Row: -  5 12.0 62.0 65.0 38.0 48.0 62.0
Row: -  6 1.0 66.0 68.0 42.0 52.0 64.0
Row: -  7 2.0 69.0 72.0 43.0 54.0 66.0
Row: -  8 3.0 72.0 74.0 43.0 57.0 68.0
Row: -  9 4.0 74.0 75.0 45.0 60.0 64.0
Row: -  10 5.0 73.0 73.0 42.0 60.0 61.0
Row: -  11 Weather Site
```

How it works...

We created a `FileInputStream` instance for the `Temperatures.xlsx` file. An instance of the `XSSFWorkbook` class was created to represent this file. At the end of the `try` block, we closed the object:

```
try (FileInputStream fileInputStream = new
FileInputStream("Temperatures.xlsx")) {
    Workbook workBook = new XSSFWorkbook(fileInputStream);
    ...
    workBook.close();
}
```

Next, nested `for` loops were used to display the contents of the spreadsheet. The outer `for` loop handled each sheet of the spreadsheet, one at a time, based on the value returned by the `getNumberOfSheets` method. A new `Sheet` object was created for each sheet:

```
for (int i = 0; i < workBook.getNumberOfSheets(); i++) {
    Sheet sheet = workBook.getSheetAt(i);
    ...
}
```

The next two `for` loops processed one row at a time, displaying the contents of each cell for that row. Each line of output was prefixed with the row number as returned by the `getRowNum` method:

```
for (Row row : sheet) {
    System.out.printf("Row: - %2d", row.getRowNum());
    for (Cell cell : row) {
        System.out.printf("\t%3s", cell);
    }
    System.out.println();
}
```

There's more...

We can specify a single cell using the `getRow` and `getCell` methods as shown next. The argument for these methods is zero-based:

```
Sheet sheet = workBook.getSheetAt(0);
Cell cell = sheet.getRow(2).getCell(2);
System.out.println("Cell: " + cell);
```

When this code is executed, you will get the following output:

```
Cell: 48.0
```

For specialized cells containing dates, we can use the `getDateCellValue` and `getNumericCellValue` methods to display their contents. The latter method provides more details about the date:

```
cell = sheet.getRow(0).getCell(0);
System.out.println("Cell: " + cell);
System.out.println("Cell: " + cell.getDateCellValue());
System.out.println("Cell: " + cell.getNumericCellValue());
```

When this code is executed, you will get the following output:

```
Cell: 25-Jan-2019
Cell: Fri Jan 25 00:00:00 CST 2019
Cell: 43490.0
```

Hyperlinks may be embedded in a spreadsheet. We can use the `getHyperlink` and `getAddress` methods to display their contents as shown here:

```
cell = sheet.getRow(11).getCell(0);
System.out.println("Hyperlink: " + cell);
System.out.println("Hyperlink: " + cell.getHyperlink().getAddress());
```

The following output is be displayed from the preceding code:

```
Hyperlink: Weather Site
Hyperlink: https://weather.com/
```

In addition, we can determine the spreadsheet version using the `getSpreadsheetVersion` method as shown next:

```
System.out.println("Spreadsheet Version: " +
workBook.getSpreadsheetVersion());
```

The output of this statement follows:

```
Spreadsheet Version: EXCEL2007
```

See also

We can use the following references for extracting text from a spreadsheet:

- The Apache PDFBox main page is found at `https://pdfbox.apache.org/`
- The JavaDocs for Apache PDFBox is found at `https://pdfbox.apache.org/docs/2.0.13/javadocs/`

Extracting metadata from a spreadsheet

In this recipe, we will demonstrate how to extract metadata from an Excel spreadsheet using the Apache PDFBox API. We will demonstrate using the Excel document created in the *Extracting text from a spreadsheet* recipe.

Getting ready

To prepare this recipe, we need to do the following:

1. Create a new Maven project.
2. Add the following dependency to the project's POM file:

```
<dependency>
    <groupId>org.apache.pdfbox</groupId>
    <artifactId>pdfbox</artifactId>
    <version>2.0.13</version>
</dependency>
```

3. Copy the spreadsheet developed in the *Extracting text from a spreadsheet* recipe to the root level of the project

How to do it...

Follow these steps:

1. Insert the following imports into the project:

```
import java.io.FileInputStream;
import java.io.FileNotFoundException;
import java.io.IOException;
import org.apache.poi.ooxml.POIXMLProperties;
import org.apache.poi.ooxml.POIXMLProperties.CoreProperties;
import org.apache.poi.ss.usermodel.Workbook;
import org.apache.poi.xssf.usermodel.XSSFWorkbook;
```

2. Add the following `try` block to the `main` method:

```
try (FileInputStream fileInputStream = new
FileInputStream("Temperatures.xlsx")) {
    Workbook workBook = new XSSFWorkbook(fileInputStream);

    ...
    workBook.close();
} catch (FileNotFoundException e) {
    // Handle exceptions
} catch (IOException e) {
    // Handle exceptions
}
```

3. Insert the next code sequence into the `try` block:

```
XSSFWorkbook xssfWorkbook = (XSSFWorkbook) workBook;
POIXMLProperties poiXMLProperties = xssfWorkbook.getProperties();
CoreProperties coreProperties =
poiXMLProperties.getCoreProperties();
System.out.println("Title: " + coreProperties.getTitle());
System.out.println("Key Words: " + coreProperties.getKeywords());
System.out.println("Status: " + coreProperties.getContentStatus());
System.out.println("Category: " + coreProperties.getCategory());
System.out.println("Subject: " + coreProperties.getSubject());
System.out.println("Creator: " + coreProperties.getCreator());
System.out.println("Last Modified: " +
coreProperties.getModified());
```

4. Execute the program. You will get output similar to the following:

```
Title: The Title
Key Words: Java NLP
Status: In progress
Category: Java
```

```
Subject: The Subject
Creator: Richard Reese
Last Modified: Tue Jan 22 14:22:09 CST 2019
```

How it works...

We created a `FileInputStream` instance for the `Temperatures.xlsx` file. An instance of the `XSSFWorkbook` class was created to represent this file. At the end of the `try` block, we close the object:

```
try (FileInputStream fileInputStream =
        new FileInputStream("Temperatures.xlsx")) {
    Workbook workBook = new XSSFWorkbook(fileInputStream);
    ...
    workBook.close();
}
```

Next, we will see an instance of the `XSSFWorkbook` class cast from the `WookBook` object. The `getProperties` method returned an instance of the `POIXMLProperties` class that was used in conjunction with the `getCoreProperties` method to return the `CoreProperties` object. A series of `get` methods returned the properties that were displayed:

```
XSSFWorkbook xssfWorkbook = (XSSFWorkbook) workBook;
POIXMLProperties poiXMLProperties = xssfWorkbook.getProperties();
CoreProperties coreProperties = poiXMLProperties.getCoreProperties();
System.out.println("Title: " + coreProperties.getTitle());
System.out.println("Key Words: " + coreProperties.getKeywords());
System.out.println("Status: " + coreProperties.getContentStatus());
System.out.println("Category: " + coreProperties.getCategory());
System.out.println("Subject: " + coreProperties.getSubject());
System.out.println("Creator: " + coreProperties.getCreator());
System.out.println("Last Modified: " + coreProperties.getModified());
```

See also

We can use the following references for extracting metadata from a spreadsheet:

- The Apache PDFBox main page is found at `https://pdfbox.apache.org/`
- The JavaDocs for Apache PDFBox is found at `https://pdfbox.apache.org/docs/2.0.13/javadocs/`

11
Creating a Chatbot

A **chatbot** is an application that interacts with a user using natural language. Chatbots have been used for many different types of user interaction including help desks, customer service, and order placements. Usually, the conversation is somewhat limited in the type and structure of the interaction.

In this chapter, we will demonstrate how to create a chatbot using Amazon's AWS. We will start with creating a simple bot using online support. This will introduce the terminology and structure of a bot.

Then, we will demonstrate how to create a bot using Java. This will be accomplished using AWS Toolkit for Eclipse. We will also demonstrate how to pass data to an AWS Lambda function. This type of function executes on an AWS server and can be written in a number of languages including Java. How this function is updated to the cloud will be shown along with how it can be executed within the Eclipse environment.

In this chapter, we will cover the following recipes:

- Creating a simple chatbot using AWS
- Creating a bot using the AWS Toolkit for Eclipse
- Creating a Lambda function
- Uploading the Lambda function
- Executing a Lambda function from Eclipse

Technical requirements

In this chapter, you will need to install the following software, if it has not already been installed:

- Eclipse Photon 4.8.0
- Java JDK 8 or later

We will be using the following APIs, which you will be instructed to add for each recipe as appropriate:

- Amazon AWS Lex
- Amazon's Corretto 8
- AWS Toolkit for Eclipse

The code files for this chapter can be found at `https://github.com/PacktPublishing/Natural-Language-Processing-with-Java-Cookbook/tree/master/Chapter11`.

Creating a simple chatbot using AWS

This recipe will not require the reader to write code but instead create the application through a series of web pages. Upon completion of the recipe, the reader will have a good idea of a bot's structure.

Getting ready

To prepare this recipe, we need to log on to the AWS account.

How to do it...

Follow these steps in order to create a simple chatbot:

1. Select **Amazon Lex** from the **Services** tab as shown in the following screenshot:

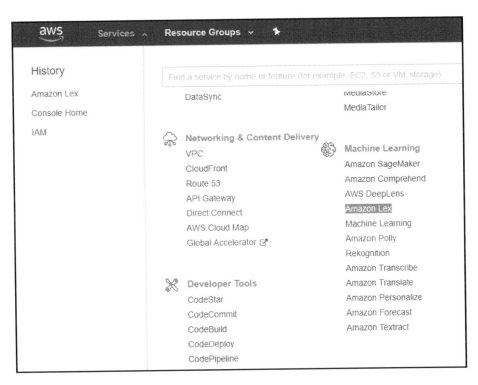

2. Once you have selected **Amazon Lex**, you will need to select the appropriate region for your location from the list shown within this screenshot:

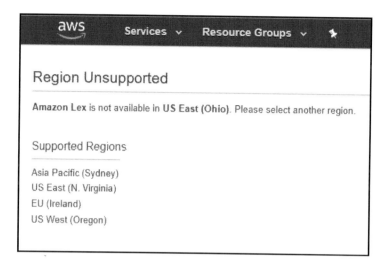

3. Click on the **Get Started** button shown in the following screenshot:

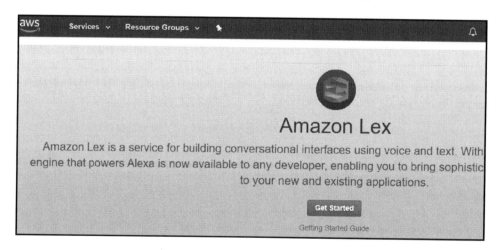

4. Next, select the **Custom bot** button as shown here:

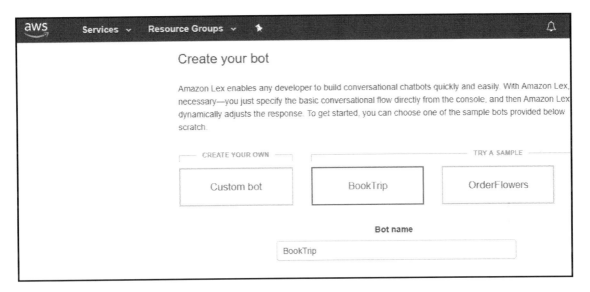

5. In the next window, enter the following values into the corresponding fields, and then select the **Create** button:

- **Bot name:** `WeatherBot`
- **Output voice:** **Salli** (this will only be used for a voice-chat version of the bot)
- **Session timeout:** 5 **min**
- **COPPA:** **No**

The following page will appear:

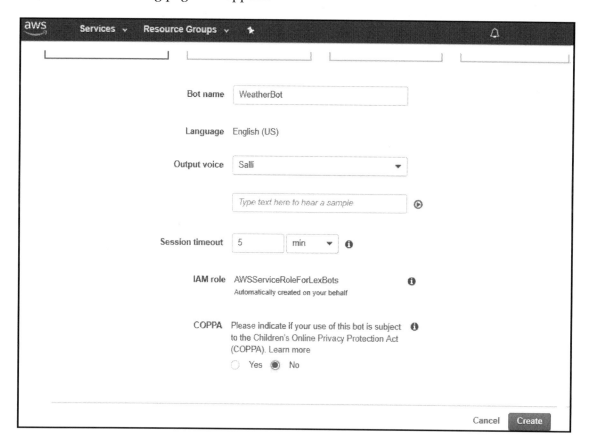

6. Select the **Create Intent** button:

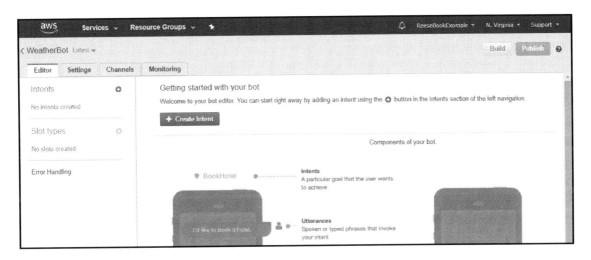

7. An **intent** is a response provided by a bot to a client message. Select **Create intent** again from the following window:

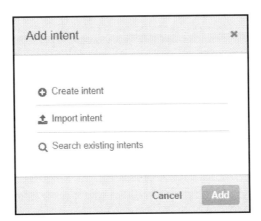

8. Use the name `WhatIsTheTemperature`, as shown next, and then select the **Add** button:

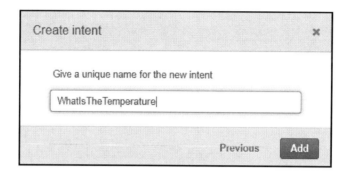

The following page will appear. **Sample utterances** are possible user queries:

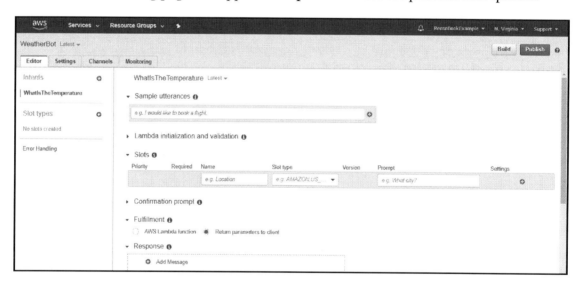

9. Add the following utterances by typing the utterance in the **Sample utterances** text field and then clicking on the + button:

    -   `What is the temperature`
    -   `What is the temperature now`
    -   `What is the temperature right now`

The page will appear as follows:

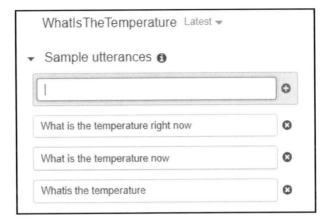

10. Add the following responses by selecting the **Add Message** field:

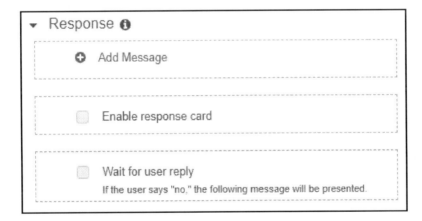

11. **Enter** `The temperature is 72 degrees.` **Next, select the + sign to the right of the text field, as shown next:**

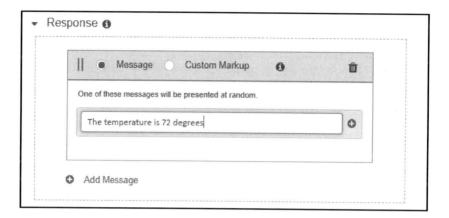

12. Add the following responses in a similar manner:
    - `It is 72 degrees`
    - `72 degrees`

    The messages will then appear as follows:

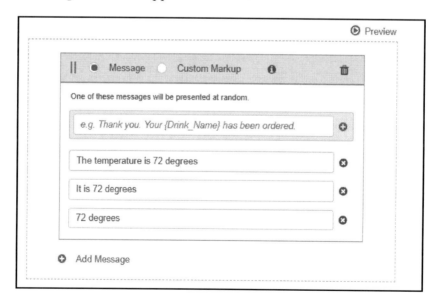

13. Select the **Save Intent** button at the bottom of the page.

14. Select the **Build** button at the top-right of the page. Then, select the **Build** button in the following dialog box:

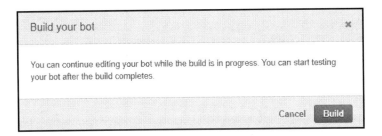

The **Build** button will appear with a rotating busy icon until the build is complete. This may take several minutes. When the build is complete, you will see the following window:

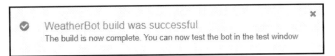

15. Close the window.
    A **Test bot** area will appear on the right-hand side of the page:

16. Enter `What is the temperature` in the text field with the microphone icon.

17. Then press the *Enter* key. The bot will respond with one of the responses such as **It is 72 degrees**, as shown next:

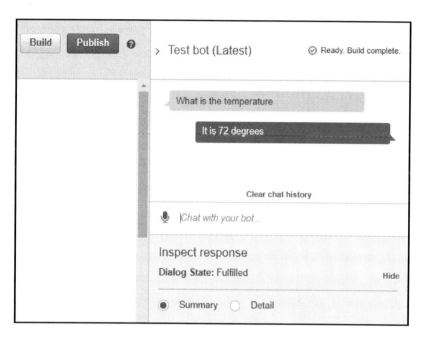

How it works...

We created a simple bot called Weatherbot. We added an intent that consisted of **utterances** and **responses**. Utterances are possible user queries and the responses are used to reply to a user query. The utterances are analyzed using various NLP technologies. This will allow Lex to recognize similar queries. Multiple responses allow Lex to randomly choose between different reply formats, making the responses seem more natural.

Once the bot was built, we were able to test its operations. There is much more to this bot than this recipe is able to demonstrate, but it provides the basic idea of how bots work.

See also

- The AWS Lex web page is found at `https://aws.amazon.com/lex/`

Creating a bot using AWS Toolkit for Eclipse

AWS Toolkit provides another technique for creating and testing bots. We will create a second weather bot using AWS Toolkit for Eclipse and Java to demonstrate how the user can pass data to our application, which allows more sophisticated processing.

Getting ready

We will follow these steps to create a bot:

1. Download Amazon's Corretto 8 found at `https://docs.aws.amazon.com/corretto/latest/corretto-8-ug/downloads-list.html`.
2. Open Eclipse and select the **Window | Preferences** menu item.
3. Select the **Java** and then **Installed JREs** categories.
4. Use the **Add ...** button to add the Corretto distribution, as shown in the following screenshot:

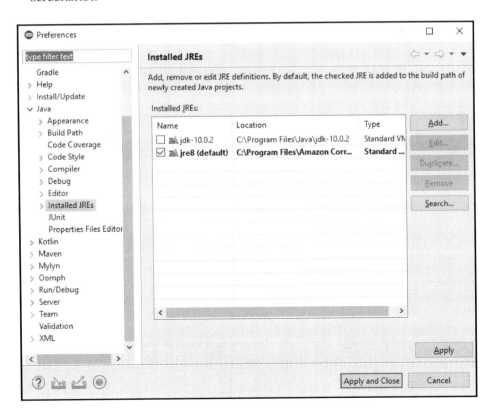

5. Configure the AWS region, as shown next, using the same **Preferences** window by selecting the **Regions** category:

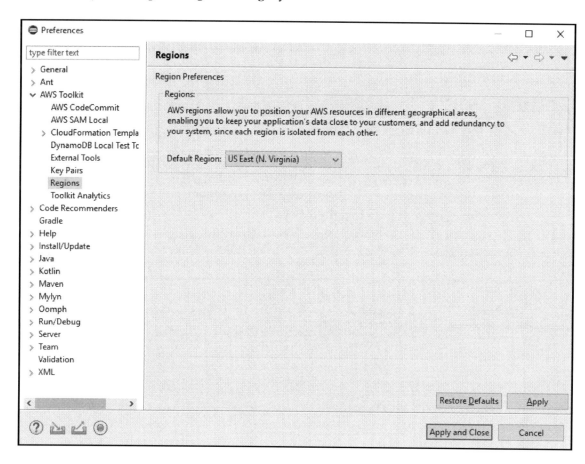

6. Ensure that the **AWS Toolkit** preferences reflect on our account, shown as follows:

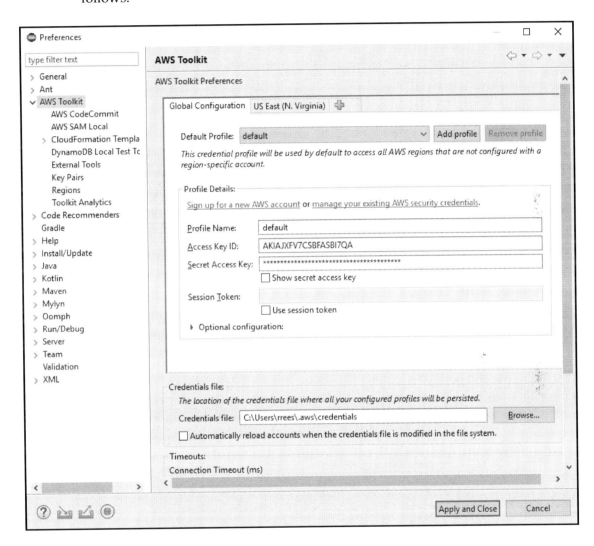

7. Select the **Apply and Close** button.

How to do it...

Follow these steps:

1. Select the **File | New** menu item.
2. Next, choose a new **AWS Java Project**, as shown:

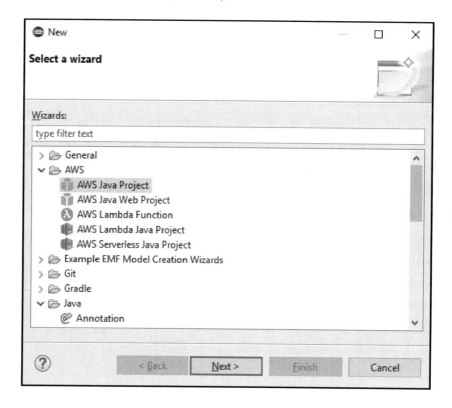

3. Select **Next**. The **New AWS Java Project** window will appear, as shown in the following screenshot:

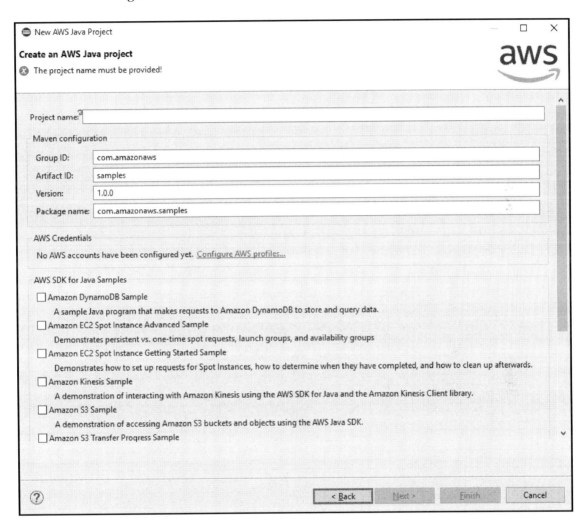

4. Complete the following fields of the window using the data specified:

- **Project name:** WeatherBot2
- **Group ID:** com.packt.weatherbot2
- **Artifact ID:** weather

The **Version** and **Package name** fields are automatically populated as shown next:

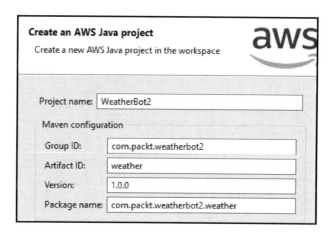

5. Select **Finish**. It may take a few minutes to create the project. When completed, open the project. You will find that the basic structure of the project has been generated, as shown in the following screenshot:

How it works...

We assigned the project a name, group ID, artifact ID, and package name using AWS Toolkit for Eclipse. We also configured the project to use our AWS account. This created the files and application structure that we will use for the subsequent recipes.

See also

- A tutorial demonstrating the process of creating a sample project is found at https://docs.aws.amazon.com/toolkit-for-eclipse/v1/user-guide/tke_java_apps.html

Creating a Lambda function

An AWS Lambda function is a code that executes in the cloud and supports operations such as those used in a chatbot. In this recipe, we will demonstrate how to create a Lambda function using AWS Toolkit for Eclipse. This function will receive data from a user and then return an appropriate response.

Getting ready

Follow the steps to create the Lambda function:

1. Complete the previous recipe, *Creating a bot using the AWS Toolkit for Eclipse*.
2. Add the following dependencies to the project's POM file:

```xml
<!-- https://mvnrepository.com/artifact/junit/junit -->
<dependency>
    <groupId>junit</groupId>
    <artifactId>junit</artifactId>
    <version>4.8.1</version>
    <scope>test</scope>
</dependency>

<dependency>
    <groupId>com.amazonaws</groupId>
    <artifactId>aws-java-sdk</artifactId>
    <version>1.11.505</version>
    <scope>compile</scope>
</dependency>
<dependency>
    <groupId>com.amazonaws</groupId>
    <artifactId>amazon-kinesis-client</artifactId>
    <version>1.2.1</version>
    <scope>compile</scope>
</dependency>
<!--
https://mvnrepository.com/artifact/com.amazonaws/aws-java-sdk-lex -
```

```
->
<dependency>
    <groupId>com.amazonaws</groupId>
    <artifactId>aws-lambda-java-core</artifactId>
    <version>1.2.0</version>
</dependency>
<dependency>
    <groupId>com.amazonaws</groupId>
    <artifactId>aws-lambda-java-events</artifactId>
    <version>2.2.5</version>
</dependency>
<dependency>
    <groupId>com.amazonaws</groupId>
    <artifactId>aws-lambda-java-log4j</artifactId>
    <version>1.0.0</version>
</dependency>
<dependency>
    <groupId>com.amazonaws</groupId>
    <artifactId>aws-lambda-java-log4j2</artifactId>
    <version>1.0.0</version>
</dependency>
```

How to do it...

The following steps will describe how to create the Lambda function:

1. Right-click on the package and select **New** and then **Other**. The **New** window will appear, as shown here:

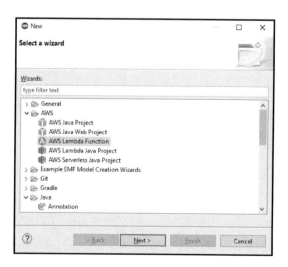

2. Select **AWS Lambda Function** and then click on **Next**. The following window is then displayed:

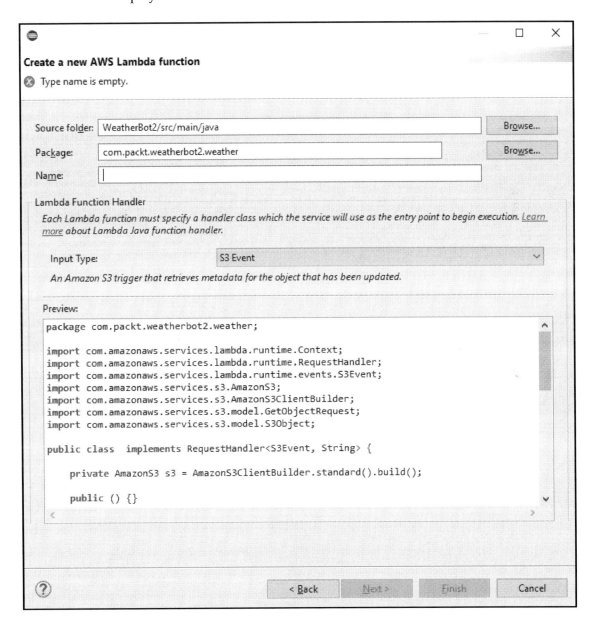

3. Enter `WeatherBot` in the **Name** field and select an **Input Type** of **Custom**, as shown next. The **Preview** window will display the code that will be created for the function:

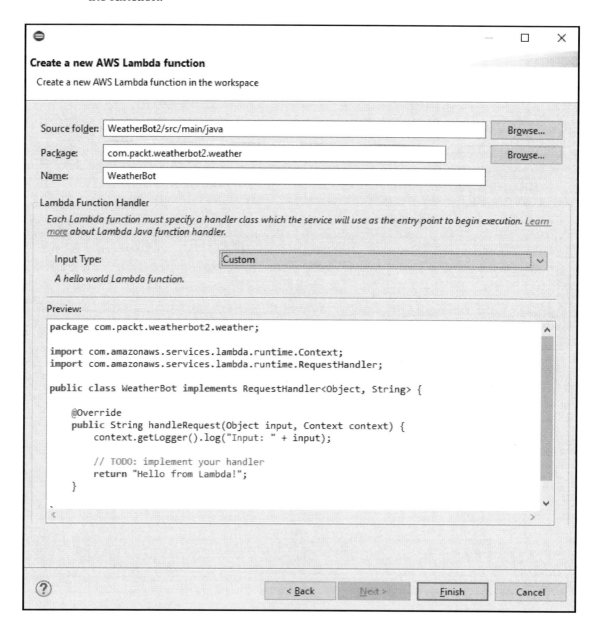

4. Next, select **Finish**. We will modify the class to handle the string input by changing the class and method declarations. Currently, we have the following code:

```
public class WeatherBot implements RequestHandler<Object, String> {

    @Override
    public String handleRequest(Object input, Context context) {
        context.getLogger().log("Input: " + input);
        // TODO: implement your handler
        return "Hello from Lambda!";
    }

}
```

5. Change the use of the `Object` class to a `String` class. This occurs in two locations: the `RequestHandler` declaration and the first argument of the `handleRequest` method. Also, change the name of the first argument to `city`. Next, replace the body of the `handleRequest` function so that it will appear as follows:

```
public class WeatherBot implements RequestHandler<String, String> {

    @Override
    public String handleRequest(String city, Context context) {
        context.getLogger().log("Input: " + city);
        // TODO: implement your handler
        switch (city) {
        case "London":
            return "The current temperature is 56";
        case "Miami":
            return "The current temperature is 86";
        case "Barrow":
            return "The current temperature is -26";
        default:
            return "Error - Unknown city";
        }
    }

}
```

How it works...

We use the Toolkit wizard to create a function with the name `WeatherBot`. We specified a custom input type to permit more controlled specification of the function. This created a `handleRequest` method that we then modified.

The method's first argument was changed from an `Object` type to a `String` type, which we used to pass the name of a city. A `switch` statement used this name to return a response with the current temperature of that city.

See also

- More information regarding Java Lambda functions is found at `https://docs.aws.amazon.com/lambda/latest/dg/java-programming-model-handler-types.html`

Uploading the Lambda function

Before we create a Lambda function using AWS Toolkit for Eclipse, the Lambda function must be uploaded on the cloud. In this recipe, we will demonstrate how this is accomplished using the Toolkit.

Getting ready

The required setup was completed earlier. Complete the previous recipe, *Creating a Lambda function*, to prepare for this recipe.

How to do it...

We will follow these steps to upload the Lambda function:

1. Right-click in in the code window and then choose **AWS Lambda**. Then, choose the **Upload function to AWS Lambda** menu option.
2. In the **Upload function to AWS Lambda** window, select an appropriate region and enter CurrentTemperatureFunction as the name of the Lambda function.
3. Select the **Next** button. The following window will appear, as shown in this screenshot:

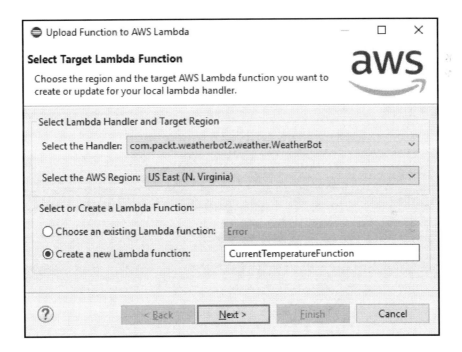

4. Select the **Create** button in the **Function Role** section:

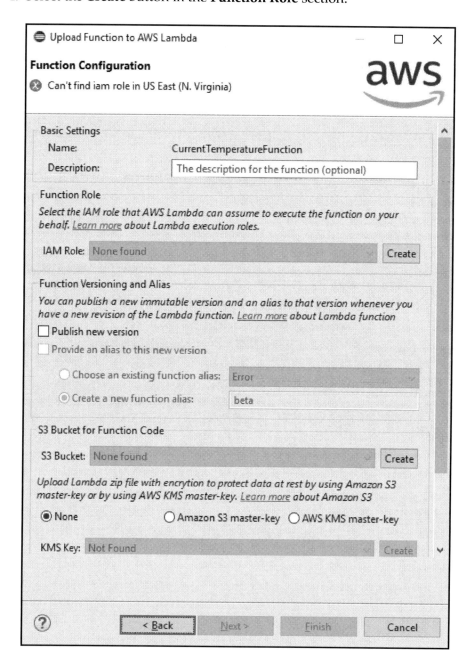

5. Ensure that the **Role Name** is `lambda_basic execution` and then select **OK:**

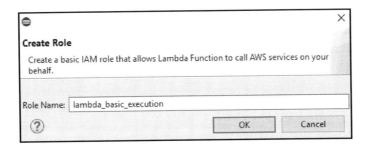

 A message indicating that the role is being created will be displayed. It may take a few minutes to complete.

6. Next, check the **Publish new version** checkbox in the **Upload Function to AWS Lambda** window. Accept the default **Bucket Name** unless you prefer to use something different.
7. Next, select the **OK** button:

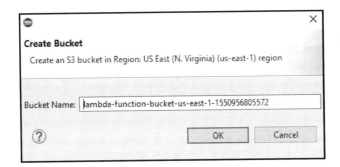

8. Select the **Finish** button.

How it works...

We used AWS Toolkit for Eclipse to select the handler function for our Lambda expression. The name, `CurrentTemperatureFunction`, was used. We specified a **Role Name** of `lambda_basic execution`, which is typically used for these types of functions. A bucket was created from the **US East (N. Virginia)** region. This is used to hold the function on the server. The function is now ready to be used.

See also

- More information regarding the upload process can be found at `https://docs.aws.amazon.com/toolkit-for-eclipse/v1/user-guide/lambda-ref-upload-function.html`

Executing a Lambda function from Eclipse

When a chatbot is running, it may use various Lambda functions to support it. In the previous recipes, we created and uploaded a Lambda function written in Java. In this recipe, we will execute the function from AWS Toolkit for Eclipse.

Getting ready

The required setup was completed earlier. Complete the previous recipe, *Uploading the Lambda function*, to prepare for this recipe.

How to do it...

We will follow these steps to execute the Lambda function from Eclipse:

1. Right-click on the code window, select **AWS Lambda**, and then select the **Run function on AWS Lambda ...** menu item.
2. In the window, enter a string such as `"Barrow"`, as shown next. Then, select the **Invoke** button:

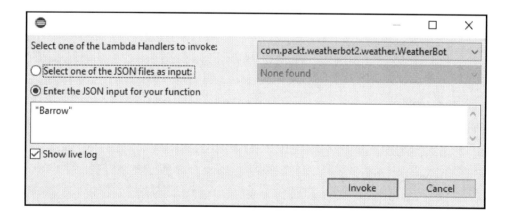

You will get the output similar to the following:

```
Skip uploading function code since no local change is found...
Invoking function...
==================== FUNCTION OUTPUT ====================
"The current temperature is -26"
==================== FUNCTION LOG OUTPUT ====================
START RequestId: c3136512-32ad-474b-9693-8c850dee8a89 Version: $LATEST
Input: BarrowEND RequestId: c3136512-32ad-474b-9693-8c850dee8a89
REPORT RequestId: c3136512-32ad-474b-9693-8c850dee8a89 Duration: 5.54 ms
Billed Duration: 100 ms Memory Size: 512 MB Max Memory Used: 43 MB
```

How it works...

We used the toolkit to choose a Lambda function to execute. This function requires data to be sent in the form of a JSON argument. Since our argument consisted of a single string value, our JSON argument used a single string enclosed in double quotes. We then invoked the function that returned the corresponding temperature for that city.

See also

- More information about JSON can be found at `https://www.json.org/`
- More information regarding Lambda function input and response formats can be found at `https://docs.aws.amazon.com/lex/latest/dg/lambda-input-response-format.html`

Installation and Configuration

In this appendix, we will cover the following recipes:

- Getting ready to use the Google Cloud Platform
- Configuring Eclipse to use the Google Cloud Platform
- Getting ready to use Amazon Web Services
- Configuring Eclipse to use Amazon Web Services

Technical requirements

In this chapter, you will need to install the following pieces of software, if they have not already been installed:

- Eclipse Photon 4.8.0
- Java JDK 8 or later

We will be using the following APIs, which you will be instructed to add for each recipe as appropriate:

- A Google Cloud Platform subscription
- An AWS subscription

Getting ready to use the Google Cloud Platform

The **Google Cloud Platform** (**GCP**) supports several types of analysis, including entity, sentiment, and content classification, and syntax analysis. For low usage, the account is free to use. However, before you can use the API, you need to set up an account.

In this recipe, we will illustrate how to create and use a Google account to perform NLP analysis.

Getting ready

To prepare, we need to do the following:

1. Create a Google account if you do not already have one. Go to `https://accounts.google.com/signup/v2/webcreateaccount?flowName=GlifWebSignIn flowEntry=SignUp`, where you will find the following page. Fill in this and the subsequent pages to create your account:

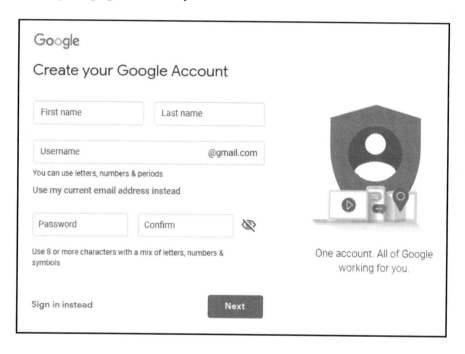

2. Once completed, you will be sent to your account page, which will appear similar to the following:

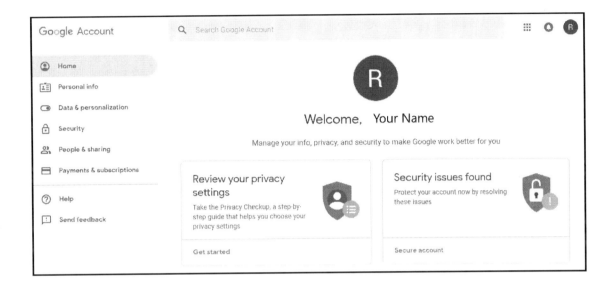

How to do it...

Let's go through the following steps:

1. Go to the GCP Cloud Developer console (`https://console.cloud.google.com/`) and agree to the service agreement.

2. Select the **ACTIVATE** button found in the upper right-hand corner of the page. The following page will appear. Select the tick box agreeing to the **Terms of service** and then select the **AGREE AND CONTINUE** button. This will be followed by a page requesting billing information, including a form of payment. Once activated, you can begin using GCP. As long as you don't exceed the limits for the free usage of GCP, you will not be charged:

Try Google Cloud Platform for free

Step 1 of 2

Country

United States ▾

Terms of service

☑ I have read and agree to the Google Cloud Platform Free Trial Terms of Service.

Required to continue

AGREE AND CONTINUE

Privacy policy | FAQs

The GCP Console navigation menu may not always be visible. Selecting the three horizontal dashes inside the circle in the upper left-hand corner of the page, as shown next, will bring up the menu:

3. Next, you will be taken to your GCP home page. At the top of the page you will see a **Select a project** drop-down menu. Select the drop-down button. Then, select the **NEW PROJECT** button found in the upper right-hand corner, as shown here:

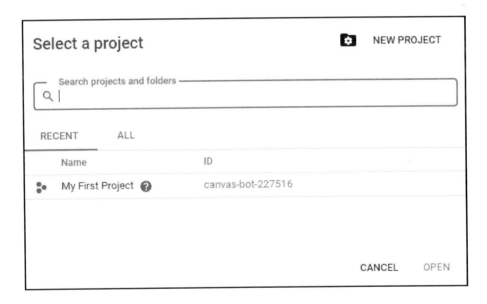

4. The following page will appear. You can change the name to a more meaningful project title if you desire. Select the **CREATE** button when done, as shown in the following screenshot:

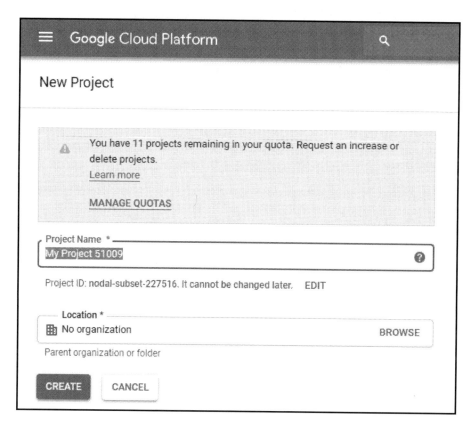

5. Select the **API & Services** menu from the GCP Console navigation menu, and then choose the **Library** submenu, as shown next:

6. Press the **Select** button on the page that follows:

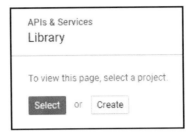

7. Select the project that you created earlier.
8. Next, select the **API & Services** menu from the GCP Console navigation menu and then the **Credentials** submenu. You will get a page containing the following:

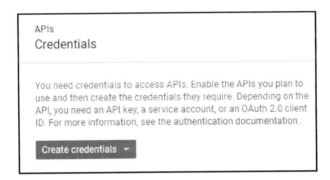

9. Select the **Create credentials** drop-down button. The following selections will appear. Select the **Service account key** option:

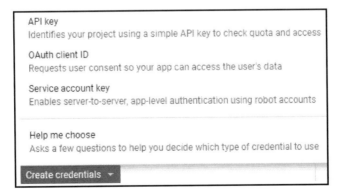

10. The following page will appear. Select the drop-down arrow and then click on **New service account**. Provide a service account name. From the **Role** drop-down menu, select **Owner**. The service account ID will be generated automatically. Leave the **JSON** option selected and then select the **Create** button:

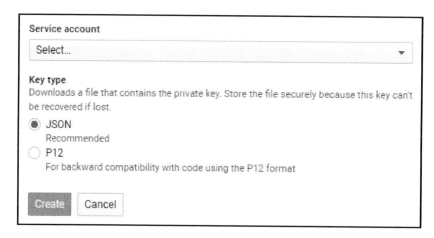

11. You will be prompted to save the **JSON** file. Select a convenient location. You are now ready to use GCP.

How it works...

The GCP uses a client/server paradigm to perform NLP tasks. Before the services could be used, it was necessary to create a Google account and then use the GCP console to configure a project.

We created a new project that will serve as the local point for access to the server. We then created a service account key, which we will use in subsequent recipes to access the server. This resulted in the creation of a JSON file, which encapsulates the information needed for your projects to access the GCP services.

See also

Important links are listed here:

- Home page: https://cloud.google.com/natural-language/
- Getting started: https://cloud.google.com/natural-language/docs/quickstart

- Java API documentation: `http://googleapis.github.io/google-cloud-java/` `google-cloud-clients/apidocs/index.html?com/google/cloud/language/v1/` `package-summary.html`

Configuring Eclipse to use the Google Cloud Platform

We used Eclipse for the examples in this book. There are a few recipes where it is necessary to reconfigure the IDE so that it can work correctly. In this recipe, we will illustrate how to configure Eclipse to work with the GCP. This involves creating a new environment variable for a specific class. You will need to perform this task for each class that will use GCP.

Getting ready

Install the Eclipse Photon version from `https://www.eclipse.org/downloads/`.

How to do it...

Let's go through the following steps:

1. From the **Run** menu, select **Run configurations...**.
2. On the left-hand side of the dialog box, you will see a Java application list.
3. Select the name of the class where you will be using the GCP. You may not be able to do this until an appropriate class is created.
4. Next, select the **Environment** tab.
5. Select the **New...** button to bring up the **New Environment Variable** dialog box:

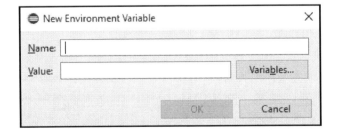

6. Add `GOOGLE_APPLICATION_CREDENTIALS` to the **Name** field.

7. Add the path and the name of your JSON file to the **Value** field. This file was downloaded as illustrated in the previous recipe, *Getting ready to use the Google Cloud Platform*.

8. Select the **OK** button. You will then see the variable added, which will look similar to the following screenshot:

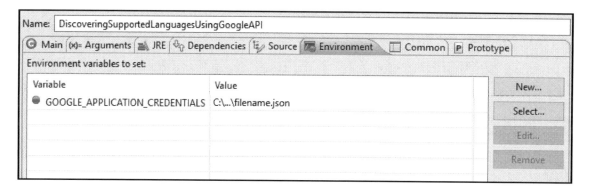

How it works...

Before you can use the GCP, it is necessary to set up the `GOOGLE_APPLICATION_CREDENTIALS` environment variable so that the GCP credentials can be accessed. These credentials are found in the JSON file created when you set up your GCP project. We used the **Run Configurations** dialog box to perform this task.

See also

- Information about how you can create your GCP credentials is detailed in the *Getting ready to use the Google Cloud Platform* recipe

Getting ready to use Amazon Web Services

We will use **Amazon Web Services** (**AWS**) in several recipes in various chapters (Chapter 7, *Language Identification and Translation*, and Chapter 11, *Creating a Chatbot*). This is a cloud-based service that provides a multitude of services, including support for various NLP tasks. A server is located in the cloud and requires a client application to connect and then request a service. The server will then respond, sending results back to the client.

In this recipe, we will demonstrate how to set up your system to use AWS. These services are free for a period of time and as long as the limits on access are not exceeded. When used for the later recipes, you should not exceed these limits. More information regarding pricing is found at `https://aws.amazon.com/pricing/?nc2=h_ql_pr`.

Getting ready

There are no explicit tasks that need to be performed.

How to do it...

Let's go through the following steps:

1. Set up your credentials by opening the page at `https://portal.aws.amazon.com/billing/signup#/start`. The following page is shown next. Fill in the required fields and select the **Continue** button:

2. Fill in the required fields for the contact page, as shown in the following screenshot. When completed, select the **Create Account and Continue** button:

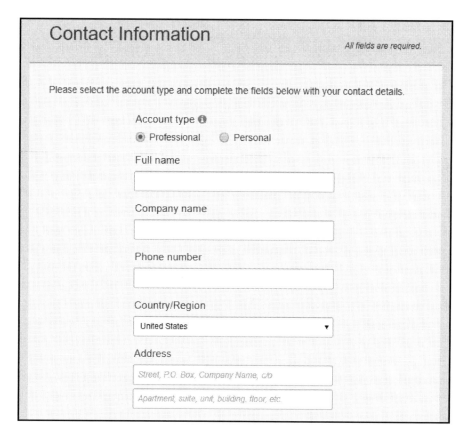

3. On the next few pages, enter the payment method. You will then encounter the page shown in the following screenshot. Now, select the appropriate plan:

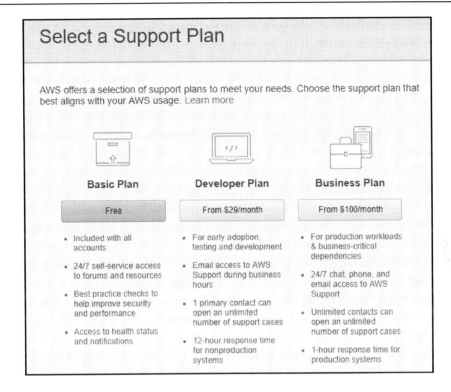

4. You will then be asked to sign into the console, as shown in the next screenshot. Select the **Sign in to the Console** button:

Once you are signed in, you will see the following page:

5. Select the **IAM** link shown on the left-hand side of the screen. This will bring up the **Welcome to Identity and Access Management** page, as shown in the next screenshot:

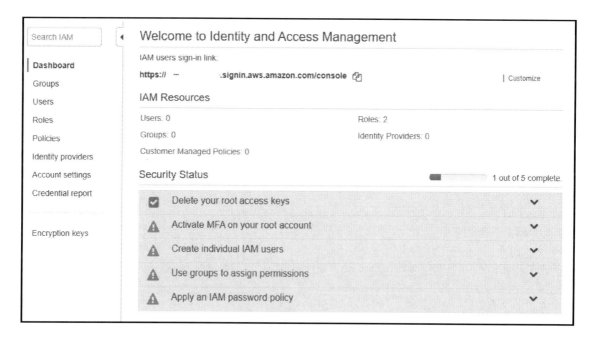

6. Select the **User** link shown on the left-hand side of the page. This will bring up the following page. Select the **Add user** button:

7. Add a user name and select the **Programmatic access** option. Then, select the **Next: Permissions** button:

8. Select the **Create group** button:

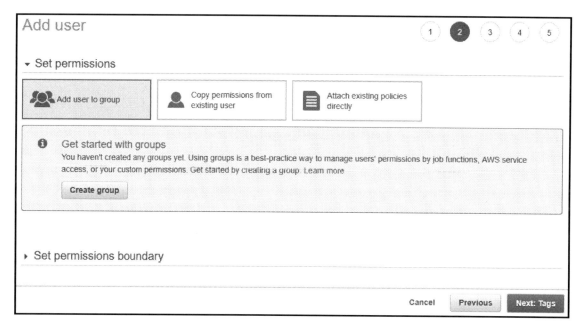

9. Enter a group name and choose the **AdministratorAccess** option. Then, select the **Create group** button:

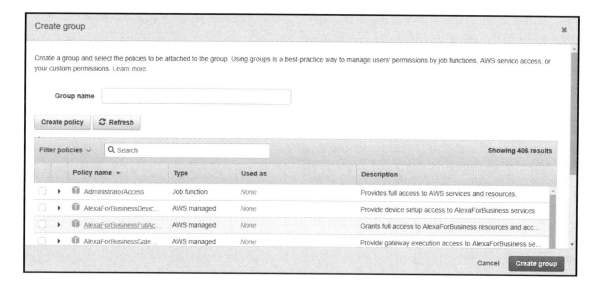

10. This will take you back to the **Add user** page. Select the **Next: Tags** button. The next page, **Add tags**, is optional. Select the **Next: Review** button:

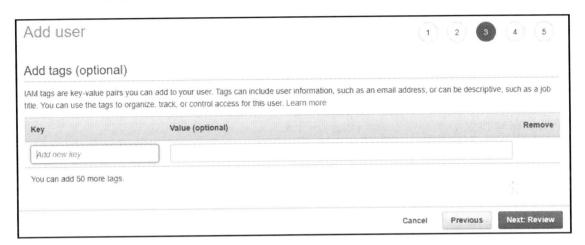

11. The next page summarizes your selections. Select the **Create user** button:

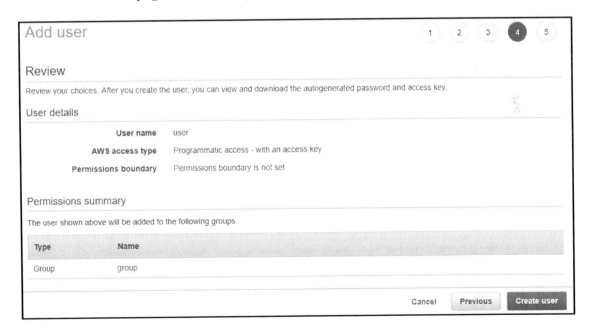

12. Next, select the **Download .csv** button. Save the file at a convenient location. Next, select the **Close** button:

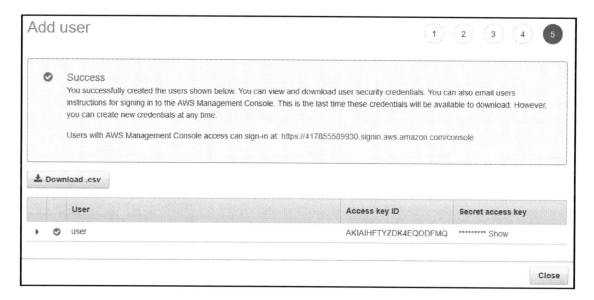

You can now access the file to utilize the AWS services.

How it works...

We created a new account for AWS. This involved creating a user account and group. We also created a `credentials.csv` file, which holds the information needed to access the services.

See also

- In the next recipe, *Configuring Eclipse to use Amazon Web Services*, we will set up Eclipse to use the credential file

Configuring Eclipse to use Amazon Web Services

Once the AWS account and credentials have been set up, we can use the credential file to access the services. In this recipe, we will demonstrate how to configure Eclipse to work with this file. The first step is to install the AWS Toolkit for Java and then specify the location of the credentials file.

Getting ready

We will get started by installing the Eclipse Photon version from `https://www.eclipse.org/downloads/`.

How to do it...

Let's go through the following steps:

1. To install the AWS Toolkit for Java, start by selecting the **Help** menu then the **Install New Software...** submenu. This will bring up the **Install** dialog box, as shown in the next screenshot.

2. Enter `https://aws.amazon.com/eclipse` in the **Work with** field and select the AWS components. Select the **Finish** button:

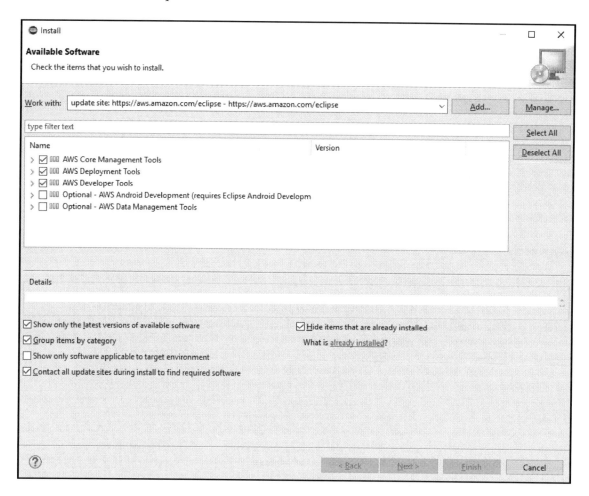

3. You may need to restart Eclipse at this point.
4. Select the **Windows** – **Preferences** menu in Eclipse. This will bring up the **Preferences** dialog box.
5. Next, select the **AWS Toolkit** menu on the left-hand side of the dialog box, as shown in the next screenshot. In the **Credentials file** field, enter the location of your `credentials.csv` file.

6. Select the **Apply and Close** button when done:

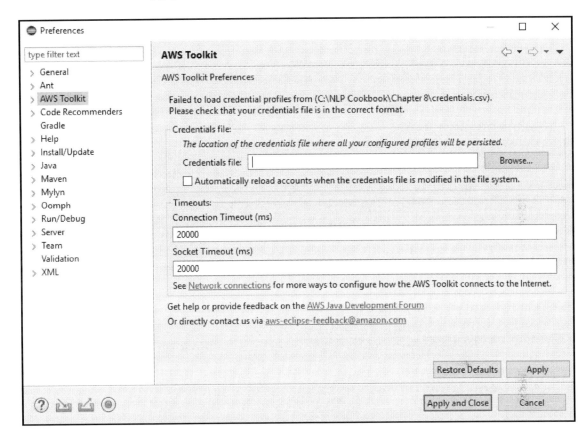

Eclipse can now be used to access the AWS services.

How it works...

We installed the AWS Toolkit for Java, which prepares the IDE to access AWS. We specified the credentials file for use within the IDE. We can now access the AWS services.

See also

- More details about how to use the AWS Toolkit for Java is found at `https://docs.aws.amazon.com/sdk-for-java/v2/developer-guide/aws-sdk-java-dg.pdf`

Other Books You May Enjoy

If you enjoyed this book, you may be interested in these other books by Packt:

Statistics for Machine Learning - Second Edition
Pratap Dangeti

ISBN: 9781789532678

- Learn Statistical and Machine Learning fundamentals necessary to build models
- Explore different Statistical techniques for Machine Learning using R and Python packages
- Learn reinforcement learning and its application in artificial intelligence domain
- Explore Probabilistic Graphical Models to create powerful Artificial Intelligence
- Learn Time Series Prediction Using Recurrent Neural Networks
- Understand Bayesian methods to estimate uncertainty in prediction

Natural Language Processing with Java - Second Edition
Richard M Reese, AshishSingh Bhatia

ISBN: 9781788993494

- Understand basic NLP tasks and how they relate to one another
- Discover and use the available tokenization engines
- Apply search techniques to find people, as well as things, within a document
- Construct solutions to identify parts of speech within sentences
- Use parsers to extract relationships between elements of a document
- Identify topics in a set of documents
- Explore topic modeling from a document

Leave a review - let other readers know what you think

Please share your thoughts on this book with others by leaving a review on the site that you bought it from. If you purchased the book from Amazon, please leave us an honest review on this book's Amazon page. This is vital so that other potential readers can see and use your unbiased opinion to make purchasing decisions, we can understand what our customers think about our products, and our authors can see your feedback on the title that they have worked with Packt to create. It will only take a few minutes of your time, but is valuable to other potential customers, our authors, and Packt. Thank you!

Index

LingPipe API documentation
  reference link 193
LingPipe
  used, for removing stop words 30, 31, 32
  used, for training model to classify text 135, 138
  used, to classify text 139, 141
  using 49, 51

M

Markov model
  used, to perform POS 113, 115
Marsaglia's KISS algorithm
  reference link 251
maximum entropy model
  used, for tokenization 12, 13, 14, 128, 130
metadata
  extracting, from HTML page 278, 280
  extracting, from PDF document 289, 292
  extracting, from spreadsheet 304, 306
  extracting, from Word document 296
model
  training, to classify text using LingPipe 135, 138
multiple entities types
  isolating 76, 79

N

Named-entity recognition (NER) 63
natural language processing (NLP) 7, 245
natural language
  detecting, in Google API 196, 199
  detecting, in LingPipe 190, 192
NER model
  training 86, 89, 91
neural machine translation (NMT) 194
neural network tokenizer
  training, for specialized text 15, 18, 20
neural network
  training, to perform SBD with specialized text 57,
    59, 62
Norwegian (NO) 262

O

OpenNLP API documentation
  reference link 168
OpenNLP API

reference link 76
OpenNLP lemmatization model
  training 22, 23, 24, 26
OpenNLP
  reference link 45
  used, for determining lexical meaning of word
    26, 27, 28
  used, for generating parse tree 165, 166, 167
  used, for tokenization 10, 11
  used, to find entities in text 71, 74, 76
  used, to perform SBD 41, 44

P

parent-child relationships
  identifying, in text 175, 177, 178, 180, 182
parse text
  Google NLP API, using to 169, 170, 171, 172,
    174
  probabilistic context-free grammar, using to 160,
    161, 162, 164
parse tree
  generating, OpenNLP used 165, 166, 167
parse trees graphically
  displaying 156, 157, 159
Part-Of-Speech (POS)
  about 93, 155
  chunks, used 97, 100
  finding, from textese 107, 110
  finding, Penn Treebank used 104, 106
  finding, tag used 94, 96
  Markov model, using 113, 115
  model, training 117, 121
PDF document
  metadata, extracting 289, 292
  text, extracting 283, 287
PDFBox 283
phrase-based machine translation (PBMT) 194
pipeline
  used, to perform tagging 110, 112
plaintext instances
  differences, finding 231, 233, 234, 235
pricing, LanguageTool
  reference link 252
probabilistic context-free grammar
  used, to parse text 160, 161, 162, 164

R

Random Numbers Generators (RNG) 246, 251
random numbers
  generating 246, 249, 251
regular expression, for sentences
  reference link 37
regular expression
  chunks, used to identify entities 68, 70
  used, to find entities 64, 66
responses 318

S

Sentence Boundary Disambiguation (SBD)
  about 33
  performing, BreakIterator class used 37, 40
  performing, on specialized text 53, 56
  performing, OpenNLP used 41, 44
  performing, Stanford NLP API used 45, 48
sentences
  co-references, searching in 182, 183, 185, 186
  finding, Java core API used 34, 36
sentiment analysis
  performing, on reviews 150, 153, 154
software development kit (SDK) 246
spam detection techniques
  reference link 150
spam
  detecting 142, 145, 148, 150
speech to text
  converting, Google Cloud Speech-to-Text API
    used 217, 220
spreadsheet
  metadata, extracting 304, 306
  text, extracting 299, 302
Stanford API
  used, for classifying documents 131, 134
Stanford NLP API documentation
  reference link 164
Stanford NLP API

  used, to perform SBD 45, 48
stem of word
  identifying 20, 22
stemming, versus lemmatization
  reference link 7
stop words
  about 143
  removing, with LingPipe 30, 31, 32
supported languages
  discovering, Google API used 194, 195

T

tag dictionary
  using 101, 103
text to speech
  converting, Google Cloud Text-to-Speech API
    used 213, 216
text
  classifying, LingPipe used 139, 141
  cosine similarity, finding of 224, 226, 227
  distance, finding between 228, 229, 230
  extracting, from HTML page 278, 280
  extracting, from PDF document 283, 287
  extracting, from spreadsheet 299, 302
  extracting, from Word document 292, 294
  parent-child relationships, identifying in 175,
    177, 178, 180, 182
  summarizing, in document 260, 262, 263
tokenization
  with Java SDK 8, 9, 10
  with maximum entropy 12, 14
  with OpenNLP 10, 11

U

utterances 318

W

Word document
  metadata, extracting 296
  text, extracting 292, 294

Made in the USA
Middletown, DE
21 May 2020

95683185R00214